CompTIA
CySA+®
Cybersecurity Analyst
Certification

PRACTICE EXAMS

Exam CS0-001

Jeff T. Parker

New York   Chicago   San Francisco
Athens   London   Madrid   Mexico City
Milan   New Delhi   Singapore   Sydney   Toronto

McGraw-Hill Education books are available at special quantity discounts to use as premiums and sales promotions, or for use in corporate training programs. To contact a representative, please visit the Contact Us pages at www.mhprofessional.com.

CompTIA CySA+® Cybersecurity Analyst Certification Practice Exams (Exam CS0-001)

1 2 3 4 5 6 7 8 9   LCR   21 20 19 18

ISBN: Book p/n 978-1-260-11698-4 and CD p/n 978-1-260-11699-1
of set 978-1-260-11701-1

MHID: Book p/n 1-260-11698-0 and CD p/n 1-260-11699-9
of set 1-260-11701-4

Sponsoring Editor	**Technical Editor**	**Production Supervisor**
Lisa McClain	Brice Kelly Sparks	Pamela Pelton
Editorial Supervisor	**Contributor**	**Composition**
Janet Walden	Bobby E. Rogers	Cenveo Publisher Services
Project Manager	**Copy Editor**	**Illustration**
Radhika Jolly,	Bart Reed	Cenveo Publisher Services
Cenveo® Publisher Services	**Proofreader**	**Art Director, Cover**
Acquisitions Coordinator	Rick Camp	Jeff Weeks
Claire Yee		

*This book is dedicated to two people. First, to Eric Korte,
my buddy with whom many movies are quoted. Second, to whomever can
correctly identify every movie (odd) and TV show (even) referenced per chapter. Good luck!*

ABOUT THE AUTHOR

Jeff Parker is a certified trainer and consultant who loves breaking, fixing, and re-breaking his home lab. His career in information security spans from engineer consulting with HP in Boston, to IT risk management with Deutsche Post in Prague, Czech Republic, and ending now in Canada, where he most enjoys teaching how security can succeed alongside business goals.

Jeff is a firm believer in the CySA+ certification for IT professionals who can recognize and respond to information security issues. Over many years, he has earned (and let lapse) several certifications, including the MCSE, CCNA, MCNE, and three from SANS Institute. Jeff does maintain his CISSP (since 2004), as well as the CompTIA ITT+ and Project+ certifications. But his new favorite is, of course, the CySA+.

About the Technical Editor

Brice Kelly Sparks is the Test Directorate Information System Security Manager for the U.S. Missile Defense Agency and has more than 30 years experience in the cybersecurity field. Kelly's experience includes 20 years in the U.S. Air Force, specializing in electronic systems security assessment, information operations, electronic warfare training, and operations security. Prior to joining the Missile Defense Agency, he served as the senior principal cybersecurity analyst with Dynetics, Inc., for nine years, specializing in certification and accreditation, network vulnerability assessment, and penetration testing, providing service to multiple Department of Defense and commercial technology clients. He has more than eight years teaching experience as an adjunct faculty member at the University of Alabama in Huntsville, the U.S. Air Force Information Operations School, and the U.S. Navy Network Security and Vulnerability technician course. Kelly has an A.S. in intelligence analysis from the Community College of the Air Force, a B.S. in computer science from Park University, and an M.S. in network security from Capitol Technical University. Kelly also holds the CISSP certification.

About the Contributor

Bobby E. Rogers is an information security engineer working as a contractor for Department of Defense agencies, helping to secure, certify, and accredit their information systems. Bobby has a master's degree in information assurance (IA) and is pursuing a doctoral degree in cybersecurity. His many certifications include CISSP-ISSEP, CEH, and MCSE: Security, as well as the CompTIA A+, Network+, Security+, and Mobility+ certifications.

Becoming a CompTIA Certified IT Professional Is Easy

It's also the best way to reach greater professional opportunities and rewards.

Why Get CompTIA Certified?

Growing Demand

Labor estimates predict some technology fields will experience growth of more than 20% by the year 2020. (Source: CompTIA 9th Annual Information Security Trends study: 500 U.S. IT and Business Executives Responsible for Security.) CompTIA certification qualifies the skills required to join this workforce.

Higher Salaries

IT professionals with certifications on their resume command better jobs, earn higher salaries, and have more doors open to new multi-industry opportunities.

Verified Strengths

Ninety-one percent of hiring managers indicate CompTIA certifications are valuable in validating IT expertise, making certification the best way to demonstrate your competency and knowledge to employers. (Source: CompTIA Employer Perceptions of IT Training and Certification.)

Universal Skills

CompTIA certifications are vendor neutral—which means that certified professionals can proficiently work with an extensive variety of hardware and software found in most organizations.

 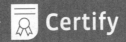 

Learn more about what
the exam covers by
reviewing the following:

- Exam objectives for
  key study points.

- Sample questions for a general
  overview of what to expect
  on the exam and examples
  of question format.

- Visit online forums, like LinkedIn, to
  see what other IT professionals say
  about CompTIA exams.

Purchase a voucher at a
Pearson VUE testing center
or at CompTIAstore.com.

- Register for your exam at a
  Pearson VUE testing center.

- Visit pearsonvue.com/CompTIA to
  find the closest testing center to you.

- Schedule the exam online. You will
  be required to enter your voucher
  number or provide payment
  information at registration.

- Take your certification exam.

Congratulations on your
CompTIA certification!

- Make sure to add your
  certification to your resume.

- Check out the CompTIA
  Certification Roadmap to plan
  your next career move.

Learn More: Certification.CompTIA.org

CompTIA Disclaimer

CONTENTS

ACKNOWLEDGMENTS

Thank you, Lisa McClain, Claire Yee, and Janet Walden for my opportunity to work with you. I look forward to continuing our relationship on future titles with McGraw-Hill Education. Thanks go to all MHE staff along the workflow who carry a book from concept to paper.

A special nod to Bart Reed for his copyedits, sense of humor, and allowing the added spirit of the book to stay. I know he was watching closely, but it took until Chapter 13 for Bart to come out and acknowledge that spirit ("Over the line!").

A massive thank you to the technical editor Kelly Sparks. Kelly kept an ever-vigilant eye on the depth and truth of every question, scenario, and explanation. As a TE new to authoring, I learned to take a deep breath before reading your comments. Sincere thanks, Kelly, for your expertise and persistence.

To Carole Jelen of Waterside Productions, my thanks for connecting me with MHE and Lisa McClain. For every project and connection, thank you Carole.

Lastly, a big thank you to my supportive family, especially to our new puppy, Abby. Abby listened to me create many questions during our walks.

INTRODUCTION

Why Go for the CySA+?

Why do people go for any certification? For recognition? For self-assurance of knowledge and experience? Job security? Maybe all the above?

Not every certification can deliver "all the above," but the CySA+ can and will. The CySA+ combines considerable difficulty, industry approval, and specialization. I know this might look like marketing hyperbole, but read on and you'll learn why getting *this* credential should be your top priority. But waste no time afterward—you need to practice and study!

The CySA+ Is Intermediate Level: Not for Beginners

You might already know CompTIA has a beginner infosec certification: Security+. Being an entry-level certification, the Security+ "casts a wide net," attracting candidates from outside information security circles, such as database admins, system admins, network engineers, and general IT professionals. For people coming from outside information security, the Security+ starts them on the path of information security professional. It's safe to assume that many Security+ candidates pass the exam based on diligent studying, but likely have minimal actual infosec experience. Getting by with just book know-how is not the case with the CySA+.

By comparison, a CySA+ candidate must possess knowledge beyond the core book knowledge. If you read the exam details, you see there is no absolute work experience prerequisite. However, CompTIA does recommend a minimum of three to four years of hands-on experience. The difference is, the CySA+ has a strong, technical, hands-on focus. You will see this in the wording of the questions and explanations.

The CySA+ Is Specialized: Not for Generalists

Exams for other information security certifications (including the Security+) will test candidates on a broad range of topics: risk and threat management, incident detection and handling, as well as penetration testing and IT auditing. The CySA+ exam does cover the first few main topics, with a deeper focus on analytics and incident response. However, penetration testing and auditing are purposefully detached from the CySA+ coverage.

Instead of generalizing the CySA+, CompTIA took penetration testing and auditing and created another separate intermediate-level cert for information security professionals: PenTest+. I would assume this was done to better reflect real life. Full-time security analysts and penetration testers are typically different people, each with a respectable depth of knowledge of their role. More about PenTest+ can be found online.

The Industry Recognizes Your Good Work

Of course, there are no guarantees or absolute job security. And adding a few letters next to your name on your resume doesn't guarantee you are a rock star. But if you seek an information security analyst position, the CySA+ credential labels your experience and value. Your employer, whether current or expected, recognizes the CySA+ and what was required from you to earn it.

What to Expect from the CySA+ Exam

To reap that sweet, sweet professional karma we talked about, you must take the CySA+ exam. Be forewarned: it isn't easy. (Why should it be?) Let's talk about what to expect when you take the CySA+ exam.

Some bullet points:

- It is composed of up to 85 questions. (You might get fewer, but doubtful.)
- The format is multiple choice, plus a few "performance-based" questions (a few comments about those later).
- You'll have 165 minutes to complete the exam. (That's 2 hours and 45 minutes.)
- To pass, you need to score a 750 or higher, out of 900.

Some quick math shows you have roughly two minutes per question. Anyone who has ever taken such an exam before knows that some questions will take you five seconds while others may plague you for five minutes.

One warning I will give: do *not* be surprised by the performance-based questions if they come early. Do not panic about them taking all your time. After you handle the performance-based questions, the standard multiple-choice questions will seem to go by quickly.

Lastly, because the exam delivers only up to 85 questions, it is not possible to be questioned on every topic and subtopic listed in the Exam Objectives map. In this book, however, you can be assured that at least one question will touch each and every bullet point on the Objective map, to help you assess your knowledge and prepare for the exam.

How to Use This Book

This is a practice exam book, not a study guide. The goal of this book is to prepare you for the CompTIA CySA+ exam. Use this book as a tool to assess your knowledge. Only after you assess what you know (and don't know), can you decide confidently whether you're ready to take the exam. Therefore, you want to use this book as your tool to gauge your readiness.

Based on the Exam Structure

This book takes a practical and systematic approach, more than other books available. This book's 15 chapters are divided into four parts:

- Threat Management
- Vulnerability Management
- Cyber Incident Response
- Security Architecture and Tool Sets

These should look familiar, as they are the same four domains found on the CySA+ exam.

Weighted by Exam Domain Distribution

There are about 300 questions in total across all four parts (and many more in the TotalTester software). Of these questions, the number allotted to each part also mimics the same percentage each domain is allotted on the CySA+ exam. As with this guide, the CompTIA exam consists of four domains (categories). CompTIA indicates the relative level of importance of each domain with the following weighting in the exam:

Domain	% of Examination
1.0 Threat Management	27 percent
2.0 Vulnerability Management	26 percent
3.0 Cyber Incident Response	23 percent
4.0 Security Architecture and Tool Sets	24 percent

And lastly, the question content and coverage were carefully written to best prepare you for the questions you will encounter on the exam. In fact, every topic, subtopic, and bullet point of the CompTIA CySA+ Exam Objectives is covered at some point within the respective chapters. This was double-checked by a third-party reviewer before this book was permitted to be published.

Taking a Practical Approach

To assess your knowledge, this book takes the simple, proven approach: you have a question and you choose among the provided answers. Like on the CySA+ exam, all of questions are multiple choice, with at least four, up to five, potential answers. The explanations given for each question do reinforce the correct answer, as well as clarify why incorrect answers are wrong.

Performance questions, very much like you'll find on the exam, are also available to you via the TotalTester software. For more information, see the "About the Digital Content" appendix.

Using the Digital Content

This book comes complete with TotalTester customizable practice exam software containing 200 multiple-choice practice exam questions, a pre-assessment test, and ten performance-based questions. For details on accessing and using the content, see the "About the Digital Content" appendix.

Using the Objective Map

The following Objective Map has been constructed to help you cross-reference the official exam objectives from CompTIA with the relevant coverage in the book. References have been provided for the exam objectives exactly as CompTIA has presented them, along with the chapter and question numbers.

 NOTE   Questions may cover more than one objective. Be sure to read the in-depth explanation of both correct and incorrect answers at the end of each chapter to understand the full context of each question.

Objective Map: Exam CS0-001

Domain, Objective, Sub-objective		Chapter Number	Question Number
1.0	**Threat Management**		
1.1	*Given a scenario, apply environmental reconnaissance techniques using appropriate tools and processes.*		
	Procedures/common tasks	1	1, 4, 5, 6, 7, 11, 16, 19, 20
	Variables	1	1, 8, 9, 10, 14, 21
	Tools	1	2, 3, 11, 12, 13, 15, 17, 18, 19, 20
1.2	*Given a scenario, analyze the results of a network reconnaissance.*		
	Point-in-time data analysis	2	5, 15, 20, 21, 22
	Data correlation and analytics	2	3, 5, 6, 7
	Data output	2	1, 4, 8, 11, 12, 13, 14, 16, 17, 19
	Tools	2	2, 9, 10, 16, 18, 19, 21
1.3	*Given a network-based threat, implement or recommend the appropriate response and countermeasure.*		
	Network segmentation	3	1, 2, 3
	Honeypot	3	6
	Endpoint security	3	12
	Group policies	3	19
	ACLs	3	7, 8, 9, 11
	Hardening	3	10, 15, 16, 17, 18
	Network Access Control (NAC)	3	4, 5, 9, 13, 14, 20
1.4	*Explain the purpose of practices used to secure a corporate environment.*		
	Penetration testing	4	2, 3, 7, 11, 14, 16, 17, 18
	Reverse engineering	4	6, 8, 9, 10, 14
	Training and exercises	4	12, 13
	Risk evaluation	4	1, 4, 5, 15, 19, 20
2.0	**Vulnerability Management**		
2.1	*Given a scenario, implement an information security vulnerability management process.*		
	Identification of requirements	5	1, 2, 3, 4, 5, 33, 39, 40
	Establish scanning frequency	5	6, 7, 8, 32, 36

Domain, Objective, Sub-objective	Chapter Number	Question Number
Configure tools to perform scans according to specification	5	9, 10, 11, 23, 24, 27, 30, 31, 34, 35
Execute scanning	5	12, 37
Generate reports	5	13, 14
Remediation	5	15, 16, 17, 18, 19, 20, 21, 22, 25, 28, 29, 38
Ongoing scanning and continuous monitoring	5	26
2.2	*Given a scenario, analyze the output resulting from a vulnerability scan.*	
Analyze reports from a vulnerability scan	6	1, 2, 3, 4, 34, 38
Validate results and correlate other data points	6	5, 7, 9, 10, 28, 29, 32, 35, 36
2.3	*Compare and contrast common vulnerabilities found in the following targets within an organization.*	
Servers	6	11
Endpoints	6	17, 27, 31
Network infrastructure	6	23
Network appliances	6	24, 37
Virtual infrastructure	6	12, 13, 18, 21, 22
Mobile devices	6	16, 30
Interconnected networks	6	15
Virtual Private Networks (VPNs)	6	14, 19
Industrial Control Systems (ICSs)	6	25
SCADA devices	6	20, 26
3.0	**Cyber Incident Response**	
3.1	*Given a scenario, distinguish threat data or behavior to determine the impact of an incident.*	
Threat classification	8	1, 2, 12
Factors contributing to incident severity and prioritization	8	3, 4, 5, 6, 7, 8, 9, 10, 11, 13, 14, 15, 16, 17
3.2	*Given a scenario, prepare a toolkit and use appropriate forensics tools during an investigation.*	
Forensics kit	9	1, 2, 5, 8, 9, 13, 14, 15, 16, 17
Forensic investigation suite	9	1, 3, 4, 6, 7, 10, 11, 12

Domain, Objective, Sub-objective		Chapter Number	Question Number
3.3	Explain the importance of communication during the incident response process.		
	Stakeholders	7	1, 8, 12, 13
	Purpose of communication processes	7	14, 17
	Role-based responsibilities	7	11, 15, 16
3.4	Given a scenario, analyze common symptoms to select the best course of action to support incident response.		
	Common network-related symptoms	10	1, 2, 3, 4, 5, 6
	Common host-related symptoms	10	7, 8, 9, 10, 12, 13, 17
	Common application-related symptoms	10	8, 11, 12, 14, 15, 16
3.5	Summarize the incident recovery and post-incident response process.		
	Containment techniques	7	2, 3, 4, 5
	Eradication techniques	7	2, 3, 4, 5
	Validation	7	3, 4, 5, 7
	Corrective actions	7	8, 9
	Incident summary report	7	10
4.0	**Security Architecture and Tool Sets**		
4.1	Explain the relationship between frameworks, common policies, controls, and procedures.		
	Regulatory compliance	11	12
	Frameworks	11	1, 2, 5
	Policies	11	3, 4, 7
	Controls	11	9, 10, 13
	Procedures	11	6, 8, 13, 14
	Verifications and quality control	11	11, 12
4.2	Given a scenario, use data to recommend remediation of security issues related to identity and access management.		
	Security issues associated with context-based authentication	12	1, 4
	Security issues associated with identities	12	2, 3, 7
	Security issues associated with identity repositories	12	5, 6

Domain, Objective, Sub-objective	Chapter Number	Question Number
Security issues associated with federation and single sign-on	12	10, 11
Exploits	12	8, 9, 12, 13
4.3 Given a scenario, review security architecture and make recommendations to implement compensating controls.		
Security data analytics	13	5, 11
Manual review	13	8, 10, 14
Defense in depth	13	1, 2, 3, 4, 5, 6, 7, 8, 9, 13, 12, 14
4.4 Given a scenario, use application security best practices while participating in the Software Development Life Cycle (SDLC).		
Best practices during software development	14	1, 2, 4, 5, 6, 7
Secure coding best practices	14	3, 8, 9
4.5 Compare and contrast the general purpose and reasons for using various cybersecurity tools and technologies.		
Preventative	15	7, 8, 10, 11, 13, 14
Collective	15	1, 2, 3, 4, 5, 6, 7, 8, 9, 13, 14
Analytical	15	1, 2, 4, 6, 8, 9
Exploit	15	1, 4, 6, 7, 14
Forensics	15	5, 6, 7

PART I

Threat Management

Applying Reconnaissance Techniques

This chapter includes questions on the following topics:

- Approaches to conducting reconnaissance
- Tasks involved in identifying and reconnoitering a target
- Variables affecting reconnaissance efforts
- Common tools used for discovery or reconnaissance

As a cybersecurity analyst, you'll need the knowledge and skills to carry out a variety of tasks. Those tasks include configuring and using threat detection tools, performing data analysis, as well as interpreting the results to identify vulnerabilities, threats, and risks to an organization. The end goal is to secure and protect the resources within the organization. Those resources include the servers, network, and data as well as the user accounts accessing and using it all.

Protecting resources starts with vulnerability management, or knowing what weaknesses exist and applying appropriate measures to minimize them. Risk management is an ongoing process. To begin, you need to identify and evaluate the assets—or in the attacker's perspective, the targets. The first part, identifying what targets exist, is done through reconnaissance. To perform reconnaissance, you need to apply several techniques and employ a variety of tools. And that is what this chapter is all about.

1. Which of the following is *not* an example of reconnaissance or gathering information of the target company through open source intelligence?

    A. Using LinkedIn and other social media to gather e-mail addresses of top executives

    B. Performing passive reconnaissance by capturing packets and scanning ports

    C. Monitoring job sites to learn what technologies are used

    D. Performing DNS harvesting of company network data from external DNS servers

2. What is the name of the command-line version of Wireshark?

    A. nmap

    B. tcpdump

    C. Nessus

    D. TShark

3. You're at an employee's workstation. You need to quickly determine what other machines this system is talking to. You don't have time to install extra tools. What command-line utility and command-line switch will reveal connections between this workstation and others?

    A. tcpdump -i -eth0

    B. nikto -host

    C. netstat -a

    D. nbtstat -A

4. You suspect an employee's workstation may be the source of malicious traffic. Which of the following steps is the best course of action to determine both the type of traffic and this workstation's participation in the traffic?

    A. Set up packet capturing on a network device upstream from the workstation.

    B. Set up packet capturing on the suspect workstation.

    C. Set up packet capturing on a small group of servers identified as targets.

    D. Install antivirus software on the suspect workstation.

5. At a few employee workstations, including a suspect system, you bring up a command window and type **arp -a** to display the cached entries of hostnames and IP addresses, as well as those IPs resolved to a MAC address. At first glance, today's entries seem normal. However, you know for a fact these MAC addresses are not how they were or should be. This illustration shows what the cache was before the suspicious behavior:

Alan's system IP address: 10.1.1.20		Gail's system IP address: 10.1.1.34		Sam's system IP address: 10.1.1.90	
IP address	Hardware address	IP address	Hardware address	IP address	Hardware address
10.1.1.34	Gail's MAC	10.1.1.20	Alan's MAC	10.1.1.20	Alan's MAC
10.1.1.90	Sam's MAC	10.1.1.90	Sam's MAC	10.1.1.34	Gail's MAC

And this illustration shows today's new cached entries:

Alan's system IP address: 10.1.1.20	
IP address	Hardware address
10.1.1.34	Sam's MAC
10.1.1.90	Sam's MAC

Gail's system IP address: 10.1.1.34	
IP address	Hardware address
10.1.1.20	Sam's MAC
10.1.1.90	Sam's MAC

Sam's system IP address: 10.1.1.90	
IP address	Hardware address
10.1.1.20	Alan's MAC
10.1.1.34	Gail's MAC

Notice the differences between the illustrations. From these differences, which is the suspect system and what technique is being used?

   A. DNS poisoning, and both Alan and Gail's systems are attacking.

   B. ARP poisoning, and Alan's system is the attacker.

   C. ARP poisoning, and Gail's system is the attacker.

   D. ARP poisoning, and Sam's system is the attacker.

6. Utilizing search sites as well as professional and social media sites with the goal of gathering contact information is an example of what?

   A. CVSS

   B. OSINT

   C. Social engineering

   D. Phishing

7. A small business is concerned about the threat of social media profiling on its employees. Which of the following actions could you take to best mitigate the threat?

   A. Demonstrate phishing examples to the users.

   B. Increase the level of detail in the system logs.

   C. Review the social media application logs with management.

   D. Review job site listings with HR and systems administrators.

8. Which of the following is *not* an example of a virtualization technology?

   A. Containers

   B. Software-defined networking

   C. Mirroring

   D. Hypervisors

9. Which of the following is a Type 2 hypervisor?

   A. VMware Player

   B. Microsoft Hyper-V

   C. VMware ESX

   D. Kernel-based Virtual Machine

10. Which of the following is *not* an actual cloud computing technology?

    A. IaaS

    B. SaaS

    C. PaaS

    D. SDN

11. You are tasked with scanning across the network space 192.168.2.x and identifying what operating systems are presently running. Select the correct tool and command-line switch necessary to determine what operating systems are running on that subnet.

    A. nikto -Version 192.168.2.0

    B. nmap -O 192.168.2.0/24

    C. syslog -network 192.168.2.0-192.168.2.254

    D. netstat -a 192.168.2.0 /24

12. Referring to Figure 1-1, select from the following actions what the person's likely intentions are.

    A. Assessing what web vulnerabilities are present

    B. Inventorying the web configuration settings

    C. Locating the host web server from the network

    D. Reviewing the web server's HTTP methods

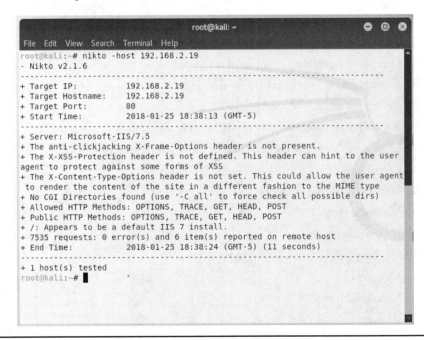

Figure 1-1   Running nikto at the command line

13. A company has suffered a recent incident where a print server was infected with malware and began aggressively scanning other machines on the network. The malware-infected server was identified only after a significant number of other machines were experiencing issues. Although the problem was contained, the timing was an issue. The company asks you to suggest how responding to problems like this could be done more quickly. What do you suggest?

   A. The company should review the firewall rules for areas to improve.

   B. The company should install an IDS on the network.

   C. The company should install an IPS on the network.

   D. The company should scan for further vulnerable print servers.

14. What is a primary challenge to using cloud storage versus on-premises storage?

   A. On-premises storage doesn't permit mobile access.

   B. Expensive software licensing and hardware for cloud services.

   C. Cloud resources put more emphasis on identity management.

   D. Limited options for cloud computing.

15. Wireshark and tcpdump are examples of what kind of application?

   A. Syslog aggregators

   B. Packet analyzers

   C. Intrusion detection systems

   D. Port scanners

16. Which of the following is not included when capturing packet headers but is provided with full packet capture?

   A. Source address

   B. Payload

   C. Protocol flags

   D. Destination address

17. Which of the following statements is not true when it comes to syslog?

   A. Syslog supports a broad range of devices and events.

   B. Messages can be aggregated into a single, nonhierarchical feed.

   C. Devices are polled for messages, echoing back to a syslog server.

   D. The syslog protocol and messaging come native in most firewalls and network devices as well as most *nix systems.

18. A company is frustrated by its firewall's inability to catch higher-level malicious attacks, such as SQL injection and cross-site scripting (XSS). The firewall is unable to distinguish between valid HTTP traffic and malicious attacks when such traffic traverses the firewall on port 80. What do you see as the primary limitation of the firewall?

   A. The firewall is an application-layer firewall, unable to identify the higher-layer data.

   B. The firewall needs to be partnered with an IDS or IPS.

   C. The firewall rules need to be reviewed and likely changed.

   D. The firewall is a layer 3 or 4 device and should be replaced with an application-layer device.

19. If an attacker is using nmap to map the network topology, which of the returned states of the port scans provides the least information?

   A. Unfiltered

   B. Filtered

   C. Closed

   D. Open

20. What would be an appropriate tool for performing service discovery on a large network?

   A. An IDS (but no IPS) placed anywhere on the servers' local subnet

   B. A HIDS placed on a target server

   C. Any tool able to review firewall logs or router ACLs

   D. A port scanner

21. When you're capturing packets on a wireless network versus a wired network, which of the following statements are true? (Choose all that apply.)

   A. Using promiscuous mode to view all packets applies on both wired and wireless networks.

   B. Being in monitor mode allows for the capture of all 802.11 activity, without connection to the access point.

   C. Wireless signals can be relatively limited beyond a physical presence such as a fence.

   D. Strong, secure encryption provides no protection against data exposed via eavesdropping.

1. B	**8.** C	**15.** B
2. D	**9.** A	**16.** B
3. C	**10.** D	**17.** C
4. B	**11.** B	**18.** D
5. D	**12.** A	**19.** B
6. B	**13.** C	**20.** D
7. A	**14.** C	**21.** A, B

1. Which of the following is *not* an example of reconnaissance or gathering information of the target company through open source intelligence?

   A. Using LinkedIn and other social media to gather e-mail addresses of top executives

   B. Performing passive reconnaissance by capturing packets and scanning ports

   C. Monitoring job sites to learn what technologies are used

   D. Performing DNS harvesting of company network data from external DNS servers

   ☑ **B** is correct. Capturing packets and scanning ports are not examples of passive reconnaissance. Scanning ports is considering active reconnaissance. If your activities could create entries in a log, then those actions are not passive.

   ☒ **A, C,** and **D** are incorrect. **A** is incorrect because LinkedIn is a site external to the company. You can interact with LinkedIn to gather information about a company without directly interacting with that company. Therefore, this is a form of open source intelligence gathering. **C** is incorrect because, like LinkedIn, the job sites are presumed to be external to the company. **D** is incorrect because DNS harvesting involves interacting with DNS servers outside the company's DNS servers, versus interacting with internal DNS servers.

2. What is the name of the command-line version of Wireshark?

   A. nmap

   B. tcpdump

   C. Nessus

   D. TShark

   ☑ **D** is correct. TShark is the command-line interface of Wireshark.

   ☒ **A, B,** and **C** are incorrect. **A** is incorrect because nmap is a port scanning tool, not a command-line interface to Wireshark. **B** is incorrect because, although tcpdump is indeed a packet capturing tool, it is not the command-line version of Wireshark. **C** is incorrect because Nessus is a vulnerability scanning tool, not a command-line packet capturing tool.

3. You're at an employee's workstation. You need to quickly determine what other machines this system is talking to. You don't have time to install extra tools. What command-line utility and command-line switch will reveal connections between this workstation and others?

   A. tcpdump -i -eth0

   B. nikto -host

   C. netstat -a

   D. nbtstat -A

☑ **C** is correct. The utility netstat is on the workstation and is already a part of the operating system. Netstat is a command-line utility for viewing network statistics information, such as what connections and protocols are in use. The command-line switch **-a** will display all connections and listening ports.

☒ **A, B,** and **D** are incorrect. **A** is incorrect because tcpdump is a packet capturing utility. The **-i** switch is for specifying an interface. **B** is incorrect because Nikto is a utility for scanning web vulnerabilities. The command-line switch **-host** will set the target host by IP or hostname. **D** is incorrect because the utility nbtstat informs you about NetBIOS connections. Although both nbtstat and netstat are available in most Windows versions, the utility netstat is best for determining all the current network connections.

4. You suspect an employee's workstation may be the source of malicious traffic. Which of the following steps is the best course of action to determine both the type of traffic and this workstation's participation in the traffic?

   A. Set up packet capturing on a network device upstream from the workstation.

   B. Set up packet capturing on the suspect workstation.

   C. Set up packet capturing on a small group of servers identified as targets.

   D. Install antivirus software on the suspect workstation.

   ☑ **B** is correct. Capturing packets from the suspect workstation will yield complete information regarding this workstation as the source, thus demonstrating both the types of traffic and how the workstation fits into the situation.

   ☒ **A, C,** and **D** are incorrect. **A** is incorrect because, although capturing packets is correct, capturing them from the network may miss traffic routed outside of the capturing device. The optimum location for capturing is on the workstation itself. **C** is incorrect because capturing packets on a few targets would likely mean missing specific traffic to unknown targets. **D** is incorrect because, although antivirus software might help identify malware, it might not help identify the type of traffic, nor will it answer whether the traffic is associated with any quarantined malware.

5. At a few employee workstations, including a suspect system, you bring up a command window and type **arp -a** to display the cached entries of hostnames and IP addresses, as well as those IPs resolved to a MAC address. At first glance, today's entries seem normal. However, you know for a fact these MAC addresses are not how they were or should be. This illustration shows what the cache was before the suspicious behavior:

Alan's system IP address: 10.1.1.20		Gail's system IP address: 10.1.1.34		Sam's system IP address: 10.1.1.90	
IP address	Hardware address	IP address	Hardware address	IP address	Hardware address
10.1.1.34	Gail's MAC	10.1.1.20	Alan's MAC	10.1.1.20	Alan's MAC
10.1.1.90	Sam's MAC	10.1.1.90	Sam's MAC	10.1.1.34	Gail's MAC

And this illustration shows today's new cached entries:

Alan's system IP address: 10.1.1.20	
IP address	Hardware address
10.1.1.34	Sam's MAC
10.1.1.90	Sam's MAC

Gail's system IP address: 10.1.1.34	
IP address	Hardware address
10.1.1.20	Sam's MAC
10.1.1.90	Sam's MAC

Sam's system IP address: 10.1.1.90	
IP address	Hardware address
10.1.1.20	Alan's MAC
10.1.1.34	Gail's MAC

Notice the differences between the illustrations. From these differences, which is the suspect system and what technique is being used?

A. DNS poisoning, and both Alan and Gail's systems are attacking.

B. ARP poisoning, and Alan's system is the attacker.

C. ARP poisoning, and Gail's system is the attacker.

D. ARP poisoning, and Sam's system is the attacker.

☑ **D is correct.** ARP poisoning is the technique, which is apparent by the changed ARP cache entries, and the second illustration shows Sam's system as the new target MAC address for traffic intended for Gail and Alan's systems. Thus, we can assume Sam's system is the culprit.

☒ **A, B,** and **C** are incorrect. **A** is incorrect because DNS poisoning or DNS spoofing involves spreading illegitimate DNS information, which isn't evident in the illustration or mentioned in the text. **B** and **C** are incorrect because the second illustration shows Sam's system as the new MAC entry, not Alan's or Gail's.

6. Utilizing search sites as well as professional and social media sites with the goal of gathering contact information is an example of what?

A. CVSS

B. OSINT

C. Social engineering

D. Phishing

☑ **B is correct.** OSINT, or open source intelligence, refers to gathering information about a target without directly interacting with that target's infrastructure.

☒ **A, C,** and **D** are incorrect. **A** is incorrect because CVSS stands for Common Vulnerability Scoring System, which is the industry standard method for ranking vulnerabilities. **C** is incorrect because social engineering involves interacting with people, not websites. **D** is incorrect because phishing involves e-mailing potential targets.

7. A small business is concerned about the threat of social media profiling on its employees. Which of the following actions could you take to best mitigate the threat?

A. Demonstrate phishing examples to the users.

B. Increase the level of detail in the system logs.

C. Review the social media application logs with management.

D. Review job site listings with HR and systems administrators.

☑ **A** is correct. Phishing e-mails are a common result of targeted social media profiling. Showing users the dangers of phishing might improve their social profiles.

☒ **B, C,** and **D** are incorrect. **B** is incorrect because system logs provide no reflection of social media profiling. **C** is incorrect because management already is aware of the problem, and reviewing application logs accomplishes little here. **D** is incorrect because job site listings are not the problem.

8. Which of the following is *not* an example of a virtualization technology?

A. Containers

B. Software-defined networking

C. Mirroring

D. Hypervisors

☑ **C** is correct. Mirroring describes a technique of fault tolerance in storage, or in the case of switch ports, it describes copying network traffic. Mirroring is not a virtualization technology.

☒ **A, B,** and **D** are incorrect. Containers, software-defined networking (SDN), and hypervisors are all virtualization technologies.

9. Which of the following is a Type 2 hypervisor?

A. VMware Player

B. Microsoft Hyper-V

C. VMware ESX

D. Kernel-based Virtual Machine

☑ **A** is correct. VMware Player is a Type 2 hypervisor, which means it runs from within an operating system.

☒ **B, C,** and **D** are incorrect. Microsoft's Hyper-V, VMware ESX, and Kernel-based Virtual Machine are all Type 1 hypervisors, also called bare-metal hypervisors because the software runs directly on the "bare metal" hardware, not within an OS.

10. Which of the following is *not* an actual cloud computing technology?

   A. IaaS

   B. SaaS

   C. PaaS

   D. SDN

   ☑ **D** is correct. Although SDN (or software-defined networking) is a virtualization technology, it is not necessarily in the cloud.

   ☒ **A, B,** and **C** are incorrect. **A** is incorrect because Infrastructure as a Service (IaaS) describes utilizing a complete infrastructure from a service provider. **B** is incorrect because Software as a Service (SaaS) describes user access to specific applications from a service provider. **C** is incorrect because Platform as a Service (PaaS) describes running a platform on top of a server operating system.

11. You are tasked with scanning across the network space 192.168.2.x and identifying what operating systems are presently running. Select the correct tool and command-line switch necessary to determine what operating systems are running on that subnet.

   A. nikto -Version 192.168.2.0

   B. nmap -O 192.168.2.0/24

   C. syslog -network 192.168.2.0-192.168.2.254

   D. netstat -a 192.168.2.0 /24

   ☑ **B** is correct. Nmap is capable of detecting operating systems, and the command-line syntax shown is correct.

   ☒ **A, C,** and **D** are incorrect. The utilities nikto, syslog, and netstat are incapable of determining the operating systems.

12. Referring to Figure 1-1, select from the following actions what the person's likely intentions are.

   A. Assessing what web vulnerabilities are present

   B. Inventorying the web configuration settings

   C. Locating the host web server from the network

   D. Reviewing the web server's HTTP methods

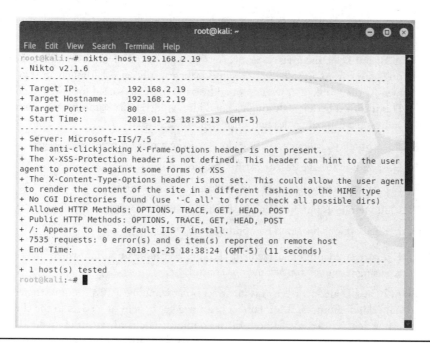

Figure 1-1   Running nikto at the command line

☑ **A** is correct. The tool shown is Nikto, a web vulnerability scanner. The person used Nikto to scan for vulnerabilities on the web server at address 192.168.2.19.

☒ **B, C,** and **D** are incorrect. **B** is incorrect because web server configuration settings are not adequately collected. **C** is incorrect because Nikto is not a network scanner, nor can it identify where is the web server is on a network. **D** is incorrect because, although Nikto does show the HTTP methods, that's not its intended purpose.

13. A company has suffered a recent incident where a print server was infected with malware and began aggressively scanning other machines on the network. The malware-infected server was identified only after a significant number of other machines were experiencing issues. Although the problem was contained, the timing was an issue. The company asks you to suggest how responding to problems like this could be done more quickly. What do you suggest?

   A. The company should review the firewall rules for areas to improve.

   B. The company should install an IDS on the network.

   C. The company should install an IPS on the network.

   D. The company should scan for further vulnerable print servers.

☑ **C** is correct. An IPS would not only identify the problem but immediately react to contain or eliminate it.

☒ **A, B,** and **D** are incorrect. **A** is incorrect because the problem was not described as originating from outside the firewall. **B** is incorrect because, although an IDS would identify the problem, it would not address the company's need for faster response. **D** is incorrect because, although a good idea, vulnerability scanning would not address the company's desire for fast response.

14. What is a primary challenge to using cloud storage versus on-premises storage?

   A. On-premises storage doesn't permit mobile access.

   B. Expensive software licensing and hardware for cloud services.

   C. Cloud resources put more emphasis on identity management.

   D. Limited options for cloud computing.

   ☑ **C** is correct. Identity management becomes ever more important when users are accessing resources away from your control.

   ☒ **A, B,** and **D** are incorrect. **A** is incorrect because mobile access is not restricted to only cloud resources. **B** is incorrect because a key benefit of services in the cloud is how inexpensive it is without the need to purchase hardware or upgrades. **D** is incorrect because cloud computing can take many forms: Infrastructure as a Service, Platform as a Service, or simply Software as a Service.

15. Wireshark and tcpdump are examples of what kind of application?

   A. Syslog aggregators

   B. Packet analyzers

   C. Intrusion detection systems

   D. Port scanners

   ☑ **B** is correct. Wireshark and tcpdump are packet capturing and analysis tools. Both will allow you to capture and view packets as well as perform varying levels of analysis on network traffic.

   ☒ **A, C,** and **D** are incorrect. Neither Wireshark nor tcpdump perform as a syslog aggregator, an intrusion detection system, or a port scanner. Although Wireshark could technically be set to alert if a particular packet or part of a packet were captured, that is far from its intended purpose.

16. Which of the following is not included when capturing packet headers but is provided with full packet capture?

   A. Source address

   B. Payload

   C. Protocol flags

   D. Destination address

☑ **B** is correct. The payload is not captured when only the packet header is captured.

☒ **A, C,** and **D** are incorrect. The header contains source and destination addresses, protocol flags, TTL, a header checksum, and protocol version—all dependent on the exact protocol in use.

17. Which of the following statements is not true when it comes to syslog?

   A. Syslog supports a broad range of devices and events.

   B. Messages can be aggregated into a single, nonhierarchical feed.

   C. Devices are polled for messages, echoing back to a syslog server.

   D. The syslog protocol and messaging come native in most firewalls and network devices as well as most *nix systems.

   ☑ **C** is correct. Syslog does not "poll" devices for event messages. Syslog messages are only sent to a syslog server, with no prompting.

   ☒ **A, B,** and **D** are incorrect. **A** is incorrect because a wide variety of devices and types of messages are supported by syslog. **B** is incorrect because syslog messages are collected and shown as a flat feed. **D** is incorrect because such network devices and *nix systems do support syslog.

18. A company is frustrated by its firewall's inability to catch higher-level malicious attacks, such as SQL injection and cross-site scripting (XSS). The firewall is unable to distinguish between valid HTTP traffic and malicious attacks when such traffic traverses the firewall on port 80. What do you see as the primary limitation of the firewall?

   A. The firewall is an application-layer firewall, unable to identify the higher-layer data.

   B. The firewall needs to be partnered with an IDS or IPS.

   C. The firewall rules need to be reviewed and likely changed.

   D. The firewall is a layer 3 or 4 device and should be replaced with an application-layer device.

   ☑ **D** is correct. The problem described seems to point to a standard firewall that's unable to inspect application-layer traffic. It should be replaced with a capable, application-layer firewall.

   ☒ **A, B,** and **C** are incorrect. **A** is incorrect because it is a false to claim the application-layer firewall is unable to identify higher-layer data. **B** is incorrect because, although an IDS/IPS would help, the firewall's shortcoming is the primary issue here. **C** is incorrect because the rules are likely not able to address the application-layer issue.

19. If an attacker is using nmap to map the network topology, which of the returned states of the port scans provides the least information?

   A. Unfiltered

   B. Filtered

   C. Closed

   D. Open

☑ **B** is correct. Filtered state means the nmap probe scan was unable to reach the port, to hear back whether the port was open or closed. This would make the attacker's efforts most difficult in mapping the network topology in order to understand the various network areas such DMZ, perimeter devices, and other key network components.

☒ **A, C,** and **D** are incorrect. **A** is incorrect because unfiltered means nmap was able to reach the port but was unable to determine conclusively whether it was open or closed. The unfiltered state only applies when an ACK scan is being performed, often to map firewall rulesets. **C** is incorrect because closed means the port was reached and was decidedly closed. **D** is incorrect because open means the port was reached and was concluded to be open or listening.

20. What would be an appropriate tool for performing service discovery on a large network?

    A. An IDS (but no IPS) placed anywhere on the servers' local subnet

    B. A HIDS placed on a target server

    C. Any tool able to review firewall logs or router ACLs

    D. A port scanner

    ☑ **D** is correct. A port scanner would quickly reveal what ports (and the services behind them) are open and listening on devices on the scanned network.

    ☒ **A, B,** and **C** are incorrect. **A** and **B** are incorrect because an IDS/HIDS (but not an IPS) should alert on valid services instead of only on detected malware traffic. **C** is incorrect because reviewing firewall logs and router ACLs will tell about flagged traffic attempts and permitted traffic, but provides little information about services and the systems providing them.

21. When you're capturing packets on a wireless network versus a wired network, which of the following statements are true? (Choose all that apply.)

    A. Using promiscuous mode to view all packets applies on both wired and wireless networks.

    B. Being in monitor mode allows for the capture of all 802.11 activity, without connection to the access point.

    C. Wireless signals can be relatively limited beyond a physical presence such as a fence.

    D. Strong, secure encryption provides no protection against data exposed via eavesdropping.

    ☑ **A** and **B** are correct. **A** is correct because promiscuous mode, if supported by the wireless card, is what allows the card to process all 802.11 activity, not just traffic targeted to that card. **B** is correct because monitor mode allows the same visibility to all activity, even without being connected to an access point.

    ☒ **C** and **D** are incorrect. **C** is incorrect because wireless signals are generally not too affected by thin physical structures such as fences. The distance from the access point has more of an effect on signal strength. **D** is incorrect because strong encryption does indeed protect against eavesdropping when data is gathered. The signal can be collected, but encryption ensures confidentiality.

Analyzing the Results of Reconnaissance

This chapter includes questions on the following topics:

- Sources of data to consider in your analysis
- Point-in-time data analysis
- Data correlation and analysis
- Common tools used in security analytics

In the prior chapter, you applied tools and techniques to conduct reconnaissance. Benefiting from reconnaissance takes more than just collecting information. To benefit, you need to both collect and analyze that information. The analysis is what changes the collected data into something useful—something that helps the security analyst identify and measure what an attacker would consider as targets.

Careful analysis involves a variety of sources and methods. Sources include various logs, devices on the perimeter or within the network, and data you've personally collected. You might analyze data from a snapshot in time or across a period of time. Depending on what you're looking for, you have an assortment of tools at your disposal—and that is what this chapter is all about.

1. Which of the following data sources would offer the least diverse, most precise kind of information?

   A. Syslogs

   B. Firewalls logs

   C. Packet captures

   D. Nmap results

2. What device combines the functionality of a traditional firewall and an IPS?

   A. Next-Generation Firewall

   B. DSN firewall

   C. Enterprise firewall

   D. Discovery firewall

3. Which of the following are the two types of approaches to analyzing data?

   A. Compare and contrast

   B. Correlation

   C. Patterned

   D. Point-in-time

4. In an IP packet header, what field value is decremented with each interface the packet goes through?

   A. Fragment offset

   B. ToS

   C. TTL

   D. IHL

5. Which of the following is an example of point-in-time analysis?

   A. Anomaly analysis

   B. Behavioral analysis

   C. Availability analysis

   D. Traffic analysis

Use the following scenario to answer Questions 6–9:

Recently, a few users have been complaining that their workstations are exhibiting some strange behavior. However, you find no obvious events showing up in system logs, and the application logs show nothing out of the ordinary. You suspect the issue could be new malware and decide to delve deeper.

6. You inspect logs from multiple sources. Your hope is to find some odd behavior. What type of analysis are you performing now?

    A. Trend

    B. Heuristics

    C. Packet capture

    D. Spatial trend

7. Based on your assumptions, how will you likely discover the malware?

    A. The packet trace will reveal a port famous for malware.

    B. The IDS log will show a matched signature.

    C. Your experience will guide your analysis.

    D. The long-term degradation in availability.

8. Select the most valuable data sources in this analysis. (Choose two.)

    A. IDS/IPS

    B. Router logs

    C. Security logs of affected servers

    D. Next-Generation Firewall

9. Which of the following would be the most valued SIEM tool in this scenario?

    A. Bro

    B. Snort

    C. Splunk

    D. ELK

10. Your company has used Splunk over many years, during a large growth in infrastructure. Lately, network engineers are complaining that Splunk requires a significant share of the network bandwidth. What might be the best course of action to resolve the network issue?

    A. Eliminate the "noisy" SIEM.

    B. Make use of heavy forwarders to index data at the source.

    C. Have the network engineer run a separate path for the Splunk data.

    D. Make the indexers fault tolerant.

11. Given an IP address, a security analyst seeks to identify and locate a system. Comparing Figures 2-1 and 2-2, select the *most* relevant difference between the two scans.

    A. The system represented in Figure 2-1 has several unknown services listening on dynamic ports.

    B. The system represented in Figure 2-2 is behind a firewall.

    C. The system represented in Figure 2-1 is behind a firewall.

    D. The scan shown in Figure 2-1 positively identifies the OS.

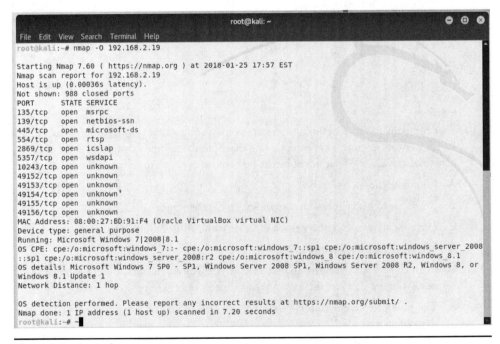

Figure 2-1 First scan

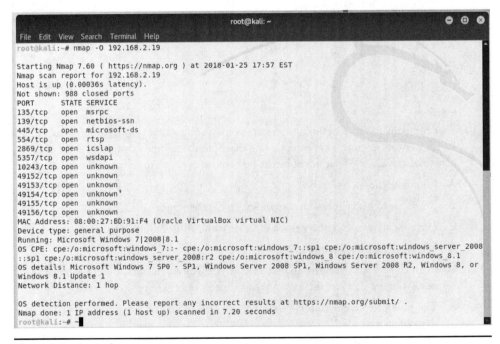

Figure 2-2 Second scan

12. Which of the following is not a valid Event Log category in Windows desktop systems?

   A. Application

   B. System

   C. Security

   D. Storage

   E. Audit

13. You are viewing the Event Log and you list the warnings from a Windows 10 machine. Referring to Figure 2-3, select the log category from which the warning came, as well as the Event ID and the machine name.

   A. Security, 1014, DNS Client

   B. Security, 1014, XERXES

   C. System, 268435456, XERXES

   D. System, 1014, XERXES

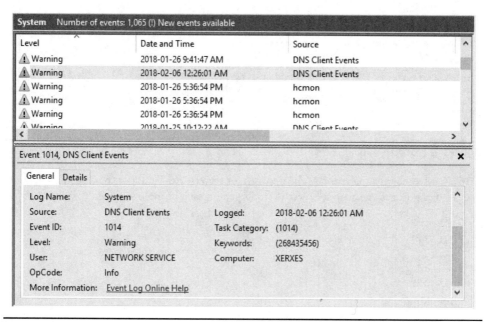

Figure 2-3   Event Viewer results

14. An analyst has launched nmap to scan an unknown machine. From the ports shown in Figure 2-4, what can the analyst assume is the operating system?

    A. Linux

    B. Windows

    C. Ubuntu

    D. OpenVMS

    E. Cisco IOS

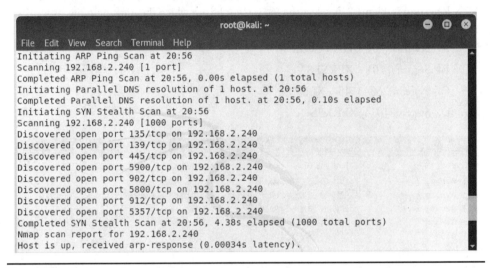

```
                              root@kali: ~                        ⊖  ⊡  ⊗
 File  Edit  View  Search  Terminal  Help
Initiating ARP Ping Scan at 20:56
Scanning 192.168.2.240 [1 port]
Completed ARP Ping Scan at 20:56, 0.00s elapsed (1 total hosts)
Initiating Parallel DNS resolution of 1 host. at 20:56
Completed Parallel DNS resolution of 1 host. at 20:56, 0.10s elapsed
Initiating SYN Stealth Scan at 20:56
Scanning 192.168.2.240 [1000 ports]
Discovered open port 135/tcp on 192.168.2.240
Discovered open port 139/tcp on 192.168.2.240
Discovered open port 445/tcp on 192.168.2.240
Discovered open port 5900/tcp on 192.168.2.240
Discovered open port 902/tcp on 192.168.2.240
Discovered open port 5800/tcp on 192.168.2.240
Discovered open port 912/tcp on 192.168.2.240
Discovered open port 5357/tcp on 192.168.2.240
Completed SYN Stealth Scan at 20:56, 4.38s elapsed (1000 total ports)
Nmap scan report for 192.168.2.240
Host is up, received arp-response (0.00034s latency).
```

Figure 2-4 nmap results

15. A cybersecurity analyst scans the network for servers with TCP port 636 open. What other port can the analyst expect to find open on each of those servers?

    A. 22

    B. 111

    C. 53

    D. 389

    E. 5000

16. What tool presents a graphical user interface for nmap?

    A. Nessus

    B. Zenmap

    C. TShark

    D. Qualys

17. An analyst is having trouble viewing the logs of a Cisco ASA firewall. What should the analyst type at the command line to verify what logging is enabled?

   A. # show running-config logging

   B. # log full show

   C. # log show all

   D. # show run all logging

18. After running tcpdump, an analyst reviews the output, which includes the following line:

   ```
   16:35:39.834754 > badguy.org.1289 > target.net.8008: FP 2921:4105(1184)
   ack 1 win 32120 (DF)
   ```

   What does the "FP" represent?

   A. Final Packet

   B. First Packet

   C. Fin Push

   D. Forward Packet

19. The director of technology has decided that the company requires an IDS. As the senior security analyst, you recommend Snort. The director requests that you flag any SSH request traffic coming from a known competitor's network. Examine the following rules and select the one that alerts if traffic originates from the network at 12.34.56.x/24 and is destined for the company's own web server (IP address 210.67.79.89).

   A. alert tcp 210.67.78.89 -> 12.34.56.0/24 80

   B. alert tcp 12.34.56.0 24 -> 210.67.79.89 21

   C. alert tcp 210.67.78.89 80 -> 12.34.56.0/24 any

   D. alert tcp 12.34.56.0 24 -> 210.67.79.89 22

20. Users inform a security analyst that network performance is poor. The security analyst takes a quick look at a packet capture to determine if anything is obvious. Based on Figure 2-5, what should be the security analyst's first impression?

   A. ARP storm

   B. DDoS

   C. DoS

   D. Broadcast storm

No.	Time	Source	Destination	Info	Protocol
1	0.000000	Cisco251_af:f…	Broadcast	Who has 24.166.173.159? Tell 24.166.172.1	ARP
2	0.098594	Cisco251_af:f…	Broadcast	Who has 24.166.172.141? Tell 24.166.172.1	ARP
3	0.110617	Cisco251_af:f…	Broadcast	Who has 24.166.173.161? Tell 24.166.172.1	ARP
4	0.211791	Cisco251_af:f…	Broadcast	Who has 65.28.78.76? Tell 65.28.78.1	ARP
5	0.216744	Cisco251_af:f…	Broadcast	Who has 24.166.173.163? Tell 24.166.172.1	ARP
6	0.307909	Cisco251_af:f…	Broadcast	Who has 24.166.175.123? Tell 24.166.172.1	ARP
7	0.330433	Cisco251_af:f…	Broadcast	Who has 24.166.173.165? Tell 24.166.172.1	ARP
8	0.408556	Cisco251_af:f…	Broadcast	Who has 24.166.175.82? Tell 24.166.172.1	ARP
9	0.455104	Cisco251_af:f…	Broadcast	Who has 69.76.220.131? Tell 69.76.216.1	ARP
10	0.486666	Cisco251_af:f…	Broadcast	Who has 24.166.173.168? Tell 24.166.172.1	ARP
11	0.504694	Cisco251_af:f…	Broadcast	Who has 69.76.221.27? Tell 69.76.216.1	ARP
12	0.510684	Cisco251_af:f…	Broadcast	Who has 24.166.174.184? Tell 24.166.172.1	ARP
13	0.540733	Cisco251_af:f…	Broadcast	Who has 24.166.173.169? Tell 24.166.172.1	ARP
14	0.587308	Cisco251_af:f…	Broadcast	Who has 24.166.174.181? Tell 24.166.172.1	ARP
15	0.662937	Cisco251_af:f…	Broadcast	Who has 69.76.223.216? Tell 69.76.216.1	ARP

Figure 2-5 Wireshark packet list pane

21. What would be an appropriate tool for analyzing bandwidth consumption on the network?

    A. Wireshark

    B. TShark

    C. NetFlow

    D. IDS

22. Which of the following are key challenges to analyzing wireless networks? (Choose all that apply.)

    A. High confidence in the hardware addresses of wireless devices

    B. Recognizing what devices are authorized

    C. Having an inventory of all WAPs

    D. Determining whether the network is in ad-hoc or infrastructure mode

1. D	**9.** A	**17.** A
2. A	**10.** B	**18.** C
3. B, D	**11.** C	**19.** D
4. C	**12.** D	**20.** A
5. D	**13.** D	**21.** C
6. B	**14.** B	**22.** A, B
7. C	**15.** D	
8. A, D	**16.** B	

1. Which of the following data sources would offer the least diverse, most precise kind of information?

   A. Syslogs

   B. Firewalls logs

   C. Packet captures

   D. Nmap results

   ☑ **D** is correct. Nmap results are particularly focused as port scans and only contain the information asked for, depending on the command-line switches the operator uses.

   ☒ **A, B,** and **C** are incorrect. **A** is incorrect because syslogs can include a very wide variety of events, such as an application faulting, a security event, or something pertaining to the system itself. **B** is incorrect because firewall logs are also more diverse than nmap results. Although only related to traffic-related events, the logs are quite a diverse mix. **C** is incorrect because the traffic seen on any network can be wide ranging.

2. What device combines the functionality of a traditional firewall and an IPS?

   A. Next-Generation Firewall

   B. DSN firewall

   C. Enterprise firewall

   D. Discovery firewall

   ☑ **A** is correct. Next-Generation Firewall combines a traditional firewall with intrusion detection and prevention.

   ☒ **B, C,** and **D** are incorrect. There are no such devices as a DSN firewall, enterprise firewall, and discovery firewall.

3. Which of the following are the two types of approaches to analyzing data?

   A. Compare and contrast

   B. Correlation

   C. Patterned

   D. Point-in-time

   ☑ **B** and **D** are correct. Point-in-time analysis describes examining data around a snapshot in time, whereas correlation analysis focuses on anomalies or changes over time, whether you're searching for abnormal behavior, some outlier, or a trend.

   ☒ **A** and **C** are incorrect. **A** is incorrect because "compare and contrast" is not the term coined for such analysis. Although you could say it describes one type of analysis, it wouldn't include all aspects of correlation analysis. **C** is incorrect for similar reasons. "Patterned" analysis is not the term used to describe a standard approach for analyzing data.

4. In an IP packet header, what field value is decremented with each interface the packet goes through?

   A. Fragment offset

   B. ToS

   C. TTL

   D. IHL

   ☑ **C** is correct. TTL stands for Time To Live, the value set for how many hops a packet has to go through before ending and expiring. The starting value for TTL varies based on operating system, but the more popular OSs use a value of either 255 or 128.

   ☒ **A, B,** and **D** are incorrect. **A** is incorrect because the fragment offset facilitates breaking up a packet into smaller, individually transmitted units. **B** is incorrect because the Type of Service field helps set a priority for or quality to the packet. **D** is incorrect because the Internet Header Length value just denotes the length of the header.

5. Which of the following is an example of point-in-time analysis?

   A. Anomaly analysis

   B. Behavioral analysis

   C. Availability analysis

   D. Traffic analysis

   ☑ **D** is correct. Traffic analysis is an example of point-in-time analysis.

   ☒ **A, B,** and **C** are incorrect. These are all forms of correlation analysis.

Use the following scenario to answer Questions 6–9:

Recently, a few users have been complaining that their workstations are exhibiting some strange behavior. However, you find no obvious events showing up in system logs, and the application logs show nothing out of the ordinary. You suspect the issue could be new malware and decide to delve deeper.

6. You inspect logs from multiple sources. Your hope is to find some odd behavior. What type of analysis are you performing now?

   A. Trend

   B. Heuristics

   C. Packet capture

   D. Spatial trend

   ☑ **B** is correct. The scenario portrays a new, unknown behavior. From that, you know you cannot rely on known threats. This will require heuristics analysis.

☒ **A, C,** and **D** are incorrect. **A** is incorrect because careful trend analysis might only show effects of the malware, but won't disclose the malware itself. **C** is incorrect because packet capture analysis is helpful after you know what you're looking for, but searching for anomalies in a packet capture is looking for the proverbial "needle in a haystack." **D** is incorrect because spatial trend analysis deals with correlating between different geographical areas.

7. Based on your assumptions, how will you likely discover the malware?

   A. The packet trace will reveal a port famous for malware.

   B. The IDS log will show a matched signature.

   C. Your experience will guide your analysis.

   D. The long-term degradation in availability.

   ☑ **C** is correct. Heuristic analysis can't rely on a signature or known behavior. Instead, experience best guides your analysis.

   ☒ **A, B,** and **D** are incorrect. **A** and **B** are incorrect because the answer suggests a known signature (famous malware port or an IDS signature). **D** is incorrect because although trend analysis might possibly point out symptomatic differences, it will not discover and identify the malware.

8. Select the most valuable data sources in this analysis. (Choose two.)

   A. IDS/IPS

   B. Router logs

   C. Security logs of affected servers

   D. Next-Generation Firewall

   ☑ **A** and **D** are correct. The intrusion detection/prevention system very likely logged information relevant for your analysis. Similarly, the firewall might show if or when malicious traffic passed through to the affected systems.

   ☒ **B** and **C** are incorrect. The router log is unlikely to reveal any information specific to the suspected malware. The security logs of affected systems might yield valuable information. However, if the system is compromised, you cannot trust its logs as complete or accurate.

9. Which of the following would be the most valued SIEM tool in this scenario?

   A. Bro

   B. Snort

   C. Splunk

   D. ELK

☑ **A** is correct. Bro is both signature- and anomaly-based. Bro will watch sessions, monitoring for strange behavior. Bro is also able to extract executables from network traffic, retaining them for forensic analysis.

☒ **B, C,** and **D** are incorrect. **B** is incorrect because Snort as an IDS would be signature-based, and as such not likely to catch the new malware. **C** is incorrect because although Splunk is incredible as a SIEM, it wouldn't necessarily be the tool able to discover and identify new malware. **D** is incorrect because ELK is a package of three open source tools (Elasticsearch, Logstash, and Kibana), which together operate similarly to the commercial product Splunk.

10. Your company has used Splunk over many years, during a large growth in infrastructure. Lately, network engineers are complaining that Splunk requires a significant share of the network bandwidth. What might be the best course of action to resolve the network issue?

   A. Eliminate the "noisy" SIEM.

   B. Make use of heavy forwarders to index data at the source.

   C. Have the network engineer run a separate path for the Splunk data.

   D. Make the indexers fault tolerant.

☑ **B** is correct. Splunk normally sends raw data onto the universal forwarder to be indexed. Using heavy forwarders instead at each source can accomplish preprocessing, before the event data is forwarded.

☒ **A, C,** and **D** are incorrect. **A** is incorrect because eliminating the SIEM causes much more harm to the company's ability to monitor security information. **C** is incorrect because running a separate network path is far more work than necessary. **D** is incorrect because fault tolerance is not a solution to the problem of heavy network usage.

11. Given an IP address, a security analyst seeks to identify and locate a system. Comparing Figures 2-1 and 2-2, select the *most* relevant difference between the two scans.

   A. The system represented in Figure 2-1 has several unknown services listening on dynamic ports.

   B. The system represented in Figure 2-2 is behind a firewall.

   C. The system represented in Figure 2-1 is behind a firewall.

   D. The scan shown in Figure 2-1 positively identifies the OS.

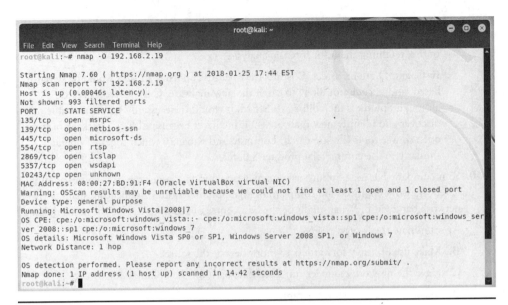

Figure 2-1   First scan

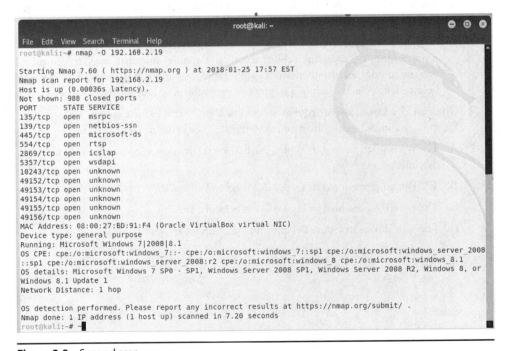

Figure 2-2   Second scan

☑ **C** is correct. Figure 2-1 shows a system that's likely behind a firewall. This is determined by noticing that the ports are reported as "filtered," as compared to "closed" in Figure 2-2.

☒ **A, B,** and **D** are incorrect. **A** is incorrect because the additional ports reported in the dynamic range (49152 to 65535) are likely not services that are listening. **B** is incorrect because Figure 2-2 reports closed ports. If the system were behind a firewall, the ports would be reported as filtered. **D** is incorrect because neither scan conclusively identifies the operating system.

12. Which of the following is not a valid Event Log category in Windows desktop systems?

   A. Application

   B. System

   C. Security

   D. Storage

   E. Audit

   ☑ **D** is correct. Storage is not an actual Event Log category.

   ☒ **A, B, C,** and **E** are incorrect. All of these answers—Application, System, Security, and Audit—are valid Event Log categories.

13. You are viewing the Event Log and you list the warnings from a Windows 10 machine. Referring to Figure 2-3, select the log category from which the warning came, as well as the Event ID and the machine name.

   A. Security, 1014, DNS Client

   B. Security, 1014, XERXES

   C. System, 268435456, XERXES

   D. System, 1014, XERXES

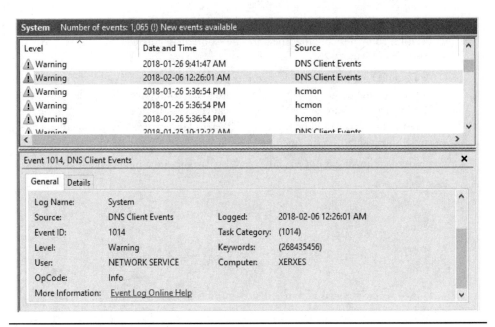

Level	Date and Time	Source
⚠ Warning	2018-01-26 9:41:47 AM	DNS Client Events
⚠ Warning	2018-02-06 12:26:01 AM	DNS Client Events
⚠ Warning	2018-01-26 5:36:54 PM	hcmon
⚠ Warning	2018-01-26 5:36:54 PM	hcmon
⚠ Warning	2018-01-26 5:36:54 PM	hcmon
⚠ Warning	2018-01-25 10:12:22 AM	DNS Client Events

Figure 2-3   Event Viewer results

☑ **D** is correct. The log name is shown as System, with an event ID of 1014. Also, the system name is shown as COMPUTER: XERXES.

☒ **A, B,** and **C** are incorrect. **A** and **B** are incorrect because of they have the wrong log category. Additionally, **A** has an incorrect system name. **C** is incorrect because it shows a numeric string from Keywords, which is not the same as the event ID (1014).

14. An analyst has launched nmap to scan an unknown machine. From the ports shown in Figure 2-4, what can the analyst assume is the operating system?

   A. Linux

   B. Windows

   C. Ubuntu

   D. OpenVMS

   E. Cisco IOS

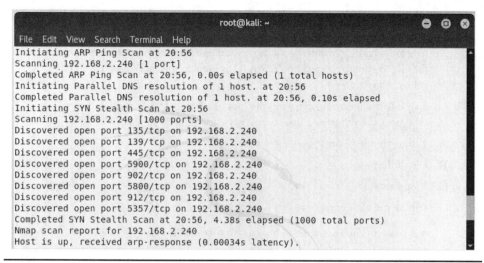

Figure 2-4 nmap results

☑ **B** is correct. The scanned system is Windows. The revealing evidence is the discovered TCP ports 135 and 139.

☒ **A, C, D,** and **E** are incorrect. Those operating systems would not show TCP ports 135 and 139 as open.

15. A cybersecurity analyst scans the network for servers with TCP port 636 open. What other port can the analyst expect to find open on each of those servers?

   A. 22

   B. 111

   C. 53

   D. 389

   E. 5000

   ☑ **D** is correct. Port 636 is open for LDAP over SSL (LDAPS). Any server that has port 636 listening very likely also has LDAP listening on port 389.

   ☒ **A, B, C,** and **E** are incorrect. **A** is incorrect because port 22 is typically for SSH. **B** is incorrect because port 111 is for MSRPC (Microsoft Remote Procedure Call). **C** is incorrect because port 53 is for DNS. Lastly, **E** is incorrect because port 5000 could be for several services, but nothing specifically associated with port 636.

16. What tool presents a graphical user interface for nmap?

   A. Nessus

   B. Zenmap

   C. TShark

   D. Qualys

☑ **B** is correct. Zenmap is the GUI version of nmap.

☒ **A, C,** and **D** are incorrect. **A** is incorrect because although Nessus is a GUI tool, it's a vulnerability scanner, not a port scanner. **C** is incorrect because TShark is the CLI version of Wireshark. Lastly, **D** is incorrect because Qualys is a GUI vulnerability scanner.

17. An analyst is having trouble viewing the logs of a Cisco ASA firewall. What should the analyst type at the command line to verify what logging is enabled?

   A. # show running-config logging

   B. # log full show

   C. # log show all

   D. # show run all logging

   ☑ **A** is correct. The command **show running-config logging** is the proper one to start with, in order to continue with a specific command for logging onto a Cisco ASA firewall.

   ☒ **B, C,** and **D** are incorrect. None of these commands is the correct one.

18. After running tcpdump, an analyst reviews the output, which includes the following line:

```
16:35:39.834754 > badguy.org.1289 > target.net.8008: FP 2921:4105(1184)
ack 1 win 32120 (DF)
```

   What does the "FP" represent?

   A. Final Packet

   B. First Packet

   C. Fin Push

   D. Forward Packet

   ☑ **C** is correct. The "F" stands for Fin, and the "P" for Push. The words Fin and Push denote what TCP flags were set (for example, Fin, Push, Urg, Syn, Reset, or Ack).

   ☒ **A, B,** and **D** are incorrect. The "P" in FP does not stand for "Packet."

19. The director of technology has decided that the company requires an IDS. As the senior security analyst, you recommend Snort. The director requests that you flag any SSH request traffic coming from a known competitor's network. Examine the following rules and select the one that alerts if traffic originates from the network at 12.34.56.x/24 and is destined for the company's own web server (IP address 210.67.79.89).

   A. alert tcp 210.67.78.89 -> 12.34.56.0/24 80

   B. alert tcp 12.34.56.0 24 -> 210.67.79.89 21

   C. alert tcp 210.67.78.89 80 -> 12.34.56.0/24 any

   D. alert tcp 12.34.56.0 24 -> 210.67.79.89 22

   ☑ **D** is correct. The Snort rule correctly alerts if an SSH request (over 22/TCP) comes from the network 12.34.56.0/24 to the company web server at 210.67.79.89.

☒ **A, B,** and **C** are incorrect. **A** is incorrect because the Snort rule has the source and destination addresses reversed and is monitoring port 80 (HTTP), when the question stated SSH traffic. **B** is incorrect because the Snort rule is monitoring for port 21 (FTP). **C** is incorrect because the Snort rule has the source and destination addresses reversed and is monitoring for traffic going to all TCP ports, not just port 22.

20. Users inform a security analyst that network performance is poor. The security analyst takes a quick look at a packet capture to determine if anything is obvious. Based on Figure 2-5, what should be the security analyst's first impression?

   A. ARP storm

   B. DDoS

   C. DoS

   D. Broadcast storm

No.	Time	Source	Destination	Info	Protocol
1	0.000000	Cisco251_af:f...	Broadcast	Who has 24.166.173.159? Tell 24.166.172.1	ARP
2	0.098594	Cisco251_af:f...	Broadcast	Who has 24.166.172.141? Tell 24.166.172.1	ARP
3	0.110617	Cisco251_af:f...	Broadcast	Who has 24.166.173.161? Tell 24.166.172.1	ARP
4	0.211791	Cisco251_af:f...	Broadcast	Who has 65.28.78.76? Tell 65.28.78.1	ARP
5	0.216744	Cisco251_af:f...	Broadcast	Who has 24.166.173.163? Tell 24.166.172.1	ARP
6	0.307909	Cisco251_af:f...	Broadcast	Who has 24.166.175.123? Tell 24.166.172.1	ARP
7	0.330433	Cisco251_af:f...	Broadcast	Who has 24.166.173.165? Tell 24.166.172.1	ARP
8	0.408556	Cisco251_af:f...	Broadcast	Who has 24.166.175.82? Tell 24.166.172.1	ARP
9	0.455104	Cisco251_af:f...	Broadcast	Who has 69.76.220.131? Tell 69.76.216.1	ARP
10	0.486666	Cisco251_af:f...	Broadcast	Who has 24.166.173.168? Tell 24.166.172.1	ARP
11	0.504694	Cisco251_af:f...	Broadcast	Who has 69.76.221.27? Tell 69.76.216.1	ARP
12	0.510684	Cisco251_af:f...	Broadcast	Who has 24.166.174.184? Tell 24.166.172.1	ARP
13	0.540733	Cisco251_af:f...	Broadcast	Who has 24.166.173.169? Tell 24.166.172.1	ARP
14	0.587308	Cisco251_af:f...	Broadcast	Who has 24.166.174.181? Tell 24.166.172.1	ARP
15	0.662937	Cisco251_af:f...	Broadcast	Who has 69.76.223.216? Tell 69.76.216.1	ARP

Figure 2-5 Wireshark packet list pane

☑ **A** is correct. The displayed packet list reveals a barrage of ARP packets. The ARP protocol resolves the hardware or MAC address to an IP address. ARP storms can be caused by malicious tools or by misconfigured network connections (for example, a bridging loop).

☒ **B, C,** and **D** are incorrect. **B** and **C** are incorrect because there is not enough evidence to believe that that many ARP packets were intended maliciously. Additionally, there are more effective ways to disrupt service than with an ARP storm. **D** is incorrect because although ARP is a protocol restricted to a broadcast domain, the more correct answer is ARP storm.

21. What would be an appropriate tool for analyzing bandwidth consumption on the network?

   A. Wireshark

   B. TShark

   C. NetFlow

   D. IDS

☑ **C** is correct. NetFlow Analyzer shows network bandwidth consumption, along with other metrics concerning the network utilization and health.

☒ **A, B,** and **D** are incorrect. **A** and **B** are packet analyzers and would illustrate the volume of packets in great detail, but would not give much insight on bandwidth consumption versus capacity. **D** is incorrect because an intrusion detection system gives very little information about the network's bandwidth, with the exception of an ongoing denial of service (DoS) attack.

22. Which of the following are key challenges to analyzing wireless networks? (Choose all that apply.)

    A. High confidence in the hardware addresses of wireless devices

    B. Recognizing what devices are authorized

    C. Having an inventory of all WAPs

    D. Determining whether the network is in ad-hoc or infrastructure mode

    ☑ **A** and **B** are correct. **A** is correct because the hardware or MAC addresses of wireless devices are fairly simple to modify. Most operating systems provide this ability without requiring special software. **B** is correct because wireless devices are so commonplace that the number of connected devices changes constantly—especially in an environment with a bring-your-own-device (BYOD) policy.

    ☒ **C** and **D** are incorrect. **C** is incorrect because having an inventory of the company's wireless access points (WAPs) should be fairly simple. It's assumed that the company installed the access points, so having that baseline is far more straightforward than having a comprehensive list of all wireless devices connected to the WAPs. **D** is incorrect because the administrator will (or should) know how the wireless network is set up.

Responding to Network-Based Threats

This chapter includes questions on the following topics:

- Practices for network and host hardening
- Deception techniques for improving security
- Common types of access controls
- Trends in threat detection and endpoint protection

If only making a network secure required the push of a button. Alas, it doesn't. The security analyst will be continually occupied with securing the network. Even after writing policy, hardening a configuration, and reviewing logs, the analyst must still make time to respond to threats as they become known. A secure network is not as much an end goal as it is a constant journey. The analyst's first goal is to ensure the network performs as the business needs, with minimal risk to confidentiality, integrity, and availability. The business needs for the network might be fairly stable, but the risks to the network are changing all the time.

To manage those risks and threats to the network, the cybersecurity analyst can respond with a variety of controls and techniques. Those controls and techniques range from additional hardware and software, to changes to the configuration and topology. Clearly, responding to network threats is a vital portion to being a cybersecurity analyst, and this chapter covers this important portion of the exam.

1. Currently a company web server is outside the company's internal network. The web server needs to be available for public access, but the external exposure poses a large, continuous risk. What is the *most* relevant recommendation for the company to mitigate risk to the web server?

   A. Implement a triple-homed firewall.

   B. Utilize IDS on the web server.

   C. Segment the internal network.

   D. Isolate the web server from the network.

2. Which of the following are benefits of network segmentation? (Choose all that apply.)

   A. Improving network traffic

   B. Mitigating risk from attackers

   C. Simpler network topology

   D. Preventing spillover of sensitive data

   E. Streamlining access to applications and services

3. On occasion, the administrators for the company servers are offsite. However, when required, they need access to the servers on the internal network. What would be your recommendation?

   A. Implement a firewall with a port of which only administrators are aware.

   B. Allow administrators to bypass the firewall only if using their own mobile devices.

   C. Configure the web server on the DMZ as a jump server.

   D. Install and configure a stand-alone jump box just inside the firewall.

4. A "captive portal" is an example of which of the following?

   A. DAC

   B. In-band NAC

   C. Out-of-band NAC

   D. Role-based NAC

5. NAC solutions grant access based on which of the following? (Choose all that apply.)

   A. Roles

   B. Rules

   C. Rates

   D. Location

   E. System patch level

   F. Time of day

6. To learn more about today's threats, a cybersecurity analyst could install a system that appears as a typical server but is available only as a lure for attackers. What is such a system called?

    A. Jump server

    B. Intrusion detection system

    C. Honeypot

    D. RBAC box

    E. Micro-segmented server

7. Which of the following are direct impacts of employing ACLs? (Choose two.)

    A. Controlling access

    B. Restricting malware from spreading

    C. Filtering specific traffic

    D. Enabling direct network routes

8. The following text is an example of a what?

    ```
    deny icmp 172.16.0.0 0.15.255.255 192.168.50.0 0.0.0.255
    ```

    A. Spam filter

    B. Access control list

    C. VPN tunnel setup

    D. IGMP setup

9. In the following ACL, what does "10.235.235.235" represent?

    ```
    permit tcp 10.15.0.0 0.255.255.255 10.235.235.235 0.255.255.255
    ```

    A. Subnet mask

    B. Source address

    C. Destination address

    D. The filtered port

10. When needing a new server, a company administrator starts with installing a pre-built server image. The image has most services running and applications already installed to make the task as easy as possible. As the cybersecurity analyst, what would be your *best* recommendation for the administrator?

    A. Rebuild the server image with as few services and applications as possible.

    B. Rebuild the server image with all services and applications installed but not running.

    C. Create several server images depending on the subnet.

    D. Run a vulnerability scanner on the already-deployed servers.

11. Which of the following are the method and purpose of a DNS sinkhole? (Choose two.)

    A. Redirecting DNS queries away from a known-malicious server

    B. Providing no DNS resolution responses

    C. Logging DNS resolution requests to determine infected hosts

    D. Logging DNS redirects to determine the infected domain

12. A company has a significant investment in network intrusion detection systems, which are able to inspect traffic with significant speed and reasonable effectiveness. However, a recent incident reveals that employees could use point-to-point encryption to mask data exfiltration. What would be the *best* recommendation for the company?

    A. Upgrade the IDS to an IPS.

    B. Employ endpoint security controls.

    C. Prohibit all uses of encryption.

    D. Replace the suspected employees.

13. What type of network access control is being demonstrated in Figure 3-1?

    A. Role-based

    B. Rule-based

    C. Time of day

    D. Location

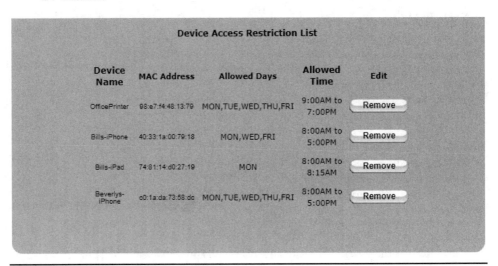

Figure 3-1 Device access restriction list

14. A cybersecurity analyst is told to enforce access control to files based on roles. Looking at the following two illustrations, select the appropriate answer when identifying an example of role-based network access control.

CySA+ Practice Exams Folder Permissions

	Read	Write	Add	Delete
Copy Editor	✓	✓	✓	
Author	✓	✓	✓	
Proj Mgr	✓	✓	✓	✓
Administrator	✓	✓	✓	✓

Illustration A

TPS Report Folder Permissions

	Read	Write	Add	Delete
P. Gibbons	✓	✓		
B. Lumbergh	✓	✓		
Bob 1	✓	✓	✓	
Bob 2	✓	✓	✓	
M. Waddams	✓			✓

Illustration B

   A. Illustration A

   B. Illustration B

   C. Both illustrations

   D. Neither illustration

15. Ensuring patches are properly tested and deployed can be a challenging but necessary task. Which of the following statements are true regarding patching? (Choose all that apply.)

   A. Patch testing should be done very soon after vendor release.

   B. Before patches are deployed, patches should be carefully tested, staged, and finally rolled out to production.

   C. If done carefully, patches can be tested, staged, and sent to production at the same time.

   D. If time is critical, patches can be tested and staged at the same time.

16. A cybersecurity analyst has identified a significant vulnerability to the company's payroll server application. The analyst's recommendation is to immediately patch the vulnerability. Unfortunately, because the application was developed internally and its developer has since left, the application cannot be patched. Without a patch, the analyst has to use other options to lessen the risk. Such options include using a host-based IDS on the application server and additional logging on upstream network devices. What is the term to describe the analyst's options?

   A. Network isolation

   B. Location-based access control

   C. Mandatory access control

   D. Compensating controls

17. What hardening technique can be described as "minimizing the attack surface"?

   A. Blocking unused ports and services

   B. Endpoint security

   C. Compensating controls

   D. Role-based access control

18. What access control model involves granting explicit authorization for a given object, per a given user?

   A. Group policies

   B. RBAC

   C. MAC

   D. Role-based

19. What is a technique that allows system administrators to apply configuration changes to several systems at once?

   A. NAC

   B. GPO

   C. ACL

   D. IDS

20. A company would like for access only to be granted if the employee's laptop meets a number of criteria. Specific conditions that each laptop must meet include only the approved version of Windows, mail application v2.5 or higher, web browser v8.0, and database application v1.18. Also, each laptop must have no unauthorized storage attached. What access control model would you recommend the company use?

   A. Location-based

   B. Rule-based

   C. Role-based

   D. Mandatory access control

1. A
2. A, B, D
3. D
4. B
5. A, B, D, E, F
6. C
7. A, C

8. B
9. C
10. A
11. A, C
12. B
13. C
14. A

15. A, B, D
16. D
17. A
18. C
19. B
20. B

1. Currently a company web server is outside the company's internal network. The web server needs to be available for public access, but the external exposure poses a large, continuous risk. What is the *most* relevant recommendation for the company to mitigate risk to the web server?

   A. Implement a triple-homed firewall.

   B. Utilize IDS on the web server.

   C. Segment the internal network.

   D. Isolate the web server from the network.

   ☑ **A** is correct. A triple-homed firewall is a firewall with three distinct networks attached—typically the external, the internal, and a DMZ. The DMZ is where the web server would be placed, accessible from the outside but more protected.

   ☒ **B, C,** and **D** are incorrect. **B** is incorrect because an IDS would alert constantly to malicious attacks while doing little to stop them or mitigate the risk of compromise. **C** is incorrect because segmenting the internal network does not help with the externally facing web server. **D** is incorrect because isolating the web server makes it inaccessible.

2. Which of the following are benefits of network segmentation? (Choose all that apply.)

   A. Improving network traffic

   B. Mitigating risk from attackers

   C. Simpler network topology

   D. Preventing spillover of sensitive data

   E. Streamlining access to applications and services

   ☑ **A, B,** and **D** are correct. Network segmentation benefits include improving traffic, mitigating network risks, and preventing spillover of sensitive traffic from one network segment to another.

   ☒ **C** and **E** are incorrect. **C** is incorrect because network segmentation does not simplify the network. **E** is incorrect because network segmentation can inadvertently stop a user on one network segment from having access to services or applications on another segment.

3. On occasion, the administrators for the company servers are offsite. However, when required, they need access to the servers on the internal network. What would be your recommendation?

   A. Implement a firewall with a port of which only administrators are aware.

   B. Allow administrators to bypass the firewall only if using their own mobile devices.

   C. Configure the web server on the DMZ as a jump server.

   D. Install and configure a stand-alone jump box just inside the firewall.

☑ **D** is correct. A jump box would give administrators special access to the internal network. A jump box should be a stand-alone server, with no unnecessary services or ports open that an attacker could possibly exploit.

☒ **A, B,** and **C** are incorrect. **A** is incorrect because having a particular "unknown" port open is not sound security. "Security through obscurity" is not good practice. **B** is incorrect because allowing any mobile device to bypass perimeter security is inviting a bad day if that mobile device falls into the wrong hands. **C** is incorrect because a jump server should not include any open ports that are unnecessary to its function as a jump box, thus ruling out the dual purpose as a web server.

4. A "captive portal" is an example of which of the following?

   A. DAC

   B. In-band NAC

   C. Out-of-band NAC

   D. Role-based NAC

   ☑ **B** is correct. A captive portal is a form of in-band network access control.

   ☒ **A, C,** and **D** are incorrect. **A** is incorrect because a captive portal is not an example of discretionary access control. **C** is incorrect because a captive portal is not out-of-band NAC. **D** is incorrect because a captive portal is not based on roles.

5. NAC solutions grant access based on which of the following? (Choose all that apply.)

   A. Roles

   B. Rules

   C. Rates

   D. Location

   E. System patch level

   F. Time of day

   ☑ **A, B, D, E,** and **F** are correct. Network access control types include role-based, rule-based, location-based, the system's health, and the time of day.

   ☒ **C** is incorrect. "Rates" is not an option for setting ACLs.

6. To learn more about today's threats, a cybersecurity analyst could install a system that appears as a typical server but is available only as a lure for attackers. What is such a system called?

   A. Jump server

   B. Intrusion detection system

   C. Honeypot

   D. RBAC box

   E. Micro-segmented server

☑ **C** is correct. The administrator wants a honeypot to lure in attackers in order to learn from their activities.

☒ **A, B, D,** and **E** are incorrect. **A** is incorrect because a jump server is for administrators to use remotely to access a protected network. **B** is incorrect because an IDS is for monitoring for and alerting on malicious traffic. **D** and **E** are incorrect because both RBAC box and micro-segmented server are nonsensical terms.

7. Which of the following are direct impacts of employing ACLs? (Choose two.)

A. Controlling access

B. Restricting malware from spreading

C. Filtering specific traffic

D. Enabling direct network routes

☑ **A** and **C** are correct. **A** is correct because an access control list is primarily for controlling access. **C** is correct because using ACLs is a primary means of filtering traffic.

☒ **B** and **D** are incorrect. **B** is incorrect because, although an ACL does facilitate filtering malware, it is a specific task for which an ACL is just one option. The primary purposes of an ACL are to control access and filter traffic, generally by address, port, or protocol. **D** is incorrect because, although an ACL can enable a direct network route (via a "permit" ACL), that is not the sole or general purpose of an ACL.

8. The following text is an example of a what?

```
deny icmp 172.16.0.0 0.15.255.255 192.168.50.0 0.0.0.255
```

A. Spam filter

B. Access control list

C. VPN tunnel setup

D. IGMP setup

☑ **B** is correct. The string "deny icmp 192.168.50.0 0.0.0.255 172.16.0.0 0.15.255.255" is an access control list that denies ICMP traffic originating from the 192.168.50.0 subnet targeting any addresses between 172.16.0.0 and 172.31.255.255.

☒ **A, C,** and **D** are incorrect. **A** is incorrect because the ACL is not filtering spam but rather Internet Control Message Protocol (ICMP) traffic. **C** is incorrect because the ACL is not setting up a VPN. **D** is incorrect because the ACL is not configuring the Internet Group Management Protocol (IGMP).

9. In the following ACL, what does "10.235.235.235" represent?

```
permit tcp 10.15.0.0 0.255.255.255 10.235.235.235 0.255.255.255
```

A. Subnet mask

B. Source address

C. Destination address

D. The filtered port

☑ **C** is correct. The 10.235.235.235 in the ACL is the destination address.

☒ **A, B,** and **D** are incorrect. **A** is incorrect because the subnet masks are 0.255.255.255. **B** is incorrect because the source address provided is 10.15.0.0 (a subnet). **D** is incorrect because no port is provided in the ACL.

10. When needing a new server, a company administrator starts with installing a pre-built server image. The image has most services running and applications already installed to make the task as easy as possible. As the cybersecurity analyst, what would be your *best* recommendation for the administrator?

A. Rebuild the server image with as few services and applications as possible.

B. Rebuild the server image with all services and applications installed but not running.

C. Create several server images depending on the subnet.

D. Run a vulnerability scanner on the already-deployed servers.

☑ **A** is correct. Certainly the best recommendation is to rebuild the image to have enabled only the minimum number of services and applications running. Then the administrator would enable or install only what is needed for the particular target system.

☒ **B, C,** and **D** are incorrect. **B** is incorrect because having all services and applications installed still provides several more attack vectors compared to not installed, even if those added are not running. **C** is incorrect because creating several images might be more work than it is worth. Having them specific to the subnet makes little practical sense. **D** is incorrect because a vulnerability scan is a good idea, but it does not address the ongoing practice of installing an image with several services running.

11. Which of the following are the method and purpose of a DNS sinkhole? (Choose two.)

A. Redirecting DNS queries away from a known-malicious server

B. Providing no DNS resolution responses

C. Logging DNS resolution requests to determine infected hosts

D. Logging DNS redirects to determine the infected domain

☑ **A** and **C** are correct. The method of a DNS sinkhole is to redirect DNS queries by infected machines away from a known malware server. The purpose of a DNS sinkhole is to log DNS resolution requests to help identify what other machines are likely infected.

☒ **B** and **D** are incorrect. **B** is incorrect because the DNS sinkhole does return DNS responses, but just to an internal server, one on which those queries are logged. **D** is incorrect because the malicious domain is already known.

12. A company has a significant investment in network intrusion detection systems, which are able to inspect traffic with significant speed and reasonable effectiveness. However, a recent incident reveals that employees could use point-to-point encryption to mask data exfiltration. What would be the *best* recommendation for the company?

   A. Upgrade the IDS to an IPS.

   B. Employ endpoint security controls.

   C. Prohibit all uses of encryption.

   D. Replace the suspected employees.

   ☑ **B** is correct. Endpoint security is a necessary complement to network security. In this case, endpoint security controls would allow inspection of network traffic before it is encrypted.

   ☒ **A, C,** and **D** are incorrect. **A** is incorrect because an IPS will also not be able to view and inspect encrypted traffic. **C** is incorrect because banning widespread use of encryption might cause more harm than good, without knowing the full impact of such a ban. **D** is incorrect because employees cannot be terminated without just cause.

13. What type of network access control is being demonstrated in Figure 3-1?

   A. Role-based

   B. Rule-based

   C. Time of day

   D. Location

Device Access Restriction List

Device Name	MAC Address	Allowed Days	Allowed Time	Edit
OfficePrinter	98:e7:f4:48:13:79	MON,TUE,WED,THU,FRI	9:00AM to 7:00PM	Remove
Bills-iPhone	40:33:1a:00:79:18	MON,WED,FRI	8:00AM to 5:00PM	Remove
Bills-iPad	74:81:14:d0:27:19	MON	8:00AM to 8:15AM	Remove
Beverlys-iPhone	c0:1a:da:73:58:dc	MON,TUE,WED,THU,FRI	8:00AM to 5:00PM	Remove

Figure 3-1   Device access restriction list

☑ **C** is correct. The device restrictions are shown to be based on the allowed days and times.

☒ **A, B,** and **D** are incorrect. **A** is incorrect because there are no roles shown as conditions for access restriction. **B** is incorrect because there is no access restriction specific to a rule. **D** is incorrect because the location is unknown and not restricting access.

14. A cybersecurity analyst is told to enforce access control to files based on roles. Looking at the following two illustrations, select the appropriate answer when identifying an example of role-based network access control.

CySA+ Practice Exams Folder Permissions

	Read	Write	Add	Delete
Copy Editor	✓	✓	✓	
Author	✓	✓	✓	
Proj Mgr	✓	✓	✓	✓
Administrator	✓	✓	✓	✓

Illustration A

TPS Report Folder Permissions

	Read	Write	Add	Delete
P. Gibbons	✓	✓		
B. Lumbergh	✓	✓		
Bob 1	✓	✓	✓	
Bob 2	✓	✓	✓	
M. Waddams	✓			✓

Illustration B

A. Illustration A
B. Illustration B
C. Both illustrations
D. Neither illustration

☑ **A** is correct. Illustration A shows roles such as author, editor, and manager.

☒ **B, C,** and **D** are incorrect. **B** is incorrect because Illustration B shows names, not roles. **C** is incorrect because Illustration B is not correct. **D** is incorrect because Illustration A an example of role-based access control.

15. Ensuring patches are properly tested and deployed can be a challenging but necessary task. Which of the following statements are true regarding patching? (Choose all that apply.)

    A. Patch testing should be done very soon after vendor release.

    B. Before patches are deployed, patches should be carefully tested, staged, and finally rolled out to production.

    C. If done carefully, patches can be tested, staged, and sent to production at the same time.

    D. If time is critical, patches can be tested and staged at the same time.

    ☑ **A, B,** and **D** are correct. **A** is correct because patches should be tested within a short time after their release. **B** is correct because patches should be tested before being installed on production systems. **D** is correct because, if time is critical, testing and staging could be done in parallel, but before a patch goes on live production systems.

    ☒ **C** is incorrect. Patches should not be put into production without at least testing first.

16. A cybersecurity analyst has identified a significant vulnerability to the company's payroll server application. The analyst's recommendation is to immediately patch the vulnerability. Unfortunately, because the application was developed internally and its developer has since left, the application cannot be patched. Without a patch, the analyst has to use other options to lessen the risk. Such options include using a host-based IDS on the application server and additional logging on upstream network devices. What is the term to describe the analyst's options?

    A. Network isolation

    B. Location-based access control

    C. Mandatory access control

    D. Compensating controls

    ☑ **D** is correct. The options cited are compensating controls, meaning controls put in place because the primary recommendation (patching) was not available or feasible.

    ☒ **A, B,** and **C** are incorrect. **A** is incorrect because the application server wasn't isolated from the network. **B** is incorrect because the options mentioned do not include any location-based access control. **C** is incorrect because no options include mandatory access control.

17. What hardening technique can be described as "minimizing the attack surface"?

    A. Blocking unused ports and services

    B. Endpoint security

    C. Compensating controls

    D. Role-based access control

    ☑ **A** is correct. Having fewer running services and open ports means fewer possible vectors for attack. Blocking unused or unnecessary ports and services minimizes the area for potential attack and exploitation.

☒ **B, C,** and **D** are incorrect. **B** is incorrect because although endpoint security means hardening the host, it's not always synonymous with minimizing the attack surface. **C** is incorrect because compensating controls can include several ways of minimizing risk beside blocking unused ports or services. **D** is incorrect because RBAC is a specialized access control, not a means of minimizing the attack surface.

18. What access control model involves granting explicit authorization for a given object, per a given user?

    A. Group policies

    B. RBAC

    C. MAC

    D. Role-based

    ☑ **C** is correct. Mandatory access control requires giving explicit authorization to a given user for a given object. Used rarely outside of military and highly sensitive organizations, the MAC model includes labels for creating levels of access, using the terms Unclassified, Confidential, Secret, and Top Secret.

    ☒ **A, B,** and **D** are incorrect. **A** is incorrect because group policies are far less explicit than MAC, allowing for access to be passed down or inherited at an admin's discretion. **B** is incorrect because role-based access control is not explicit per user, but instead per role. **D** is incorrect because role-based is a form of network access control, controlling access by a role; it is not explicit to the user.

19. What is a technique that allows system administrators to apply configuration changes to several systems at once?

    A. NAC

    B. GPO

    C. ACL

    D. IDS

    ☑ **B** is correct. Group Policy Objects allow Windows system admins to push system changes to several machines at once.

    ☒ **A, C,** and **D** are incorrect. **A** is incorrect because network access control is more about facilitating access, not pushing system changes. **C** is incorrect because access control lists also manage access, not system changes. **D** is incorrect because an intrusion detection system does not make system changes.

20. A company would like for access only to be granted if the employee's laptop meets a number of criteria. Specific conditions that each laptop must meet include only the approved version of Windows, mail application v2.5 or higher, web browser v8.0, and database application v1.18. Also, each laptop must have no unauthorized storage attached. What access control model would you recommend the company use?

   A. Location-based

   B. Rule-based

   C. Role-based

   D. Mandatory access control

   ☑ **B** is correct. Rule-based access control allows for granting access based on all those criteria. Rules are created to identify and determine all the system health and configuration criteria mentioned.

   ☒ **A, C,** and **D** are incorrect. **A** is incorrect because location is unimportant. **C** is incorrect because no user roles were mentioned. **D** is incorrect because mandatory access control involves granting explicit access to specific users, not access based on system configuration.

Securing a Corporate Network

This chapter includes questions on the following topics:

- Penetration testing
- Reverse engineering
- Training and exercises
- Risk evaluation

Keeping the corporate environment secure can be a formidable task. Assuming the cybersecurity team has already hardened the network and hosts as covered in earlier chapters, there is already an established level of assurance of the environment's security. The next task is maintaining or raising that level. Fortunately, there are approaches and practices that work well.

Penetration testing can be a highly effective process at identifying and prioritizing needs to improve security at a company's environment. Penetration testing, beginning with top-level authorization and ending with a full briefing to management, pushes the cybersecurity analyst to react and defend against attacks without the real-world exposure of an actual attack. Coordinated training and exercises, along with other means of risk evaluation, will raise the environment's security level. Also discussed in this chapter are processes and practices to raise assurance in present hardware and software.

1. At the company where you lead the cybersecurity team, a junior analyst misunderstands risk evaluation. You begin explaining how risk evaluation is performed by assessing probability and impact. You end with explaining the main purpose of risk evaluation as a balance between which of the following factors? (Choose two.)

   A. Value of a risk

   B. Potential cost of a risk

   C. Cost of the control to mitigate the risk

   D. Potential annual revenue lost

   E. Probability of a risk occurring

2. What levels of company management can provide authorization to conduct penetration testing? (Choose all that apply.)

   A. Director of IT security.

   B. Chief executive officer or a similar senior executive.

   C. Owner(s) of the data.

   D. Most senior cybersecurity analyst.

   E. Approval is optional until testing results show a need for further analysis.

3. Guidelines are to be drawn up prior any penetration testing can begin, and they determine the exact nature and scope of the testing. What are these guidelines called?

   A. Penetration TTP (Tactics, Techniques, and Procedures) document

   B. ROE (rules of engagement)

   C. Scope and Invoicing document

   D. Discovery

4. The company CEO recently came back from a conference about cybersecurity. He learned that operational control reviews are important to conduct from time to time. The CEO even offered the following answers as ideas to review. Select from the following ideas which are applicable for an operational control review. (Choose all that apply.)

   A. Intrusion detection system

   B. RADIUS authentication server

   C. Security awareness training

   D. Acceptable use policy

5. The company has employed the same encryption methods for a considerably long time. As a new security analyst, you question the effectiveness and strength of the encryption. What is the *best* recommendation for how to proceed?

   A. Conduct a technical control review of encryption as a technical control.

   B. Conduct an operational control review of encryption as an operational control.

   C. Perform a risk assessment of the encryption strength.

   D. Perform a vulnerability assessment of a server and the data now encrypted.

6. The idea of examining a finished product in order to determine what its parts are and how they work together is called what?

   A. Process isolation

   B. Sandboxing

   C. Reverse engineering

   D. Risk evaluation

7. A company hires an outside penetration testing team. A scope is agreed upon, dictating what systems may be involved and what systems may not. The penetration team proceeds with its tasks, all the way up to exploitation, when suddenly a production server is knocked offline. With the possible exception of the authorization, what aspect of penetration testing is now the most critical?

   A. Reconnaissance

   B. Exploitation

   C. Communication

   D. Reporting

8. The act of using a one-way function to create a unique, fixed-length value from a variable-length file or string of data is called what?

   A. Fingerprinting or hashing

   B. Decomposition

   C. Qualitative analysis

   D. Reverse engineering

9. Reverse engineering is done on counterfeit hardware, but what is far more often the object being taken apart?

   A. OEM hardware

   B. Software or malware

   C. Applications developed in-house

   D. Sandboxed network devices

10. During an extensive review of military assets, a cybersecurity analyst discovered that at least one piece of hardware was counterfeit. Although there were no issues that made the counterfeit hardware seem suspicious, there remains a question about expected quality and unknown hidden "features." It was later revealed that the hardware was purchased from a different manufacturer than the one normally used. What is the primary issue at fault here?

   A. OEM documentation

   B. Trusted foundry

   C. Poorly executed technical control review

   D. Source authenticity

11. At the conclusion of a penetration test, what phase involves communicating to management about the results and lessons learned?

   A. Exploitation

   B. Reporting

   C. Authorization

   D. Lateral movement

12. On what type (or types) of training exercises do red, blue, and white teams perform?

   A. Tabletop exercises

   B. Tabletop and live-fire exercises

   C. Live-fire exercises and Tactics, Techniques, and Procedural

   D. Live-fire exercises

13. In live-fire exercises, three teams play different roles. The first team performs as the exercise moderator, documenting and evaluating the progress of the other two teams. The second team functions as attackers, reconnoitering and exploiting the corporate environment. Finally, the third team is composed of the "good guys," protecting the environment and countering the activities of the second team. When these teams perform together, this exercise can produce a great deal of lessons learned and actions (hopefully) to better protect the network. From the following answers, select the team color order associated with the respective teams described.

   A. White, blue, red

   B. Red, blue, white

   C. Blue, white, red

   D. White, red, blue

   E. Red, white, blue

   F. Blue, red, white

14. When a company is ready to challenge its cybersecurity team in order to determine its strengths and weaknesses, as well as to identify through a "live-fire" exercise what risks should be addressed next, the company would sanction a what?

    A. Penetration testing

    B. Security awareness training

    C. Risk evaluation

    D. Hardware review

15. Both qualitative analysis and quantitative analysis are approaches to evaluate what aspects of a risk? (Choose two.)

    A. Potential monetary loss to the company

    B. Likelihood of the risk occurring

    C. Severity of impact of the realized risk

    D. Material exposure

16. Which of the following are valid concerns when considering the timing of penetration testing? (Choose all that apply.)

    A. Availability of the defenders to react to attacks

    B. Impact on business operations during normal hours

    C. Availability of executive management for reporting

    D. Size and scope of the penetration test

17. An organization owns systems that are to be probed during a penetration test. Some of the systems intended for testing are production systems containing protected health information (PHI). What aspect of penetration testing is *most* in jeopardy of breaking the law due to regulatory compliance?

    A. Timing

    B. Scope

    C. Exploitation

    D. Reconnaissance

18. From all the penetration testing phases listed, select the phase that can be described as the riskiest and one where the situation can turn into a crisis *most* quickly.

    A. Reconnaissance

    B. Exploitation

    C. Timing

    D. Report to management

    E. Scope

19. Cybersecurity analyst Hank is conducting a risk assessment of the personnel data on an HR server. Obviously, any breach in confidentiality of that data would carry a critical impact. However, the server is hardened and maintained by junior analysts Walt and Jessie. Given the rating of "unlikely" for the likelihood of a confidentiality breach, what is the overall risk rating? (Refer to Figure 4-1.)

    A. The risk rating cannot be calculated.

    B. Low.

    C. Medium.

    D. High.

Figure 4-1 Qualitative risk matrix. The impact axis and likelihood axis show an established overall risk rating at each square where those axes meet.

20. Regarding the same server, a significant rise in utilization has prompted cybersecurity analyst Hank to investigate personally. To his surprise, illegal crypto-mining software is discovered running on the server. Given the nature of the software, its unauthorized installation, and its unknown origin, Hank immediately assesses that the critical data is at least likely to be jeopardized in a confidentiality breach. What is the overall risk rating now? (Refer to Figure 4-1.)

    A. The risk rating cannot be calculated.

    B. Low.

    C. Medium.

    D. High.

1. A, C	**8.** A	**15.** B, C
2. B, C	**9.** B	**16.** A, B, D
3. B	**10.** D	**17.** B
4. C, D	**11.** B	**18.** B
5. A	**12.** B	**19.** C
6. C	**13.** D	**20.** D
7. C	**14.** A	

1. At the company where you lead the cybersecurity team, a junior analyst misunderstands risk evaluation. You begin explaining how risk evaluation is performed by assessing probability and impact. You end with explaining the main purpose of risk evaluation as a balance between which of the following factors? (Choose two.)

   A. Value of a risk

   B. Potential cost of a risk

   C. Cost of the control to mitigate the risk

   D. Potential annual revenue lost

   E. Probability of a risk occurring

   ☑ **A** and **C** are correct. The purpose of risk evaluation is to strike a balance between the determined value of a risk and the determined cost of whatever control is used to mitigate the risk.

   ☒ **B, D,** and **E** are incorrect. **B** is incorrect because the potential cost of a realized risk is only part of the risk value. **D** is incorrect because annualized loss expectancy is one factor of quantitatively calculating risk, along with rate of occurrence. **E** is incorrect because probability is just part of the risk value.

2. What levels of company management can provide authorization to conduct penetration testing? (Choose all that apply.)

   A. Director of IT security.

   B. Chief executive officer or a similar senior executive.

   C. Owner(s) of the data.

   D. Most senior cybersecurity analyst.

   E. Approval is optional until testing results show a need for further analysis.

   ☑ **B** and **C** are correct. Typically in a medium- to large-sized company, a senior executive or the CEO would be aware of and sanction the penetration testing. In much smaller or private environments, the owner of the data, as the most senior person, can make the decision. In any case, strict rules of engagement would be key to approval.

   ☒ **A, D,** and **E** are incorrect. **A** is incorrect because the IT security director is not senior enough to accept liability for possible negative impacts from testing. Similarly, **D** is incorrect because the role of senior cybersecurity analyst is not senior enough. **E** is incorrect because approval is absolutely necessary. Without approval, penetration testing is unethical, if not illegal.

3. Guidelines are to be drawn up prior any penetration testing can begin, and they determine the exact nature and scope of the testing. What are these guidelines called?

   A. Penetration TTP (Tactics, Techniques, and Procedures) document

   B. ROE (rules of engagement)

C. Scope and Invoicing document

D. Discovery

☑ **B** is correct. Having the rules of engagement (ROE) is an absolute necessity before beginning any phase of a penetration test. The ROE determine what is within bounds, out of bounds, with whom to communicate, and so on. Most importantly, the approved rules of engagement function as your "get out of jail free" card, considering that without them, the penetration test is likely illegal.

☒ **A, C,** and **D** are incorrect. **A** is incorrect because TTP does not reference a standard document, but instead refers to the general techniques and processes of conducting the test. **C** is incorrect because there is no standard document called a "Scope and Invoicing" document. **D** is incorrect because discovery is an early phase of a penetration test, not some procedural document.

4. The company CEO recently came back from a conference about cybersecurity. He learned that operational control reviews are important to conduct from time to time. The CEO even offered the following answers as ideas to review. Select from the following ideas which are applicable for an operational control review. (Choose all that apply.)

A. Intrusion detection system

B. RADIUS authentication server

C. Security awareness training

D. Acceptable use policy

☑ **C** and **D** are correct. Both the security awareness training and the acceptable use policy (AUP) are examples of operational controls. Operational controls, also called administrative or policy controls, are security controls put into practice from business processes or policies and standards.

☒ **A** and **B** are incorrect. **A** is incorrect because an IDS is an example of a technical control. **B** is incorrect because the RADIUS server is also a technical control.

5. The company has employed the same encryption methods for a considerably long time. As a new security analyst, you question the effectiveness and strength of the encryption. What is the *best* recommendation for how to proceed?

A. Conduct a technical control review of encryption as a technical control.

B. Conduct an operational control review of encryption as an operational control.

C. Perform a risk assessment of the encryption strength.

D. Perform a vulnerability assessment of a server and the data now encrypted.

☑ **A** is correct. Encryption is a technical control. Conducting a technical control review is the best course of action when the long-term effectiveness of a technical control comes into question.

☒ **B, C,** and **D** are incorrect. **B** is incorrect because encryption is a technical control, not an operation control. **C** is incorrect because performing a risk assessment is important, but is only part of a technical control review. **D** is incorrect because performing a vulnerability assessment of the encryption in use might not produce a valid representation of the encryption's effectiveness.

6. The idea of examining a finished product in order to determine what its parts are and how they work together is called what?

   A. Process isolation

   B. Sandboxing

   C. Reverse engineering

   D. Risk evaluation

   ☑ **C** is correct. Taking a finished product apart in order to determine what its parts are and how they work is called reverse engineering.

   ☒ **A, B,** and **D** are incorrect. **A** is incorrect because process isolation speaks to quarantining a running process, not breaking it down into its components. **B** is incorrect because sandboxing refers to isolating a system from the network as a form of containment. **D** is incorrect because risk evaluation is about measuring a risk's impact and probability.

7. A company hires an outside penetration testing team. A scope is agreed upon, dictating what systems may be involved and what systems may not. The penetration team proceeds with its tasks, all the way up to exploitation, when suddenly a production server is knocked offline. With the possible exception of the authorization, what aspect of penetration testing is now the most critical?

   A. Reconnaissance

   B. Exploitation

   C. Communication

   D. Reporting

   ☑ **C** is correct. Communication is critically important for a penetration test, especially during a crisis, as described.

   ☒ **A, B,** and **D** are incorrect. **A** is incorrect because reconnaissance is performed at the beginning of the penetration test and is not appropriate when a production system fails. **B** is incorrect because exploitation was done just before the production system failed. **D** is incorrect because reporting is performed after the test is completed, when management can be calmly informed of the results.

8. The act of using a one-way function to create a unique, fixed-length value from a variable-length file or string of data is called what?

   A. Fingerprinting or hashing

   B. Decomposition

C. Qualitative analysis

D. Reverse engineering

☑ **A** is correct. The process to take a string of data or any file of any length through a one-way function to produce a unique fixed-length value is called fingerprinting or hashing.

☒ **B, C,** and **D** are incorrect. **B** is incorrect because decomposition refers to the principle of deconstructing something into its parts. **C** is incorrect because qualitative analysis refers to a subjective form of evaluating risks. **D** is incorrect because reverse engineering, performed by decomposition, means taking a finished product and learning what its made of as well as how it works.

9. Reverse engineering is done on counterfeit hardware, but what is far more often the object being taken apart?

A. OEM hardware

B. Software or malware

C. Applications developed in-house

D. Sandboxed network devices

☑ **B** is correct. The typical object being reverse engineered is a piece of software that's suspected to be or identified as malware.

☒ **A, C,** and **D** are incorrect. **A** is incorrect because OEM hardware is highly likely to be genuine and not counterfeit. **C** is incorrect because applications developed in-house might not always be perfect, but it's unlikely that they are compromised. **D** is incorrect because a network device, whether sandboxed or not, is unlikely to be taken apart under suspicion of being Trojaned or compromised.

10. During an extensive review of military assets, a cybersecurity analyst discovered that at least one piece of hardware was counterfeit. Although there were no issues that made the counterfeit hardware seem suspicious, there remains a question about expected quality and unknown hidden "features." It was later revealed that the hardware was purchased from a different manufacturer than the one normally used. What is the primary issue at fault here?

A. OEM documentation

B. Trusted foundry

C. Poorly executed technical control review

D. Source authenticity

☑ **D** is correct. The primary issue is an absence of source authenticity, or assurance that the source of the asset is reputable and authentic.

☒ **A, B,** and **C** are incorrect. **A** is incorrect because OEM documentation describes the documentation from the original equipment manufacturer. **B** is incorrect because trusted foundry is a U.S. government program that inspects and approves a manufacturer as authentic. **C** is incorrect because the problem was discovered by an "extensive hardware review," which leads one to think the review was at least somewhat successful.

11. At the conclusion of a penetration test, what phase involves communicating to management about the results and lessons learned?

A. Exploitation

B. Reporting

C. Authorization

D. Lateral movement

☑ **B** is correct. The phase of penetration testing that involves communicating results and lessons learned to management is called reporting.

☒ **A, C,** and **D** are incorrect. **A** is incorrect because the exploitation phase involves manipulating the discovered weaknesses in target systems. **C** is incorrect because authorization involves gaining executive support and approval for conducting the penetration test. **D** is incorrect because lateral movement refers to compromising systems "laterally" from the originally compromised system.

12. On what type (or types) of training exercises do red, blue, and white teams perform?

A. Tabletop exercises

B. Tabletop and live-fire exercises

C. Live-fire exercises and Tactics, Techniques, and Procedural

D. Live-fire exercises

☑ **B** is correct. The teams referred to as "red," "blue," and "white" are used during both live-fire exercises and table-top exercises.

☒ **A, C,** and **D** are incorrect. **A** is incorrect because teams are involved in more than just tabletop exercises. Tabletop exercises are an organized event with various roles involved to test out procedures. The tabletop exercises are intended for people to work through a simulated event as a "dry run." **C** is incorrect because "Tactics, Techniques, and Procedural" is not a form of exercise. **D** is incorrect because teams perform for more than just live-fire exercises.

13. In live-fire exercises, three teams play different roles. The first team performs as the exercise moderator, documenting and evaluating the progress of the other two teams. The second team functions as attackers, reconnoitering and exploiting the corporate environment. Finally, the third team is composed of the "good guys," protecting the environment and countering the activities of the second team. When these teams perform together, this exercise can produce a great deal of lessons learned and actions (hopefully) to better protect the network. From the following answers, select the team color order associated with the respective teams described.

A. White, blue, red

B. Red, blue, white

C. Blue, white, red

D. White, red, blue

E. Red, white, blue

F. Blue, red, white

☑ **D** is correct. The correct team color order is white, red, and blue (that is, the moderators, attackers, and defenders, respectively).

☒ **A, B, C, E,** and **F** are incorrect. All other color arrangements apart from "white, red, and blue" are incorrect. The moderators are referred to as the "white team." The attackers are referred to as the "red team," and the defenders (or "good guys") are referred to as the "blue team."

14. When a company is ready to challenge its cybersecurity team in order to determine its strengths and weaknesses, as well as to identify through a "live-fire" exercise what risks should be addressed next, the company would sanction a what?

A. Penetration testing

B. Security awareness training

C. Risk evaluation

D. Hardware review

☑ **A** is correct. Penetration testing is the process whereby a company seeks to test and challenge its cybersecurity team with a simulated attack.

☒ **B, C,** and **D** are incorrect. **B** is incorrect because security awareness training is an operational control to minimize risk. **C** is incorrect because risk evaluation is the measuring of a risk. **D** is incorrect because hardware review is hardly a challenge, but instead something the cybersecurity team may perform as part of a technical control review.

15. Both qualitative analysis and quantitative analysis are approaches to evaluate what aspects of a risk? (Choose two.)

A. Potential monetary loss to the company

B. Likelihood of the risk occurring

C. Severity of impact of the realized risk

D. Material exposure

☑ **B** and **C** are correct. The likelihood of a risk occurring and the impact severity are the two aspects of any risk.

☒ **A** and **D** are incorrect. **A** is incorrect because potential monetary loss is a quantitative factor of risk evaluation. **D** is incorrect because material exposure can be considered another form of potential loss.

16. Which of the following are valid concerns when considering the timing of penetration testing? (Choose all that apply.)

    A. Availability of the defenders to react to attacks

    B. Impact on business operations during normal hours

    C. Availability of executive management for reporting

    D. Size and scope of the penetration test

    ☑ **A, B,** and **D** are correct. The timing of a penetration test is guided by several factors. The most important of those factors are the size and scope of the test, the availability of the cybersecurity staff, and the potential impact on production systems.

    ☒ **C** is incorrect. Reporting to the executive management would occur at the conclusion of the penetration test. The reporting meeting is likely to be held weeks after the penetration exercise has been completed, to allow time for preparing the report.

17. An organization owns systems that are to be probed during a penetration test. Some of the systems intended for testing are production systems containing protected health information (PHI). What aspect of penetration testing is *most* in jeopardy of breaking the law due to regulatory compliance?

    A. Timing

    B. Scope

    C. Exploitation

    D. Reconnaissance

    ☑ **B** is correct. The scope of the penetration testing is largely defined by which systems are to be tested, and which systems are *not* to be tested. The system containing PHI cannot be included within the scope of to-be-tested systems. If penetration testers were to successfully probe for and exfiltrate healthcare information, it would be in violation of federal law.

    ☒ **A, C,** and **D** are incorrect. **A** is incorrect because the timing is not an issue with regard to the servers containing PHI. **C** is incorrect because exploitation isn't the aspect of testing that permitted the systems to be included. **D** is incorrect because reconnaissance might be helpful in determining the contents of the PHI server. However, the problem of scope is more directly at fault.

18. From all the penetration testing phases listed, select the phase that can be described as the riskiest and one where the situation can turn into a crisis *most* quickly.

    A. Reconnaissance

    B. Exploitation

    C. Timing

    D. Report to management

    E. Scope

☑ **B is correct.** The process of exploitation during a penetration test can be and often is quite risky. Penetration testers plan and prepare as much as possible for such events, but occasionally systems can give unanticipated responses. This is why authorization is of paramount importance.

☒ **A, C, D,** and **E** are incorrect. **A** is incorrect because reconnaissance is quite benign, save for the risk of being discovered by cybersecurity team members unaware of the authorized test. **C** is incorrect because timing is hardly risky, except to proceed carefully but efficiently through the exploitation phase with minimal effect on business operations. **D** is incorrect because reporting to management is not quite as risky as exploitation. **E** is incorrect because scope is not risky at all, unless it is ill-conceived to begin with.

19. Cybersecurity analyst Hank is conducting a risk assessment of the personnel data on an HR server. Obviously, any breach in confidentiality of that data would carry a critical impact. However, the server is hardened and maintained by junior analysts Walt and Jessie. Given the rating of "unlikely" for the likelihood of a confidentiality breach, what is the overall risk rating? (Refer to Figure 4-1.)

A. The risk rating cannot be calculated.

B. Low.

C. Medium.

D. High.

Likelihood		Negligible	Minor	Moderate	Major	Critical
	Very Likely	Medium	Medium	High	High	High
	Likely	Low	Medium	Medium	High	High
	Possible	Low	Low	Medium	Medium	High
	Unlikely	Low	Low	Low	Medium	Medium
	Negligible	Low	Low	Low	Low	Medium
				Impact		

Figure 4-1 Qualitative risk matrix. The impact axis and likelihood axis show an established overall risk rating at each square where those axes meet.

☑ **C** is correct. Given that the impact of a data breach is evaluated as "critical" and the likelihood is "unlikely," the overall risk rating is "medium."

☒ **A, B,** and **D** are incorrect. **A** is incorrect because the overall risk rating can be determined from the provided impact and likelihood risk factors of "critical" and "unlikely," respectively. **B** and **D** are incorrect because the overall risk rating is "medium."

20. Regarding the same server, a significant rise in utilization has prompted cybersecurity analyst Hank to investigate personally. To his surprise, illegal crypto-mining software is discovered running on the server. Given the nature of the software, its unauthorized installation, and its unknown origin, Hank immediately assesses that the critical data is at least likely to be jeopardized in a confidentiality breach. What is the overall risk rating now? (Refer to Figure 4-1.)

A. The risk rating cannot be calculated.

B. Low.

C. Medium.

D. High.

☑ **D** is correct. Given that the likelihood has risen from "unlikely" to at least "likely," with the impact evaluated as "critical," the overall risk rating is now "high."

☒ **A, B,** and **C** are incorrect. **A** is incorrect because the overall risk rating can be determined from the provided impact and likelihood risk factors of "critical" and "likely," respectively. **B** and **C** are incorrect because the overall risk rating is "high."

PART II

Vulnerability Management

Implementing Vulnerability Management Processes

This chapter includes questions on the following topics:

- The requirements for a vulnerability management process
- How to determine the frequency of your vulnerability scans
- The types of vulnerabilities found in various systems
- Considerations for configuring tools for scanning

Vital to strong security is being able to identify and understand the vulnerabilities in your environment. Identifying vulnerabilities requires knowing how to search and what to search for. To do this, you will need tools and methods as well as a process to identify them. Lastly, you need to effectively keep track of what vulnerabilities you find. Understanding vulnerabilities starts with what you're doing now—learning and applying the principles of information security.

The cybersecurity analyst can find and understand vulnerabilities in general, but to manage those vulnerabilities requires knowing the business they affect. This means understanding how the business's systems interact with one another, what data they use, and what processes are required for the business to function. Once some vulnerability is found, that vulnerability might be eliminated at one company but another company's operations must allow the vulnerability to stay. The vulnerabilities you must face are caused by the nature of your business and your data. (Wouldn't turning off all the servers eliminate many vulnerabilities?) Regulatory requirements and policy requirements will impact vulnerability management further. In this chapter, implementing a vulnerability management process is at the core of the questions provided.

1. A company needs a vulnerability scan performed on its internal network. After the company consults with an external cybersecurity analyst, the analyst immediately begins drafting a contract to outline conditions to be met for the scan. These conditions include limiting who is allowed to view the results, specifying what servers and data must not be accessed under any circumstances, and satisfying the company's need for two types of scans to be done quarterly. Which of the following is the *most* likely reason behind these conditions?

    A. Regulatory requirements

    B. Security policy

    C. Analyst's recommendation

    D. Past experience deems the contract prudent

2. Regulatory requirements can specify the need for vulnerability scanning when a company is in the financial or health industry. However, what *best* specifies vulnerability scanning as a requirement without regulatory requirement?

    A. CISO mandate

    B. Local and/or national legislation

    C. Corporate policy

    D. NIST 800-53

3. What is a technique that allows a company to vary resources spent toward protecting data according to a set value?

    A. Data encryption

    B. Data classification

    C. Data criticality

    D. Data storage location

4. With regard to asset inventory, how would a cybersecurity analyst classify assets such as financial systems, intellectual property, and a customer-facing ordering system?

    A. Noncritical

    B. Sensitive

    C. Credentialed

    D. Critical

5. When a company is developing a vulnerability management plan, its assets must be inventoried. Which of the following asset types would be included? (Choose all that apply.)

    A. Noncritical

    B. Critical

    C. Critical only

    D. On-site and assets of partners and suppliers

6. The frequency with which a company performs vulnerability scanning is dependent upon which of the following criteria? (Choose all that apply.)

   A. Scanning policy

   B. Vulnerability management planning

   C. Risk appetite

   D. Regulatory requirements

   E. Limitations of time, tools, and personnel

7. The cybersecurity analyst must consider several factors when determining vulnerability scanning frequency. Criteria such as network bandwidth, systems' CPU capacity, and number of qualified personnel are examples of which of the following?

   A. Soft restrictions

   B. Regulatory requirements

   C. Technical constraints

   D. Budgetary limitations

8. Apart from policies and regulatory requirements, what creates the largest impact on establishing an effective vulnerability scanning process?

   A. Regular routine and workflow of personnel

   B. Management style of the IT director or head of security

   C. Mandates from the chief of information security

   D. Personal whims of the CEO

9. When a company is configuring tools to perform vulnerability scans, which of the following would be the earliest step?

   A. Choosing the tool plug-ins

   B. Generating reports

   C. Establishing permissions and scanning credentials

   D. Establishing scanning criteria

10. A cybersecurity analyst is performing a vulnerability scan of a few systems, including a server processing protected health information (PHI). The scan of all servers completed successfully, with no interruption of service. To demonstrate proof of weaknesses found during the vulnerability scan, the analyst manages to exfiltrate documents from each server. Which of the following specifications of vulnerability scanning did the analyst likely breach?

    A. Using credentials when a noncredentialed scan would suffice.

    B. No vulnerability feed was evidenced.

    C. Permissions set incorrectly.

    D. Considering the sensitivity of the data on the scanned systems.

    E. Using agents when a server-based scan would suffice.

11. Which of the following reasons are valid arguments for using server-based vulnerability scanning instead of agent-based scanning? (Choose all that apply.)

    A. Erratic connectivity to remote and mobile devices

    B. Limited bandwidth

    C. Limited personnel availability for maintenance

    D. Occasional rogue device connecting to the network

12. When it comes time to execute a vulnerability scan, what are optional tools you might use to launch it? (Choose all that apply.)

    A. Nessus

    B. Burp Suite

    C. OpenVAS

    D. Vega

    E. FTK

    F. Nikto

13. After you complete your scan, creating heaps of output, you need to prepare a report. What are your options?

    A. As vulnerability tools rarely generate reports, there's no need for a report.

    B. It's common to pipe vulnerability tool output to a report generation tool.

    C. Nearly all vulnerability scanners generate standardized reports via XML.

    D. Every vulnerability tool generates some kind of report, but not using a standardized format.

14. It's time to deliver a vulnerability report to the stakeholders. What are your options for distribution? (Choose all that apply.)

    A. Automated delivery via the report generation component of the vulnerability scanner

    B. Delivered entirely via e-mail to all administrators

    C. Delivered manually, through face-to-face meetings

    D. E-mailing only the portions immediately relevant to the individual

15. What remediation step requires careful discussion concerning the scan results, with the goal of satisfying both the concerns of technical staff and the organization's business objectives?

    A. Validation of the results

    B. Prioritization of the results

    C. Distribution of the results

    D. Categorization of the results

16. Figure 5-1 shows the top portion of the results screen in Nessus when a scan has completed. The wide bar across the top separates quantities of results in varying colors. What is Nessus distinguishing by using colors?

   A. Scope

   B. Chronological order of the scan execution

   C. Association to the vulnerability feeds used

   D. Criticality of the findings

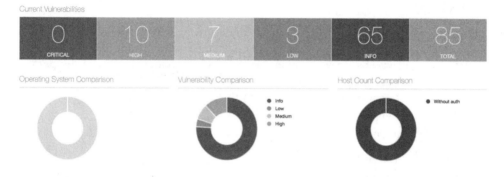

Figure 5-1 Nessus results screen

17. The chief information security officer is among many at a meeting about the vulnerability scan results. Everyone has the same table, shown in Figure 5-2. The discussion is focused on how to order the findings to remediate. The cybersecurity analyst focuses on criticality, wanting to fix the findings in the order shown: A, B, C, then D. The CISO instead wants the remediation order to be C, B, A, then D. What aspect caused the CISO to change the order of remediation?

   A. Criticality

   B. Cost

   C. Effort to fix

   D. Alphabetical

Finding	Risk	Effort to Fix	Cost
A	High	7 months	$4,500
B	Medium	2 weeks	$1,000
C	Medium	1 week	$8,500
D	Low	1 month	$6,000

Figure 5-2 Results to remediate

18. Patching is an important preventative control in ensuring a system's security. Patches generally improve the stability of a system and, in the case of security patches, remediate a vulnerability. However, on the rare occasion a patch gets released that opens up a different vulnerability, perhaps more severe than the weakness the patch originally aimed to strengthen. What is the suggested method for mitigating the risk of an errant patch?

   A. Communicate directly with the patch vendor.

   B. Wait for others to install the patch, in case of bad news.

   C. Have a safe environment as a sandbox for testing patched systems.

   D. Don't install patches.

19. After the results of a vulnerability scan were prioritized into remediation steps, a company's cybersecurity team began working on implementing those steps. All systems that were affected by the remediation team continued operating as expected, except for one. One server's application stopped functioning, no longer able to reach others systems. The system owner could not figure out why or how the system just stopped working. What overall process seems *most* at fault here?

   A. Communication/change control

   B. Patching/remediation

   C. Business continuity

   D. Systems administration

20. A cybersecurity analyst is hired by a company to conduct a vulnerability scan on its servers. In the process of scanning a particular server, the analyst comes across evidence that suggests the system has a great many open vulnerabilities. What should the analyst do to properly respond to this?

   A. Speak to the CISO in confidence about the server.

   B. Speak to the internal information security team.

   C. Consult the MOU or ROE.

   D. Write up a formal SLA specific that that server.

21. Soon after prioritizing remediation steps, the team receives an unexpected memo from executive management. The chief information officer now expresses concerns that remediation will have unforeseen effects on operations, and therefore would like the team to delay its efforts and further discuss evaluating the risks. Which terms describe the source of the memo as well as the source of the problem? (Choose two.)

   A. Business process interruption

   B. Corporate governance

   C. Continuous monitoring

   D. Service level agreement

22. What term is used to describe a contract made between units within an organization (for example, between IT and HR) to outline the service expectations, including roles and responsibilities?

   A. MOU

   B. SLA

   C. IOU

   D. ROE

23. For years, vulnerability scanning tools output their findings with no standardization, resulting in an array of reporting styles, inconsistent levels of detail, and no guarantee a particular element was included. This was tolerated until the demand for policy compliance pushed vendors and NIST to form a solution to this problem. What was the result?

   A. FISMA

   B. NIST 800-53

   C. SCAP

   D. ARF

   E. CVE

24. When you're configuring vulnerability scanners, what most influences the types of data you will gather? (Choose all that apply.)

   A. The tool's capabilities

   B. Regulatory requirements

   C. Scope

   D. SCAP

25. A company is starting the process of remediating issues discovered in a vulnerability scan. One of the more severe vulnerabilities was found on a server that happens to contain highly sensitive data and is business critical. The vulnerability would permit exfiltration of the sensitive data across the network. A possible remediation would be implementing DLP. However, being such an important system, its remediation was halted by the chief information officer. In the context of degrading functionality, what might be a good course of action?

   A. Do not implement DLP, but do place a sniffer upstream to monitor for exfiltration. Inform the CIO.

   B. Cease and desist remediation.

   C. Resume remediation after the CIO goes home for the day.

   D. Discuss with the CEO.

   E. Check to confirm that the CIO is not on the ROE and then proceed with the original remediation.

26. The terms "ongoing scanning" and "continuous monitoring" refer to what in the context of vulnerability scanning?

   A. Simultaneous scanning and monitoring during a scheduled vulnerability scan

   B. Scanning occurring regularly, such as daily

   C. Agent-based scanning, instead of server-based, to provide continual availability

   D. Full-time staff available to perform vulnerability scanning as needed

27. What vulnerability scanner provides its own scripting language with which to customize plug-ins?

   A. Klaatu

   B. Barada

   C. Necturn

   D. Nikto

   E. Nessus

28. Which of the following would be an inhibitor to remediation?

   A. Organizational governance

   B. NASL

   C. SCAP

   D. CSF

29. Which of the following is a well-known framework for quantifying severity or the criticality of vulnerabilities?

   A. OpenVAS

   B. CVE

   C. CVSS

   D. CSV

30. What aspect about performing a noncredentialed vulnerability scan is not as common as when performing a credentialed vulnerability scan?

   A. Higher level of detail

   B. Higher number of false positives

   C. Higher number of true negatives

   D. Higher number of verifiable results

31. When configuring a vulnerability scanning tool, you may utilize at least one additional vulnerability feed beyond the product's own source. Selecting a feed that matches your needs is important. Which of the following will *most* influence your selection of vulnerability feed?

   A. Scanning frequency

   B. Company policy

C. Regulatory requirements

D. Senior management risk appetite

32. A B2B health information exchange provider has hired a new cybersecurity team to perform a vulnerability scan. A junior analyst eager to make a good impression raises the point that PCI DSS standard requirement 11.2 directly affects vulnerability scanning. What specific aspect of this scan will the analyst's reference affect?

A. Scope

B. Frequency

C. Sensitivity

D. DAR encryption

E. None of the above

33. At the earliest stages of a vulnerability scan, which of the following would be the *first* step?

A. Draft the ROE.

B. Identify the requirements.

C. Sign the MOU.

D. Configure the scanning tool.

34. A hospital is interested in having an external ASV perform a vulnerability scan, from the perspective of an attacker. What is the scanning criteria that *most* satisfies the hospital's needs?

A. Agent-based, instead of server-based

B. Minimum of two vulnerability feeds

C. Extreme care for scope to avoid accessing PHI

D. Noncredentialed scan, instead of credentialed

35. What is the most important reason why vulnerability tools require feeds and updates?

A. If the tool is unaware of a vulnerability, it cannot detect the vulnerability.

B. Without updates, the tool reports more false negatives.

C. Vulnerability tools come with a vendor-provided feed. No extra feed is required.

D. If a tool receives no updates, regulatory compliance scans may be outdated.

36. A security team was hired to conduct a large-scale vulnerability scan at multiple sites. The team begins at the smallest facility. In the process of launching the vulnerability scanner, an analyst soon gets word that users are starting to complain the network seems slow or unreliable. What might likely be the cause of the problem?

A. Sensitivity level

B. Risk appetite

C. Permissions

D. Technical constraints

37. What is a benefit of utilizing a cloud-based web application security scanner, versus scanning at the site?

   A. Less network perimeter traffic.

   B. More control on the hardware.

   C. Less operations and maintenance.

   D. Frequency can be half as often when launched from the cloud.

38. Prioritizing vulnerabilities is made standard and fair given the Common Vulnerability Scoring System (CVSS). The CVSS ranks vulnerabilities on a 10-point scale using an equation based on several metrics. Which of the following is not a group of metrics used in scoring vulnerabilities?

   A. Attack Complexity/Attack Vector/Privileges Required/User Interaction

   B. Confidentiality Impact/Integrity Impact/Availability Impact

   C. Exploit Code Maturity/Remediation Level/Report Confidence

   D. Exploit Age/Attack Speed/Ease of Exploitation

39. In the process of working with a vulnerability scanning tool, which of the following shows the correct order of steps?

   A. Requirements identification, scan execution, report distribution, report generation

   B. Requirements identification, scan execution, report generation, report distribution

   C. Requirements identification, scan execution, report distribution, report generation

   D. Requirements identification, report generation, scan execution, report distribution

40. At the retailer S-Mart, a security analyst named Ash is familiar with dealing with local nefarious characters trying to exploit the point-of-sale (POS) machines. The POS machines are required for the retailer to operate. Further, data in the POS systems includes financial transaction information. Ash is now developing a data classification system and asset inventory. How should Ash classify S-Mart's POS machines and the data held inside them?

   A. Information: private, Asset: critical

   B. Information: private, Asset: noncritical

   C. Information: public, Asset: critical

   D. Information: proprietary, Asset: noncritical

1. A	**15.** B	**29.** C
2. C	**16.** D	**30.** B
3. B	**17.** C	**31.** A
4. D	**18.** C	**32.** E
5. A, B	**19.** A	**33.** B
6. A, B, C, D, E	**20.** C	**34.** D
7. C	**21.** A, B	**35.** A
8. A	**22.** B	**36.** D
9. D	**23.** C	**37.** C
10. D	**24.** A, B, C	**38.** D
11. C, D	**25.** A	**39.** B
12. A, C, F	**26.** B	**40.** A
13. D	**27.** E	
14. A, C	**28.** A	

1. A company needs a vulnerability scan performed on its internal network. After the company consults with an external cybersecurity analyst, the analyst immediately begins drafting a contract to outline conditions to be met for the scan. These conditions include limiting who is allowed to view the results, specifying what servers and data must not be accessed under any circumstances, and satisfying the company's need for two types of scans to be done quarterly. Which of the following is the *most* likely reason behind these conditions?

   A. Regulatory requirements

   B. Security policy

   C. Analyst's recommendation

   D. Past experience deems the contract prudent

   ☑ **A** is correct. Regulatory requirements are by far the most likely driver of the contract. The conditions stated are examples of regulatory requirements.

   ☒ **B, C,** and **D** are incorrect. **B** is incorrect because although security policy is also a likely reason behind the contract, the sample requirements are similar to HIPAA and PCI DSS requirements. **C** is incorrect because the analyst would offer the suggestion but not likely draft a contract with those specific conditions. **D** is incorrect because experience would not be the most likely cause.

2. Regulatory requirements can specify the need for vulnerability scanning when a company is in the financial or health industry. However, what *best* specifies vulnerability scanning as a requirement without regulatory requirement?

   A. CISO mandate

   B. Local and/or national legislation

   C. Corporate policy

   D. NIST 800-53

   ☑ **C** is correct. Corporate policy is the most likely internal source of such requirements.

   ☒ **A, B,** and **D** are incorrect. **A** is incorrect because a CISO could require the scanning but would do so via policy. **B** is incorrect because legislation suggests regulatory requirements. **D** is incorrect because NIST 800-53 suggests but does not mandate vulnerability scanning.

3. What is a technique that allows a company to vary resources spent toward protecting data according to a set value?

   A. Data encryption

   B. Data classification

   C. Data criticality

   D. Data storage location

☑ **B** is correct. Data classification provides a method of allocating resources in varying amounts based on the criticality or sensitivity of the data.

☒ **A, C,** and **D** are incorrect. **A** is incorrect because encryption does protect data but not according to its value. **C** is incorrect because criticality is an attribute that can classify the data, not a means to protect it. **D** is incorrect because storage location is not a practical primary means of protecting data according to its value.

4. With regard to asset inventory, how would a cybersecurity analyst classify assets such as financial systems, intellectual property, and a customer-facing ordering system?

   A. Noncritical

   B. Sensitive

   C. Credentialed

   D. Critical

   ☑ **D** is correct. Those asset examples should be deemed critical, versus noncritical.

   ☒ **A, B,** and **C** are incorrect. **A** is incorrect because those assets are certainly critical assets. **B** is incorrect because while the assets might have sensitive data, the assets themselves are critical. **C** is incorrect because credentialed is not a type of asset.

5. When a company is developing a vulnerability management plan, its assets must be inventoried. Which of the following asset types would be included? (Choose all that apply.)

   A. Noncritical

   B. Critical

   C. Critical only

   D. On-site and assets of partners and suppliers

   ☑ **A** and **B** are correct. Critical and noncritical assets both should be inventoried when developing a vulnerability management plan.

   ☒ **C** and **D** are incorrect. **C** is incorrect because a company can inventory all its assets, whether on-site, mobile, or company assets currently at remote locations. **D** is incorrect because partner and supplier assets are not within a company's scope to be tracked.

6. The frequency with which a company performs vulnerability scanning is dependent upon which of the following criteria? (Choose all that apply.)

   A. Scanning policy

   B. Vulnerability management planning

   C. Risk appetite

   D. Regulatory requirements

   E. Limitations of time, tools, and personnel

☑ **A, B, C, D,** and **E** are correct. All of those criteria are important factors in determining vulnerability scanning frequency.

☒ None are incorrect.

7. The cybersecurity analyst must consider several factors when determining vulnerability scanning frequency. Criteria such as network bandwidth, systems' CPU capacity, and number of qualified personnel are examples of which of the following?

   A. Soft restrictions

   B. Regulatory requirements

   C. Technical constraints

   D. Budgetary limitations

   ☑ **C** is correct. These are examples of technical constraints.

   ☒ **A, B,** and **D** are incorrect. **A** is incorrect because "soft restrictions" is not a commonly used term, and it suggests something other than hardware anyway. **B** is incorrect because regulatory requirements would not include these sample criteria to determine frequency. **D** is incorrect because although a budgetary limitation might impact these technical aspects, it would not positively help to determine scanning frequency.

8. Apart from policies and regulatory requirements, what creates the largest impact on establishing an effective vulnerability scanning process?

   A. Regular routine and workflow of personnel

   B. Management style of the IT director or head of security

   C. Mandates from the chief of information security

   D. Personal whims of the CEO

   ☑ **A** is correct. The regular routine of personnel has a huge enabling impact on vulnerability scanning and management.

   ☒ **B, C,** and **D** are incorrect. The management style of and mandates from supervisory staff and executives are effectively the same as policy.

9. When a company is configuring tools to perform vulnerability scans, which of the following would be the earliest step?

   A. Choosing the tool plug-ins

   B. Generating reports

   C. Establishing permissions and scanning credentials

   D. Establishing scanning criteria

☑ **D** is correct. Establishing scanning criteria would come before the other options.

☒ **A, B,** and **C** are incorrect. **A** is incorrect because choosing the correct plug-ins would come after determining what plug-ins are needed—after establishing the scanning criteria. **B** is incorrect because reports aren't generated before scanning. **C** is incorrect because credentials and permissions would follow deciding which systems to scan and other criteria.

10. A cybersecurity analyst is performing a vulnerability scan of a few systems, including a server processing protected health information (PHI). The scan of all servers completed successfully, with no interruption of service. To demonstrate proof of weaknesses found during the vulnerability scan, the analyst manages to exfiltrate documents from each server. Which of the following specifications of vulnerability scanning did the analyst likely breach?

    A. Using credentials when a noncredentialed scan would suffice.

    B. No vulnerability feed was evidenced.

    C. Permissions set incorrectly.

    D. Considering the sensitivity of the data on the scanned systems.

    E. Using agents when a server-based scan would suffice.

    ☑ **D** is correct. The sensitivity of the data, particularly the PHI, means no exfiltration can happen.

    ☒ **A, B, C,** and **E** are incorrect. **A** is incorrect because there is no mention of credentials. **B** is incorrect because, while the vulnerability scan specification might have detailed the requirement for a vulnerability feed, there is no evidence this was ignored or violated. **C** is incorrect because permissions didn't seem to impact the success of the scan. **E** is incorrect because the scan was completely successfully, regardless of whether agents were used.

11. Which of the following reasons are valid arguments for using server-based vulnerability scanning instead of agent-based scanning? (Choose all that apply.)

    A. Erratic connectivity to remote and mobile devices

    B. Limited bandwidth

    C. Limited personnel availability for maintenance

    D. Occasional rogue device connecting to the network

    ☑ **C** and **D** are correct. Less availability of security staff to maintain the scanning agents would be a vote in favor of server-based scanning. Also, a server-based architecture would scan the entire network space and thus be able to detect rogue devices without an agent being installed.

    ☒ **A** and **B** are incorrect. **A** is incorrect because erratic connectivity equates to erratic accessibility of the server-based scan; therefore, agent-based scanning is best for devices not consistently connected to the company network. **B** is incorrect because agent-based scanning sends only results; therefore, it requires less bandwidth, meaning any limitation on network capacity favors agent-based scanning.

12. When it comes time to execute a vulnerability scan, what are optional tools you might use to launch it? (Choose all that apply.)

   A. Nessus

   B. Burp Suite

   C. OpenVAS

   D. Vega

   E. FTK

   F. Nikto

   ☑ **A, C,** and **F** are correct. Nessus, Open Vulnerability Scanner, and Nikto are all top-rate vulnerability scanning tools, with varying levels of options, detailed analysis, and reporting.

   ☒ **B, D,** and **E** are incorrect. **B** and **D** are incorrect because Burp Suite and Vega are exploit tools. **E** is incorrect because FTK is a forensics tool.

13. After you complete your scan, creating heaps of output, you need to prepare a report. What are your options?

   A. As vulnerability tools rarely generate reports, there's no need for a report.

   B. It's common to pipe vulnerability tool output to a report generation tool.

   C. Nearly all vulnerability scanners generate standardized reports via XML.

   D. Every vulnerability tool generates some kind of report, but not using a standardized format.

   ☑ **D** is correct. Essentially every vulnerability scanner has a way of reporting on the results. Whereas some send output to the screen, others can package results in a PDF, CSV, XML, or other format.

   ☒ **A, B,** and **C** are incorrect. **A** is incorrect because a report is necessary, regardless whether the scanning tool itself generates it. **B** is incorrect because it's not common to direct results to a separate reporting tool. **C** is incorrect because XML is not a standardized format for results.

14. It's time to deliver a vulnerability report to the stakeholders. What are your options for distribution? (Choose all that apply.)

   A. Automated delivery via the report generation component of the vulnerability scanner

   B. Delivered entirely via e-mail to all administrators

   C. Delivered manually, through face-to-face meetings

   D. E-mailing only the portions immediately relevant to the individual

   ☑ **A** and **C** are correct. There are two ways to distribute scan results: automated and manual distribution. Some vulnerability tools possess the means to automatically distribute reporting. Still, for the sake of confidentiality, delivering via a face-to-face meeting is preferred, if practical.

⊠ **B** and **D** are incorrect. A vulnerability report contains sensitive information, including the organization's security weaknesses. No part of a vulnerability report should be delivered via e-mail due to the open nature of such communications.

15. What remediation step requires careful discussion concerning the scan results, with the goal of satisfying both the concerns of technical staff and the organization's business objectives?

   A. Validation of the results

   B. Prioritization of the results

   C. Distribution of the results

   D. Categorization of the results

   ☑ **B** is correct. Prioritization is the goal—that is, to discuss the results and decide on the next steps in remediation. Far too often results can be overwhelming if the focus is to "fix everything now."

   ⊠ **A, C,** and **D** are incorrect. **A** is incorrect because, although validation is a correct step, it's generally a task done by an internal technical team, not shared among management. **C** is incorrect because distribution was already carefully decided upon and can be found in the statement of work. **D** is incorrect because categorization is not such a delicate discussion.

16. Figure 5-1 shows the top portion of the results screen in Nessus when a scan has completed. The wide bar across the top separates quantities of results in varying colors. What is Nessus distinguishing by using colors?

   A. Scope

   B. Chronological order of the scan execution

   C. Association to the vulnerability feeds used

   D. Criticality of the findings

Figure 5-1   Nessus results screen

☑ **D** is correct. The colors separating the results are used to distinguish between the criticality or severity levels of the results.

☒ **B, C,** and **D** are incorrect. **B** is incorrect because the colors have nothing to do with scope. **C** is incorrect because the order in which the scan was done has little to no impact on the end results or how they are presented. **D** is incorrect because vulnerability feeds are irrelevant to the presentation of the results.

17. The chief information security officer is among many at a meeting about the vulnerability scan results. Everyone has the same table, shown in Figure 5-2. The discussion is focused on how to order the findings to remediate. The cybersecurity analyst focuses on criticality, wanting to fix the findings in the order shown: A, B, C, then D. The CISO instead wants the remediation order to be C, B, A, then D. What aspect caused the CISO to change the order of remediation?

   A. Criticality

   B. Cost

   C. Effort to fix

   D. Alphabetical

Finding	Risk	Effort to Fix	Cost
A	High	7 months	$4,500
B	Medium	2 weeks	$1,000
C	Medium	1 week	$8,500
D	Low	1 month	$6,000

Figure 5-2 Results to remediate

☑ **C** is correct. Based on the order the CISO prefers (C, B, A, D), it seems difficulty of implementation is the guiding factor. A good strategy is to follow up on the "low-hanging fruit," or perform fairly simple remediation first.

☒ **A, B,** and **D** are incorrect. **A** is incorrect because criticality would be A, B, C, D order. **B** is incorrect because cost would be B, D, A, C order. **D** is incorrect because remediating by alphabetical order, in addition to being a bit silly, would be A, B, C, D.

18. Patching is an important preventative control in ensuring a system's security. Patches generally improve the stability of a system and, in the case of security patches, remediate a vulnerability. However, on the rare occasion a patch gets released that opens up a different vulnerability, perhaps more severe than the weakness the patch originally aimed to strengthen. What is the suggested method for mitigating the risk of an errant patch?

   A. Communicate directly with the patch vendor.

   B. Wait for others to install the patch, in case of bad news.

C. Have a safe environment as a sandbox for testing patched systems.

D. Don't install patches.

☑ **C** is correct. Patching is necessary, but there are rare times when patching goes bad. Always have a sandbox or testing stage for monitoring the effect of patches on systems.

☒ **A, B,** and **D** are incorrect. **A** is incorrect because the vendor will naturally say the patch is fine. **B** is incorrect because waiting for others isn't a viable strategy, especially for critical patches. **D** is incorrect because not patching isn't going to work in the long run.

19. After the results of a vulnerability scan were prioritized into remediation steps, a company's cybersecurity team began working on implementing those steps. All systems that were affected by the remediation team continued operating as expected, except for one. One server's application stopped functioning, no longer able to reach others systems. The system owner could not figure out why or how the system just stopped working. What overall process seems *most* at fault here?

A. Communication/change control

B. Patching/remediation

C. Business continuity

D. Systems administration

☑ **A** is correct. Communication and practicing proper change control are very likely the cause for the unexpected application disconnect. Whether a previously open network port was closed or a service deemed unnecessary was shut down is in the past. Change control, if done correctly, should have alerted the systems owner to changes impacting the application.

☒ **B, C,** and **D** are incorrect. **B** is incorrect because patching and remediation are too granular. Yes, remediation was the direct cause, but not the shortfall that allowed remediation to become a problem. **C** is incorrect because business continuity deals with resuming operations after a significant outage. **D** is incorrect because system administration wasn't at fault but rather likely what helped resolve the problem.

20. A cybersecurity analyst is hired by a company to conduct a vulnerability scan on its servers. In the process of scanning a particular server, the analyst comes across evidence that suggests the system has a great many open vulnerabilities. What should the analyst do to properly respond to this?

A. Speak to the CISO in confidence about the server.

B. Speak to the internal information security team.

C. Consult the MOU or ROE.

D. Write up a formal SLA specific that that server.

☑ **C** is correct. The memorandum of understanding (MOU), or scope of the vulnerability scan, would include details on how to respond to finding evidence. The rules of engagement (ROE) should also specify detailed expectations on interacting with systems. The MOU and ROE contain the answers to questions such as "What do we do now?"

☒ **A, B,** and **D** are incorrect. **A** is incorrect, unless the MOU and ROE specifically named the CISO as the point of contact for such findings. **B** is incorrect for the same reason—the MOU and ROE would need to name that team as the contact in order for this to be the correct answer. **D** is incorrect because an SLA has no relevance here.

21. Soon after prioritizing remediation steps, the team receives an unexpected memo from executive management. The chief information officer now expresses concerns that remediation will have unforeseen effects on operations, and therefore would like the team to delay its efforts and further discuss evaluating the risks. Which terms describe the source of the memo as well as the source of the problem? (Choose two.)

    A. Business process interruption

    B. Corporate governance

    C. Continuous monitoring

    D. Service level agreement

    ☑ **A** and **B** are correct. This issue hits on corporate governance and its influence on the remediation team, as well as on business process interruption, or the tendency of upper management to be a drag on remediation efforts based on fear of instability in operations.

    ☒ **C** and **D** are incorrect. **C** is incorrect because continuous monitoring has nothing to do with the executive being concerned. **D** is incorrect because there is no mention of an SLA here.

22. What term is used to describe a contract made between units within an organization (for example, between IT and HR) to outline the service expectations, including roles and responsibilities?

    A. MOU

    B. SLA

    C. IOU

    D. ROE

    ☑ **B** is correct. A service level agreement (SLA) is a contract between units within an organization, or even between an organization and third party, to specify the service's availability, response, and other expectations.

☒ **A, C,** and **D** are incorrect. **A** is incorrect because a memorandum of understanding (MOU) is an agreement that's more about expectations for an event or partnership, such as a vulnerability scan. **C** is incorrect because an IOU, or "I owe you," does not apply here. **D** is incorrect because the ROE (rules of engagement) is a formal set of rules that, in the case of a vulnerability scan, specify what will happen, who is involved, and what to do when a vulnerability is discovered.

23. For years, vulnerability scanning tools output their findings with no standardization, resulting in an array of reporting styles, inconsistent levels of detail, and no guarantee a particular element was included. This was tolerated until the demand for policy compliance pushed vendors and NIST to form a solution to this problem. What was the result?

    A. FISMA

    B. NIST 800-53

    C. SCAP

    D. ARF

    E. CVE

    ☑ **C** is correct. SCAP, or Security Content Automation Protocol, is a product of NIST and industry leaders that provides some standardization around how vulnerability reporting is presented and managed.

    ☒ **A, B, D,** and **E** are incorrect. **A** is incorrect because FISMA is the Federal Information Security Management Act—just one of the sets of requirements that SCAP helps to present. **B** is incorrect because NIST 800-53 is the Security and Privacy Controls special publication from NIST. **D** is incorrect because ARF, or asset reporting format, is only one of many components contained SCAP. Finally, **E** is incorrect because CVE is the Common Vulnerabilities Exposure system for standardizing how vulnerabilities are catalogued.

24. When you're configuring vulnerability scanners, what most influences the types of data you will gather? (Choose all that apply.)

    A. The tool's capabilities

    B. Regulatory requirements

    C. Scope

    D. SCAP

    ☑ **A, B,** and **C** are correct. **A** is correct because a vulnerability scanner's capabilities by definition influence what the tool can do and gather. **B** is correct because the regulatory requirements of the company to be scanned would influence what data you seek to collect, in order to determine compliance. **C** is correct because what the company deems "in scope" will impact what types of data are gathered.

    ☒ **D** is incorrect. SCAP would impact how the results are presented, but not directly change the types of data you intend to find.

25. A company is starting the process of remediating issues discovered in a vulnerability scan. One of the more severe vulnerabilities was found on a server that happens to contain highly sensitive data and is business critical. The vulnerability would permit exfiltration of the sensitive data across the network. A possible remediation would be implementing DLP. However, being such an important system, its remediation was halted by the chief information officer. In the context of degrading functionality, what might be a good course of action?

A. Do not implement DLP, but do place a sniffer upstream to monitor for exfiltration. Inform the CIO.

B. Cease and desist remediation.

C. Resume remediation after the CIO goes home for the day.

D. Discuss with the CEO.

E. Check to confirm that the CIO is not on the ROE and then proceed with the original remediation.

☑ **A** is correct. Just because the CIO demands that remediation stop, this does not erase the responsibility to mitigate the risk. If the original steps are called off due to impacting the server's operation, then compensating controls such as implementing data loss prevention (DLP) and/or an intrusion detection system (IDS) would lessen the exposure.

☒ **B, C, D,** and **E** are incorrect. **B** is incorrect because simply doing nothing is not an option. **C** is incorrect because it's likely the CIO would be displeased when returning the next morning. **D** is incorrect because this might displease the CIO even more than option **C**. Finally, **E** is incorrect because dismissing the CIO's concerns is just as unwise a career move as the other incorrect answers.

26. The terms "ongoing scanning" and "continuous monitoring" refer to what in the context of vulnerability scanning?

A. Simultaneous scanning and monitoring during a scheduled vulnerability scan

B. Scanning occurring regularly, such as daily

C. Agent-based scanning, instead of server-based, to provide continual availability

D. Full-time staff available to perform vulnerability scanning as needed

☑ **B** is correct. Ongoing scanning and continuous monitoring refer to having scanning being a part of the company's routine operation. Daily is suggested as an optimal frequency, if it can be noninvasive to the environment, because it's very responsive to newly discovered vulnerabilities.

☒ **A, C,** and **D** are incorrect. **A** is incorrect because ongoing and continuous does not suggest "simultaneous." **C** is incorrect because whether the scan is performed by agent-based or server-based components is not relevant. **D** is incorrect because although having adequate staff does factor into managing ongoing scanning, it is not the defining characteristic.

27. What vulnerability scanner provides its own scripting language with which to customize plug-ins?

   A. Klaatu

   B. Barada

   C. Necturn

   D. Nikto

   E. Nessus

   ☑ **E** is correct. Okay then, that's it—Nessus has NASL, the Nessus Attack Scripting Language. Nessus plug-ins are written in NASL. This allows you to configure Nessus to perform the scan exactly as your specifications require.

   ☒ **A, B, C,** and **D** are incorrect. **A, B,** and **C** are incorrect because these are not vulnerability scanners. **D** is incorrect because Nikto, a command-line web vulnerability scanner, does not utilize a scripting language.

28. Which of the following would be an inhibitor to remediation?

   A. Organizational governance

   B. NASL

   C. SCAP

   D. CSF

   ☑ **A** is correct. Organizational governance can sometimes impede remediation efforts, based on senior management wanting to ensure operations suffer no unexpected outages.

   ☒ **B, C,** and **D** are incorrect because neither NASL (Nessus Attack Scripting Language), the SCAP (Security Content Automation Protocol), nor the CSF (Cyber Security Framework) inhibit remediation.

29. Which of the following is a well-known framework for quantifying severity or the criticality of vulnerabilities?

   A. OpenVAS

   B. CVE

   C. CVSS

   D. CSV

   ☑ **C** is correct. The CVSS, or Common Vulnerability Scoring System, is a framework for standardizing ratings for vulnerabilities, including severity.

   ☒ **A, B,** and **D** are incorrect. **A** is incorrect because OpenVAS is a vulnerability scanner. **B** is incorrect because CVE is a vulnerability and exposure database. **D** is incorrect because CSV is a file format, common with spreadsheet software.

30. What aspect about performing a noncredentialed vulnerability scan is not as common as when performing a credentialed vulnerability scan?

   A. Higher level of detail

   B. Higher number of false positives

   C. Higher number of true negatives

   D. Higher number of verifiable results

   ☑ **B** is correct. A noncredential scan produces more false positives, takes more network bandwidth, and would produce fewer verifiable results.

   ☒ **A, C,** and **D** are incorrect. **A** is incorrect because credentialed scans provide more relevant and deeper detail, whereas noncredentialed scans tend to produce more general, unverified findings. **C** is incorrect because credentialed scans will provide the greater percentage of true negatives due to the ability to log in for validation. **D** is incorrect because the credentialed scan is able to verify the results by virtue of having authenticated.

31. When configuring a vulnerability scanning tool, you may utilize at least one additional vulnerability feed beyond the product's own source. Selecting a feed that matches your needs is important. Which of the following will *most* influence your selection of vulnerability feed?

   A. Scanning frequency

   B. Company policy

   C. Regulatory requirements

   D. Senior management risk appetite

   ☑ **A** is correct. The scanning frequency most affects your vulnerability feed needs. Vulnerability feeds differ in a number of ways, such as providing only analyzed vulnerabilities versus vulnerabilities as they are discovered, or vulnerabilities every few hours versus within minutes.

   ☒ **B, C,** and **D** are incorrect. **B** is incorrect because company policy shouldn't dictate such a specific technical detail as vulnerability feed requirements. **C** is incorrect because regulatory requirements will affect the need for periodic scanning but won't have a specialized feed requirement. **D** is incorrect because the risk appetite affects the scanning frequency and scope, but has little impact on feed choice.

32. A B2B health information exchange provider has hired a new cybersecurity team to perform a vulnerability scan. A junior analyst eager to make a good impression raises the point that PCI DSS standard requirement 11.2 directly affects vulnerability scanning. What specific aspect of this scan will the analyst's reference affect?

   A. Scope

   B. Frequency

C. Sensitivity

D. DAR encryption

E. None of the above

☑ **E** is correct. Being a health information exchange, operating between businesses, it's very unlikely to be operating as a credit card merchant on any level. Therefore, there's no issue with maintaining PCI DSS compliance. (Sorry for the trick question.)

☒ **A, B, C,** and **D** are incorrect. **A, C,** and **D** are incorrect because PCI DSS 11.2 has no effect on scope, sensitivity, or data-at-rest encryption. **B** is incorrect but it would be relevant only if the company required PCI DSS compliance, in which case scanning frequency is required to be quarterly per PCI DSS requirement 11, section 2.

33. At the earliest stages of a vulnerability scan, which of the following would be the *first* step?

A. Draft the ROE.

B. Identify the requirements.

C. Sign the MOU.

D. Configure the scanning tool.

☑ **B** is correct. The first step is to identify requirements. From there, a memorandum of understanding can be signed. Upon further detailing the engagement expectations, the rules of engagement can be established. Then it's tool-configuration time.

☒ **A, C,** and **D** are incorrect. **A** is incorrect because drafting the ROE would follow the step of identifying the requirements. **C** is incorrect because signing the MOU follows knowing what to put in the MOU (identifying the requirements). **D** is incorrect because configuring the tool comes after all the paperwork is final.

34. A hospital is interested in having an external ASV perform a vulnerability scan, from the perspective of an attacker. What is the scanning criteria that *most* satisfies the hospital's needs?

A. Agent-based, instead of server-based

B. Minimum of two vulnerability feeds

C. Extreme care for scope to avoid accessing PHI

D. Noncredentialed scan, instead of credentialed

☑ **D** is correct. Choosing to run a noncredentialed scan causes the vulnerability scan to report with results that most closely resemble what an attacker would see.

☒ **A, B,** and **C** are incorrect. **A** is incorrect because an agent-based scan is certainly not what an attacker would see. **B** is incorrect because the number of feeds is not relevant to the question. **C** is incorrect because although not accessing PHI (protected health information) is very important, it's not as relevant to the question.

35. What is the most important reason why vulnerability tools require feeds and updates?

   A. If the tool is unaware of a vulnerability, it cannot detect the vulnerability.

   B. Without updates, the tool reports more false negatives.

   C. Vulnerability tools come with a vendor-provided feed. No extra feed is required.

   D. If a tool receives no updates, regulatory compliance scans may be outdated.

   ☑ **A** is correct. Similar to other signature-based products like antivirus and intrusion detection systems, a vulnerability scanning tool is only capable of scanning for what it's aware of.

   ☒ **B, C,** and **D** are incorrect. **B** is incorrect because it's true the tool requires updates to have visibility of vulnerabilities. Therefore, no updates would not produce false negatives. **C** is incorrect because the vulnerability scanning tool probably does make use of a source, but still should be configured with one or two other feeds. **D** is incorrect because it's likely the regulatory compliance aspect is not a concern when updates are lacking.

36. A security team was hired to conduct a large-scale vulnerability scan at multiple sites. The team begins at the smallest facility. In the process of launching the vulnerability scanner, an analyst soon gets word that users are starting to complain the network seems slow or unreliable. What might likely be the cause of the problem?

   A. Sensitivity level

   B. Risk appetite

   C. Permissions

   D. Technical constraints

   ☑ **D** is correct. Experiencing a sluggish network given a large vulnerability scan launched at a small facility seems to point to technical constraints.

   ☒ **A, B,** and **C** are incorrect. Sensitivity levels, risk appetite, and permissions are all very unlikely related to the network issues.

37. What is a benefit of utilizing a cloud-based web application security scanner, versus scanning at the site?

   A. Less network perimeter traffic.

   B. More control on the hardware.

   C. Less operations and maintenance.

   D. Frequency can be half as often when launched from the cloud.

   ☑ **C** is correct. Cloud-based scanning also transfers maintenance to the scanning provider.

   ☒ **A, B,** and **D** are incorrect. **A** is incorrect because you could expect an external scan to create more traffic across the perimeter. **B** is incorrect because you would have more control over infrastructure if the scanning were done on-site. **D** is incorrect because the scanning frequency is not altered based on the scanning origin.

38. Prioritizing vulnerabilities is made standard and fair given the Common Vulnerability Scoring System (CVSS). The CVSS ranks vulnerabilities on a 10-point scale using an equation based on several metrics. Which of the following is not a group of metrics used in scoring vulnerabilities?

   A. Attack Complexity/Attack Vector/Privileges Required/User Interaction

   B. Confidentiality Impact/Integrity Impact/Availability Impact

   C. Exploit Code Maturity/Remediation Level/Report Confidence

   D. Exploit Age/Attack Speed/Ease of Exploitation

   ☑ **D** is correct. Exploit age, attack speed, and ease of exploitation not actual named factors.

   ☒ **A, B,** and **C** are incorrect. All these are actual base metrics in the CVSS equation for determining severity.

39. In the process of working with a vulnerability scanning tool, which of the following shows the correct order of steps?

   A. Requirements identification, scan execution, report distribution, report generation

   B. Requirements identification, scan execution, report generation, report distribution

   C. Requirements identification, scan execution, report distribution, report generation

   D. Requirements identification, report generation, scan execution, report distribution

   ☑ **B** is correct. The correct order is, of course, requirements identification, scan execution, report generation, report distribution.

   ☒ **A, C,** and **D** are incorrect. All other variations of the process order are not correct.

40. At the retailer S-Mart, a security analyst named Ash is familiar with dealing with local nefarious characters trying to exploit the point-of-sale (POS) machines. The POS machines are required for the retailer to operate. Further, data in the POS systems includes financial transaction information. Ash is now developing a data classification system and asset inventory. How should Ash classify S-Mart's POS machines and the data held inside them?

   A. Information: private, Asset: critical

   B. Information: private, Asset: noncritical

   C. Information: public, Asset: critical

   D. Information: proprietary, Asset: noncritical

   ☑ **A** is correct. The data should be classified as private, meaning its disclosure could cause privacy issues. The POS system is required for the business to operate, so it is a critical asset.

   ☒ **B, C,** and **D** are incorrect. All these variations of the data and asset classifications are not correct.

Vulnerability Scanning

This chapter includes questions on the following topics:

- Best practices for executing vulnerability scans
- Remediation techniques for uncovering vulnerabilities
- How to review and interpret results of vulnerability scan reports
- Trend analysis techniques for vulnerability management

The cybersecurity analyst needs to be able to understand the output of vulnerability scans. With a comprehensive vulnerability management process in place, the cybersecurity analyst will regularly scan for vulnerabilities. The output of these scans includes a wide range of results. Some of the results might not be legitimate, and some might not require action. But for all the results, the cybersecurity analyst must be prepared to review, analyze, and reconcile them.

The vulnerabilities found are dependent on the types of targets within the organization where these vulnerabilities are discovered. As one would expect, vulnerabilities found on servers differ from those found on network devices or endpoints. Understanding the type of device and its purpose goes a long way in understanding weaknesses as possible avenues for attack. This chapter focuses on how to analyze vulnerability scan output and the variety of vulnerabilities across the many types of targets in an organization.

1. What are the most important types of results to identify from a vulnerability scan report? (Choose two.)

    A. False positives

    B. False negatives

    C. Policy validation

    D. Exceptions to policy

2. What is the main purpose of the report after a vulnerability scan is complete?

    A. It is to be analyzed by the cybersecurity team responsible for the scan.

    B. It is used to evaluate the team responsible for the target environment.

    C. It is included in the full report given to executive management.

    D. It is used as a baseline for future vulnerability scans.

3. A report outcome that at first seems suspicious but later proves to be neutral is called a what?

    A. False negative

    B. True positive

    C. True negative

    D. False positive

4. When it comes to prioritizing report outcomes, which of the following would you consider when deciding on response actions? (Select all that apply.)

    A. True negatives

    B. False positives

    C. Policy exceptions

    D. Validated vulnerabilities

5. Vulnerability scanning does not always return reliable and accurate results. The results depend heavily on the systems being scanned. Which of the following systems would be the least likely to be identified and return genuine scan results? (Choose two.)

    A. CCTV camera, web-enabled with embedded Apache

    B. An open source firewall, customized by the scan target client

    C. Windows 2012 server, missing three months of patches and the latest Service Pack

    D. Novell NetWare 6.5

6. Alongside results in the scan report, it's common to see references to external sources such as OSVDB and NVD. What is the reason for vulnerability scanners to include information from those databases?

    A. The sources provide validation to the scan results.

    B. The sources offer additional information and possibly mitigating actions.

C. The sources provide links to upload sanitized data from the scan.

D. The sources specify whether a result is a false positive or a genuine vulnerability.

7. What is primary value of STIGs and NSA guides?

    A. They are a source of "best practice" principles.

    B. They are a proven source of vulnerability validation steps.

    C. They provide checklists detailing regulatory compliance.

    D. They specify configuration steps for secure networking.

8. Which of the following are good sources of validating scan results? (Choose all that apply.)

    A. Interviewing the system's owner

    B. Reviewing the system's event log

    C. Comparing against past vulnerability reports and results

    D. Examining system and network data such as open ports and services

9. What method allows the internal security team to tailor threat mitigation strategies, evaluate how effective those strategies are, and see the change of controls over time?

    A. Comparing a system against similar systems in the environment

    B. Comparing the current system against the original image, when available

    C. Comparing the system's trend in reported vulnerabilities

    D. Comparing the results with the system's logs

10. What is best described as comparing a scan report against the personal and documented notes of the scan operator? Such notes would include scanning steps as well as observations around the scan devices' configuration and operation.

    A. Trending the results

    B. Validating the results

    C. Reconciling the results

    D. Managing the results

11. What type of scanning target would commonly have vulnerabilities due to the existence of unnecessary services and open ports?

    A. IDS

    B. SCADA device

    C. VPN

    D. Server

12. For which type of scanning target is it particularly easy to show duplicate vulnerabilities?

    A. VPN

    B. Virtual infrastructure

    C. Mobile device

    D. SCADA device

13. A vulnerability found in a hypervisor threatens the security of what devices? (Choose two.)

    A. Endpoint

    B. Host server

    C. Virtual machine

    D. Network device

14. A cybersecurity analyst is briefing the CEO on the encrypted nature of VPNs. The CEO, understanding how well VPNs protect confidentiality, asks what their primary vulnerability is. What should be the cybersecurity analyst's response?

    A. VPNs connect external devices to the internal network.

    B. VPNs mask network traffic from monitoring.

    C. VPN encryption is difficult to configure.

    D. VPNs have no vulnerabilities.

15. An attacker seeks to enter a protected corporate network. Fortunately, the company's cybersecurity team has locked down the network well. Instead, the attacker discovers an open port in a maintenance-related network. Moving laterally, the attacker then moves onto the protected network. What is the source of the vulnerability overlooked by the cybersecurity team?

    A. VPN connection

    B. Virtualized switch

    C. No encryption on either network

    D. Interconnected networks

16. What type of scanning target would commonly have vulnerabilities due to limitations imposed by carriers?

    A. Mobile device

    B. Virtual network infrastructure

    C. Server

    D. Industrial control system

17. What is a source of vulnerabilities for essentially all devices?

    A. No encryption

    B. Patch updates and upgrades

    C. Low memory and/or storage space

    D. Policy exceptions

18. Which term describes what permits a VM to connect to an outside network?

    A. Management interface

    B. Interconnected network

    C. Virtual private network

    D. Virtual network

19. What do the network protocols IPSec, L2TP, TLS, and DTLS have in common?

    A. They facilitate virtual private networks.

    B. All are Layer 2 protocols.

    C. They are used exclusively for virtual networks.

    D. They build interconnections between protected and peripheral networks.

20. Which of the following characteristics is prominent in Supervisory Control and Data Acquisition systems?

    A. They typically cover a wide geographical area.

    B. They contain several types of control systems, including ICS (industry control systems).

    C. They are common, with only one person operating them locally.

    D. They rely on obscure networking protocols such as IPX/SPX.

21. After creating several virtual machines, a system administrator took great effort to harden the virtual systems. When finished, the administrator sought approval from the security team and asked the cybersecurity analyst to try to compromise any one of the machines. Within a short amount of time, the administrator noticed that all the machines were running with great difficulty. A little investigation revealed the virtual systems were running with only one-fourth of the original memory. The host system was operating normally. When asked, the administrator claimed no machine was accessed. Where was the likely vulnerability?

    A. Virtual network

    B. Management interface

    C. Host system physical memory

    D. WAP

22. What is the term used to describe when an attacker is able to leap from a virtual machine to the host machine?

    A. Lateral move

    B. Virtual interruption

    C. Escape

    D. Sandbox jump

23. What are the most common vulnerabilities found in a network infrastructure? (Select two)

    A. Misconfiguration

    B. Broadcast storms

    C. WAP

    D. Enabled COM port

24. In terms of mitigating vulnerabilities, network appliances should be treated as specialized forms of what type of device?

    A. WAP

    B. Endpoint

    C. Server

    D. Virtual host

25. Stuxnet, which targeted the uranium enrichment centrifuges run in Iran, was an example of malware targeting what type of system?

    A. VM

    B. ICS

    C. HMI

    D. NAC

26. What type of system presents a unique challenge in updating due to how critical its uptime is?

    A. HVAC

    B. Finance server

    C. SCADA

    D. Perimeter network protection

27. An employee has come to you with concerns about installing a software package on their desktop. When you ask how confident they are that the software is secure and from a safe vendor, the employee assures you the package was "signed by a certificate." However, the employee mentioned that during the installation an error appeared, complaining about the signing certificate, but they clicked the error too quickly to actually understand it. A dialog box is still on the desktop screen, showing additional information about the certificate. From Figure 6-1, can you determine what the likely error was?

A. The certificate has expired.

B. The certificate is from an untrusted source.

C. The certificate is based on inadequate encryption.

D. The certificate fingerprint is invalid.

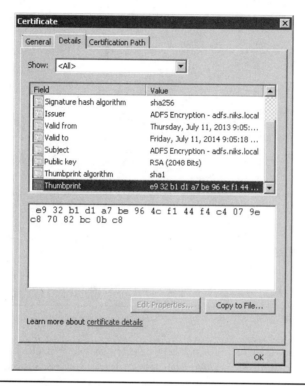

Figure 6-1   Certificate details

28. Over the past year, a few significant changes occurred in a company's IT environment. See Figure 6-2 for a list of those changes. Each change had an effect on vulnerability scan reporting. Looking at Figure 6-3, can you determine what change most affected the trend of critical vulnerabilities?

A. BYOD policy update

B. Firewall update

C. Router update

D. New AVS

Time	Policy Change
Dec-17	BYOD policy update
Mar-18	Firewall update
Mar-18	Router update
May-18	New AVS

Figure 6-2 Documented changes

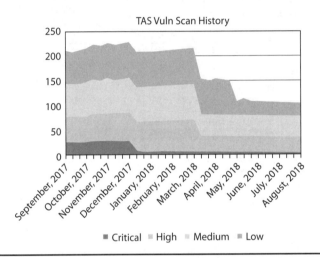

Figure 6-3 Vulnerability scan history

29. On "Bring Your Daughter to Work Day," cybersecurity analyst Elizabeth brings her daughter Paige to the data center. Paige is curious why analysts across different companies and countries take the same steps to harden their infrastructures. What is Elizabeth's likely explanation?

   A. Requirements are forced by regulatory compliance.

   B. Policy is dictated by trends.

   C. All analysts trust each other's good judgment.

   D. Best practices are being widely adopted.

30. A company is experiencing a substantial increase in incidents since allowing employees to connect their own mobile devices to the internal network. What is the key vulnerability behind this scenario?

   A. Mobile devices are being allowed without any corporate policies.

   B. Mobile devices are being used without a VPN connection.

   C. Mobile devices are allowed to be plugged into USB ports on desktop PCs

   D. The network infrastructure is burdened with additional traffic.

31. Using the Windows registry editor, a security analyst navigates to the following key:

    HKLM\Software\Policies\Microsoft\Windows\CurrentVersion\Internet Settings

    At that key, the analyst sets the value **PreventIgnoreCertErrors** to **REG_DWORD = 1**. What is the key vulnerability that encouraged this setting?

    A. The Certificate Authority is employing too weak a cryptographic cipher.

    B. Users are ignoring certificate errors.

    C. The Certificate Authority is untrusted.

    D. Users' devices are unable to send an OSCP status request.

32. You've just learned of a new, critical vulnerability that was discovered late last night. You suspect your infrastructure is particularly vulnerable. You need to perform an immediate scan to identify all the affected servers that will require action. What has your attention first?

    A. SIEM

    B. VM management interface

    C. Vulnerability feed

    D. CVSS

33. The Authentication metric, the Access Complexity metric, and the Access Vector metric are all scoring factors used for what system?

    A. NVD

    B. PCI DSS

    C. Nessus

    D. CVSS

34. Soon after completing a vulnerability scan, you review the most critical findings on your Nginx web server. From the following list, which is the likely false positive?

    A. CVE-2016-1247 Nginx Root Privilege Escalation

    B. CVE-2017-0278 Windows SMB Remote Code Execution

    C. CVE-2017-7529 Nginx Remote Integer Overflow

    D. CVE-2018-7584 PHP Stack Buffer Overflow

    E. CVE-2017-14176 Bazaar with Subprocess SSH, allows Remote Execution

35. A vulnerability scan reports a web service running on a server. However, you only know of an application developed in-house running on that server. Additionally, the server is not external facing, and you're fairly confident there is no web service running. What is the likely port of that internally developed application?

    A. 445

    B. 69

    C. 110

    D. 80

36. A vulnerability scan reports a web service running on a server, but you were unaware of any web service or anything running on port 80. What might be your next step?

   A. Scan the server with a port scanner to see if port 80 is listening.

   B. Write a policy that web services must be approved before an installation.

   C. E-mail employees to find out the website's administrator.

   D. Re-run the vulnerability scan.

37. A specialized web proxy device has been flagged by a vulnerability scanner for several scanning periods for the same vulnerability. The cybersecurity team is asked why this vulnerability persists. What are the likely causes? (Choose two.)

   A. Being a vendor-specific network appliance, its patch management was overlooked.

   B. This network appliance is on the DMZ and therefore left unmanaged.

   C. The vendor is responsible for patching, but for reasons unknown has been unable to do so.

   D. The network appliance is compromised.

38. After a vulnerability scan is completed, what's the "best practice" for prioritizing response actions?

   A. Absolutely start with the highest CVSS rating and work toward the lower-rated vulnerabilities.

   B. Start with the response with the shortest implementation time and work toward the more involved responses.

   C. All scan reports are unique, but in general you should balance least disruption with risk mitigation.

   D. First validate and reconcile all vulnerabilities and then start to remediate.

1. A, D
2. A
3. D
4. A, D
5. A, B
6. B
7. A
8. B, D
9. C
10. C
11. D
12. B
13. B, C

14. A
15. D
16. A
17. B
18. D
19. A
20. A
21. B
22. C
23. A, C
24. C
25. B
26. C

27. A
28. A
29. D
30. A
31. B
32. C
33. D
34. B
35. D
36. A
37. A, C
38. C

1. What are the most important types of results to identify from a vulnerability scan report? (Choose two.)

    A. False positives

    B. False negatives

    C. Policy validation

    D. Exceptions to policy

    ☑ **A** and **D** are correct. The two early results to identify in a scan report are false positives and policy exceptions. After factoring out false positives (those that seem like a vulnerability but are not) and policy exceptions (those that are authorized), then the remaining vulnerabilities need responses.

    ☒ **B** and **C** are incorrect. **B** is incorrect because false negatives are not identified and hence not to be found on the report. **C** is incorrect because policy validation does not make sense.

2. What is the main purpose of the report after a vulnerability scan is complete?

    A. It is to be analyzed by the cybersecurity team responsible for the scan.

    B. It is used to evaluate the team responsible for the target environment.

    C. It is included in the full report given to executive management.

    D. It is used as a baseline for future vulnerability scans.

    ☑ **A** is correct. The first goal is to analyze the report. That is done by the team responsible for the scan.

    ☒ **B, C,** and **D** are incorrect. **B** is incorrect because evaluating the internal team is not a responsibility of the scan team. **C** is incorrect because although the results will go in the final report, merely inserting the results is obviously not the primary goal. **D** is incorrect because, again, it's not a primary goal, even though the scan might act as a baseline for future scans, or be compared against a prior scan.

3. A report outcome that at first seems suspicious but later proves to be neutral is called a what?

    A. False negative

    B. True positive

    C. True negative

    D. False positive

    ☑ **D** is correct. A false positive is a result that seems suspicious or valid at first, but when later investigated is deemed not an issue.

    ☒ **A, B,** and **C** are incorrect. **A** is incorrect because a false negative is a genuine vulnerability that escapes being reported. **B** is incorrect because a true positive is a silly answer. **C** is incorrect because a true negative is also a silly answer.

4. When it comes to prioritizing report outcomes, which of the following would you consider when deciding on response actions? (Select all that apply.)

   A. True negatives

   B. False positives

   C. Policy exceptions

   D. Validated vulnerabilities

   ☑ **A** and **D** are correct. True negatives (genuine, reported vulnerabilities) will be evaluated for responses. The same goes for validated vulnerabilities.

   ☒ **B** and **C** are incorrect. **B** is incorrect because false positives should be identified and removed from consideration because they are not actual vulnerabilities. The same goes for **C**, policy exceptions, because they are authorized to remain as vulnerabilities.

5. Vulnerability scanning does not always return reliable and accurate results. The results depend heavily on the systems being scanned. Which of the following systems would be the least likely to be identified and return genuine scan results? (Choose two.)

   A. CCTV camera, web-enabled with embedded Apache

   B. An open source firewall, customized by the scan target client

   C. Windows 2012 server, missing three months of patches and the latest Service Pack

   D. Novell NetWare 6.5

   ☑ **A** and **B** are correct. Devices with embedded Apache server or lightweight versions of Linux tend to be especially challenging targets. Likewise, the firewall, customized by the customer, might present a unique profile to the scanner.

   ☒ **C** and **D** are incorrect. **C** is incorrect because the Windows server is a standard, well-known system for the scanner, and likely to produce fairly reliable results. Similarly for **D**, the NetWare system should be a recognizable target.

6. Alongside results in the scan report, it's common to see references to external sources such as OSVDB and NVD. What is the reason for vulnerability scanners to include information from those databases?

   A. The sources provide validation to the scan results.

   B. The sources offer additional information and possibly mitigating actions.

   C. The sources provide links to upload sanitized data from the scan.

   D. The sources specify whether a result is a false positive or a genuine vulnerability.

   ☑ **B** is correct. These databases provide additional information and sometimes even mitigating solutions.

   ☒ **A**, **C**, and **D** are incorrect. **A** is incorrect because the databases cannot validate your findings. **C** is incorrect because the results would not be uploaded to such sources. **D** is incorrect because such databases do not help validate or confirm a result as a false positive.

7. What is primary value of STIGs and NSA guides?

   A. They are a source of "best practice" principles.

   B. They are a proven source of vulnerability validation steps.

   C. They provide checklists detailing regulatory compliance.

   D. They specify configuration steps for secure networking.

   ☑ **A** is correct. The STIGs (Security Technical Implementation Guides) and NSA guides are configuration guides on how to harden government information systems; hence, they provide excellent reference for "best practices."

   ☒ **B, C,** and **D** are incorrect. **B** is incorrect because these guides do not offer steps on how to validate vulnerability scan results. **C** is incorrect because they might offer checklists to a degree, but such checklists are not their primary value. **D** is incorrect because, although some guides may offer hardening steps for networking devices, this is not their primary value.

8. Which of the following are good sources of validating scan results? (Choose all that apply.)

   A. Interviewing the system's owner

   B. Reviewing the system's event log

   C. Comparing against past vulnerability reports and results

   D. Examining system and network data such as open ports and services

   ☑ **B** and **D** are correct. Reviewing the system's logs is a good way of actually validating results. Also, checking system- and network-related data such as what ports are open or what services are actually running is another method for validating report results.

   ☒ **A** and **C** are incorrect. **A** is incorrect because the system's owner might really believe an additional service isn't running, but it is. **C** is incorrect because although comparing against past reports may show a trend, it doesn't really validate results.

9. What method allows the internal security team to tailor threat mitigation strategies, evaluate how effective those strategies are, and see the change of controls over time?

   A. Comparing a system against similar systems in the environment

   B. Comparing the current system against the original image, when available

   C. Comparing the system's trend in reported vulnerabilities

   D. Comparing the results with the system's logs

   ☑ **C** is correct. Comparing the system over time, or how the vulnerabilities trend, is a likely feature in the vulnerability scanner.

   ☒ **A, B,** and **D** are incorrect. **A** is incorrect because every system is unique. Comparing against other systems to make decisions is not recommended. **B** is incorrect because comparing against the original image would likely be very misleading. **D** is incorrect because comparing reported results with system logs helps validate the results but doesn't give much value over time.

10. What is best described as comparing a scan report against the personal and documented notes of the scan operator? Such notes would include scanning steps as well as observations around the scan devices' configuration and operation.

    A. Trending the results

    B. Validating the results

    C. Reconciling the results

    D. Managing the results

    ☑ **C** is correct. Reconciling results involves comparing the scan report findings with the scan operator's notes and observations. It is critical to take detailed notes; these are invaluable for verifying and validating the report.

    ☒ **A, B,** and **D** are incorrect. **A** is incorrect because trending the results is not the same as comparing results to notes. **B** is incorrect because validating the results sounds reasonable but is not as thorough as reconciling against the operator's notes. **D** is incorrect because managing the results is not a sensible term.

11. What type of scanning target would commonly have vulnerabilities due to the existence of unnecessary services and open ports?

    A. IDS

    B. SCADA device

    C. VPN

    D. Server

    ☑ **D** is correct. A common vulnerability in servers is having unnecessary services running or open ports.

    ☒ **A, B,** and **C** are incorrect. **A** is incorrect because an IDS doesn't run services like a server. **B** is incorrect because it is less common for SCADA devices to be running unnecessary services than it is for servers. SCADA devices will typically run only the essential services, albeit unpatched. **C** is incorrect because VPNs don't include services and open ports.

12. For which type of scanning target is it particularly easy to show duplicate vulnerabilities?

    A. VPN

    B. Virtual infrastructure

    C. Mobile device

    D. SCADA device

    ☑ **B** is correct. A virtual infrastructure such as a virtual machine (VM) starts with a VM image. VMs are far more easily copied and replicated. A vulnerability in the origin VM image is simply copied to the replicated VMs, making vulnerabilities easily duplicated across many machines.

☒ **A, C,** and **D** are incorrect. **A** is incorrect because VPNs are typically not as common as virtual infrastructure. **C** is incorrect because mobile devices can be unique, with vulnerabilities varied between vendors and owners. **D** is incorrect because although SCADA devices may have vulnerabilities due to infrequent updates, those vulnerabilities are not commonly duplicated across devices.

13. A vulnerability found in a hypervisor threatens the security of what devices? (Choose two.)

   A. Endpoint

   B. Host server

   C. Virtual machine

   D. Network device

   ☑ **B** and **C** are correct. The hypervisor sits between a host server and the virtual machines. Therefore, a vulnerability in the hypervisor can potentially affect both host and guest machines.

   ☒ **A** and **D** are incorrect. Network devices and endpoints are not dependent on a hypervisor (unless they are virtual devices).

14. A cybersecurity analyst is briefing the CEO on the encrypted nature of VPNs. The CEO, understanding how well VPNs protect confidentiality, asks what their primary vulnerability is. What should be the cybersecurity analyst's response?

   A. VPNs connect external devices to the internal network.

   B. VPNs mask network traffic from monitoring.

   C. VPN encryption is difficult to configure.

   D. VPNs have no vulnerabilities.

   ☑ **A** is correct. VPNs can introduce vulnerabilities because they connect unsecured devices to the protected, internal network.

   ☒ **B, C,** and **D** are incorrect. **B** is incorrect because although VPNs do mask network monitoring, if need be a host-based or server-based IDS can monitor traffic. **C** is incorrect because encryption should not be difficult for the person responsible for setting it up. **D** is incorrect because every cybersecurity analyst knows that every device has vulnerabilities.

15. An attacker seeks to enter a protected corporate network. Fortunately, the company's cybersecurity team has locked down the network well. Instead, the attacker discovers an open port in a maintenance-related network. Moving laterally, the attacker then moves onto the protected network. What is the source of the vulnerability overlooked by the cybersecurity team?

   A. VPN connection

   B. Virtualized switch

C. No encryption on either network

D. Interconnected networks

☑ **D** is correct. Networks that are unrelated but connected can provide pathways for persistent attackers. Interconnected networks are an often-overlooked vulnerability.

☒ **A, B,** and **C** are incorrect. **A** is incorrect because it's unlikely that a VPN was involved. **B** is incorrect because there was no mention of a virtualized switch. **C** is incorrect because encryption probably wouldn't have helped here.

16. What type of scanning target would commonly have vulnerabilities due to limitations imposed by carriers?

A. Mobile device

B. Virtual network infrastructure

C. Server

D. Industrial control system

☑ **A** is correct. Mobile device owners can find they are limited by their carrier in terms of upgrading or updating their operating systems.

☒ **B, C,** and **D** are incorrect. Carriers have little to no influence on virtualized network infrastructures, servers, and industrial control systems.

17. What is a source of vulnerabilities for essentially all devices?

A. No encryption

B. Patch updates and upgrades

C. Low memory and/or storage space

D. Policy exceptions

☑ **B** is correct. Being slow to patch or update is a vulnerability common to nearly every device or platform.

☒ **A, C,** and **D** are incorrect. **A** is incorrect because encryption is not common enough that a lack of it is considered a universal vulnerability. **C** is incorrect because memory and storage space are cheap and are not a common problem. **D** is incorrect because although policy exceptions may be an accepted vulnerability, they are not so common.

18. Which term describes what permits a VM to connect to an outside network?

A. Management interface

B. Interconnected network

C. Virtual private network

D. Virtual network

☑ **D** is correct. It is the virtual network that enables the VM to communicate with the outside world.

    ☒ **A, B,** and **C** are incorrect. **A** is incorrect because a management interface is not what connects a VM to a network; rather, it manages the connection. **B** is incorrect because "interconnected network" refers to more than one network type being connected. **C** is incorrect because a VPN is a means of connecting two devices and segregating traffic from their network. However, VPNs are not restricted to virtual machines.

19. What do the network protocols IPSec, L2TP, TLS, and DTLS have in common?

    A. They facilitate virtual private networks.

    B. All are Layer 2 protocols.

    C. They are used exclusively for virtual networks.

    D. They build interconnections between protected and peripheral networks.

    ☑ **A** is correct. These protocols all can be found when you're setting up a VPN.

    ☒ **B, C,** and **D** are incorrect. These protocols are not exclusively Layer 2 protocols and are not found only on virtual networks. Also, they are not intended for linking dissimilar networks.

20. Which of the following characteristics is prominent in Supervisory Control and Data Acquisition systems?

    A. They typically cover a wide geographical area.

    B. They contain several types of control systems, including ICS (industry control systems).

    C. They are common, with only one person operating them locally.

    D. They rely on obscure networking protocols such as IPX/SPX.

    ☑ **A** is correct. SCADA systems are known for covering a large geographical area.

    ☒ **B, C,** and **D** are incorrect. **B** is incorrect because SCADA does not include ICS systems; instead, it's the other way around. SCADA is a subset of industry control systems. **C** is incorrect because SCADA systems are typically unmanned, with no one operating them locally. **D** is incorrect because, up until recently, the security of SCADA systems relied on the obscurity of its communications. However, IPX/SPX, the NetWare protocols of the 1990s, were not the protocols used.

21. After creating several virtual machines, a system administrator took great effort to harden the virtual systems. When finished, the administrator sought approval from the security team and asked the cybersecurity analyst to try to compromise any one of the machines. Within a short amount of time, the administrator noticed that all the machines were running with great difficulty. A little investigation revealed the virtual systems were running with only one-fourth of the original memory. The host system was operating normally. When asked, the administrator claimed no machine was accessed. Where was the likely vulnerability?

    A. Virtual network

    B. Management interface

C. Host system physical memory

D. WAP

☑ **B** is correct. The cybersecurity analyst accessed the unprotected management interface, then reduced the memory of the VMs to demonstrate access to the interface.

☒ **A, C,** and **D** are incorrect. **A** is incorrect because accessing the virtual network would not have effectively removed three-fourths of the memory in all VMs. **C** is incorrect because changing the host system's memory would not have affected the VM memory this way. **D** is incorrect because accessing a wireless access point would not have changed the VM memory.

22. What is the term used to describe when an attacker is able to leap from a virtual machine to the host machine?

A. Lateral move

B. Virtual interruption

C. Escape

D. Sandbox jump

☑ **C** is correct. Leaving the VM and accessing the host system is called an escape.

☒ **A, B,** and **D** are incorrect. None of these is the correct term to describe moving from the VM to the host.

23. What are the most common vulnerabilities found in a network infrastructure? (Select two)

A. Misconfiguration

B. Broadcast storms

C. WAP

D. Enabled COM port

☑ **A** and **C** are correct. The misconfiguration of network devices and the wireless access point are the biggest vulnerabilities.

☒ **B** and **D** are incorrect. Broadcast storms and having unprotected COM ports are both fairly rare events for network devices. And when they do occur, we can likely blame misconfiguration.

24. In terms of mitigating vulnerabilities, network appliances should be treated as specialized forms of what type of device?

A. WAP

B. Endpoint

C. Server

D. Virtual host

☑ **C** is correct. A network appliance is essentially a customized server, performing some specialized function, such as web proxy or caching server.

☒ **A, B,** and **D** are incorrect. Network appliances are generally servers, more so than wireless access points, endpoints, or virtual hosts.

25. Stuxnet, which targeted the uranium enrichment centrifuges run in Iran, was an example of malware targeting what type of system?

   A. VM

   B. ICS

   C. HMI

   D. NAC

   ☑ **B** is correct. The malware Stuxnet, written solely to attack the uranium enrichment program in Iran, specifically targeted the industry control system (ICS) running within the facility.

   ☒ **A, C,** and **D** are incorrect. Stuxnet didn't target a VM (virtual machine), a human-machine interface (HMI), or any network access control (NAC).

26. What type of system presents a unique challenge in updating due to how critical its uptime is?

   A. HVAC

   B. Finance server

   C. SCADA

   D. Perimeter network protection

   ☑ **C** is correct. SCADA systems typically allow for no downtime because they provide critical services. No allowable downtime means no maintenance for updates or patching.

   ☒ **A, B,** and **D** are incorrect. **A** is incorrect because HVAC (heating, ventilation, and air conditioning) is not exactly critical infrastructure. **B** is incorrect because finance servers would be permitted some downtime for patching. **D** is incorrect because perimeter network protection devices would certainly need to be kept up to date and would probably include some level of redundancy to allow for downtime.

27. An employee has come to you with concerns about installing a software package on their desktop. When you ask how confident they are that the software is secure and from a safe vendor, the employee assures you the package was "signed by a certificate." However, the employee mentioned that during the installation an error appeared, complaining about the signing certificate, but they clicked the error too quickly to actually understand it. A dialog box is still on the desktop screen, showing additional information about the certificate. From Figure 6-1, can you determine what the likely error was?

A. The certificate has expired.

B. The certificate is from an untrusted source.

C. The certificate is based on inadequate encryption.

D. The certificate fingerprint is invalid.

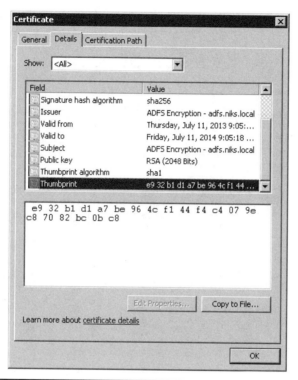

Figure 6-1   Certificate details

☑ **A is correct.** From the dates, you see the certificate has expired.

☒ **B, C,** and **D** are incorrect. **B** is incorrect because the certificate is from a known issuer. **C** is incorrect because SHA256 is an adequate level of encryption. **D** is incorrect because there is no way to determine whether the fingerprint is fine just from viewing this dialog box.

28. Over the past year, a few significant changes occurred in a company's IT environment. See Figure 6-2 for a list of those changes. Each change had an effect on vulnerability scan reporting. Looking at Figure 6-3, can you determine what change most affected the trend of critical vulnerabilities?

A. BYOD policy update

B. Firewall update

C. Router update

D. New AVS

Time	Policy Change
Dec-17	BYOD policy update
Mar-18	Firewall update
Mar-18	Router update
May-18	New AVS

Figure 6-2 Documented changes

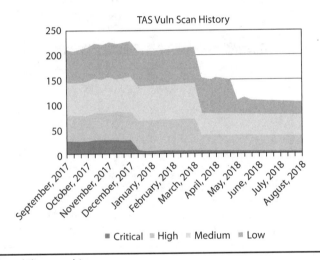

Figure 6-3 Vulnerability scan history

☑ **A** is correct. Trend analysis shows a sharp decline in critical vulnerabilities in December 2017. That month correlates to an update in the BYOD (bring your own device) policy.

☒ **B, C,** and **D** are incorrect. Critical vulnerabilities showed no increases or declines during these other changes.

29. On "Bring Your Daughter to Work Day," cybersecurity analyst Elizabeth brings her daughter Paige to the data center. Paige is curious why analysts across different companies and countries take the same steps to harden their infrastructures. What is Elizabeth's likely explanation?

A. Requirements are forced by regulatory compliance.

B. Policy is dictated by trends.

C. All analysts trust each other's good judgment.

D. Best practices are being widely adopted.

☑ **D** is correct. A general adoption of best practices means similar implementation of steps toward hardening the environment, regardless of location and industry.

☒ **A, B,** and **C** are incorrect. **A** is incorrect because only a subset of environments would be bound by regulatory compliance. **B** is incorrect because trends may influence policy changes but wouldn't create some worldwide common trend. **C** is incorrect because security is not inspired or strengthened by trust.

30. A company is experiencing a substantial increase in incidents since allowing employees to connect their own mobile devices to the internal network. What is the key vulnerability behind this scenario?

A. Mobile devices are being allowed without any corporate policies.

B. Mobile devices are being used without a VPN connection.

C. Mobile devices are allowed to be plugged into USB ports on desktop PCs

D. The network infrastructure is burdened with additional traffic.

☑ **A** is correct. The main vulnerability with starting a BYOD policy is the unknown status of all those personally managed devices. Some will not be adequately patched or updated. Some will have malware already installed. And some may be compromised.

☒ **B, C,** and **D** are incorrect. **B** is incorrect because having a VPN still means you're connected to the network, whether on-site or remotely. **C** is incorrect because although this USB policy for desktop PCs would further increase the vulnerability of rogue devices on the network, it's not the primary concern. **D** is incorrect because the additional load on the network is likely not that significant.

31. Using the Windows registry editor, a security analyst navigates to the following key:

HKLM\Software\Policies\Microsoft\Windows\CurrentVersion\Internet Settings

At that key, the analyst sets the value **PreventIgnoreCertErrors** to **REG_DWORD = 1**. What is the key vulnerability that encouraged this setting?

A. The Certificate Authority is employing too weak a cryptographic cipher.

B. Users are ignoring certificate errors.

C. The Certificate Authority is untrusted.

D. Users' devices are unable to send an OSCP status request.

☑ **B** is correct. This registry entry, when set to 1, stops users from bypassing certificate errors. A certificate error could be due to any number of issues, such as a name mismatch on the certificate, the certificate having expired, or the certificate having an inadequate cryptographic strength.

☒ **A, C,** and **D** are incorrect. **A** is incorrect because an overly weak cipher is only one of several reasons an error is getting raised. But the registry change directly changes users' ability to ignore errors. **C** is incorrect because an untrusted CA is only one of many possible causes for errors shown to users. The registry change affects the users' ability to ignore those errors. **D** is incorrect because OSCP request failures are not likely to prompt a registry change as a fix.

32. You've just learned of a new, critical vulnerability that was discovered late last night. You suspect your infrastructure is particularly vulnerable. You need to perform an immediate scan to identify all the affected servers that will require action. What has your attention first?

    A. SIEM

    B. VM management interface

    C. Vulnerability feed

    D. CVSS

    ☑ **C** is correct. You first need to find out if your vulnerability feed already has the ability to scan for and identify this vulnerability. Regardless of whether your external AVS (authorized vulnerability scanner) or in-house scanner is used, it is not guaranteed the scan will be up to date on the most recent vulnerabilities.

    ☒ **A, B,** and **D** are incorrect. **A** is incorrect because SIEM might inform you of incidents caused as a result of the new vulnerability, but that would be a job for incident response. Your job is to identify and mitigate the new critical vulnerability. **B** is incorrect because you do not need to manage the VMs right now. **D** is incorrect because CVSS probably hasn't had a chance to analyze the new vulnerability yet. There will be time to read up on that later.

33. The Authentication metric, the Access Complexity metric, and the Access Vector metric are all scoring factors used for what system?

    A. NVD

    B. PCI DSS

    C. Nessus

    D. CVSS

    ☑ **D** is correct. The Common Vulnerability Scoring System uses these metrics, among others, to calculate a rating for every vulnerability.

    ☒ **A, B,** and **C** are incorrect. **A** is incorrect because NVD provides two vulnerability feeds but is not a scoring authority like CVSS is. **B** is incorrect because PCI DSS is a set of requirements for businesses that deal with credit card data. **C** is incorrect because Nessus is a vulnerability scanner that rates its findings based on their CVSS score.

34. Soon after completing a vulnerability scan, you review the most critical findings on your Nginx web server. From the following list, which is the likely false positive?

A. CVE-2016-1247 Nginx Root Privilege Escalation

B. CVE-2017-0278 Windows SMB Remote Code Execution

C. CVE-2017-7529 Nginx Remote Integer Overflow

D. CVE-2018-7584 PHP Stack Buffer Overflow

E. CVE-2017-14176 Bazaar with Subprocess SSH, allows Remote Execution

☑ **B** is correct. This is the lone Windows vulnerability and therefore the likely false positive.

☒ **A, C, D,** and **E** are incorrect. These are all Nginx or Linux vulnerabilities. Because the odd one is a Windows vulnerability, it's safe to assume the Windows finding is the false positive.

35. A vulnerability scan reports a web service running on a server. However, you only know of an application developed in-house running on that server. Additionally, the server is not external facing, and you're fairly confident there is no web service running. What is the likely port of that internally developed application?

A. 445

B. 69

C. 110

D. 80

☑ **D** is correct. If a scanner reports a web service running, it might have only detected port 80 as open and listening.

☒ **A, B,** and **C** are incorrect. Ports 445, 69, and 110 are not associated with HTTP traffic.

36. A vulnerability scan reports a web service running on a server, but you were unaware of any web service or anything running on port 80. What might be your next step?

A. Scan the server with a port scanner to see if port 80 is listening.

B. Write a policy that web services must be approved before an installation.

C. E-mail employees to find out the website's administrator.

D. Re-run the vulnerability scan.

☑ **A** is correct. The next step would be to scan the server, paying particular attention to port 80. If port 80 is open, perhaps a web service is listening.

☒ **B, C,** and **D** are incorrect. **B** is incorrect because writing a policy does not help validate the finding. **C** is incorrect because e-mailing everyone only distracts employees. And, if the port is somehow connected to malicious activity, then a broadcast e-mail only reveals your discovery. **D** is incorrect because it may be more helpful to attempt to validate the finding before rescanning.

37. A specialized web proxy device has been flagged by a vulnerability scanner for several scanning periods for the same vulnerability. The cybersecurity team is asked why this vulnerability persists. What are the likely causes? (Choose two.)

   A. Being a vendor-specific network appliance, its patch management was overlooked.

   B. This network appliance is on the DMZ and therefore left unmanaged.

   C. The vendor is responsible for patching, but for reasons unknown has been unable to do so.

   D. The network appliance is compromised.

   ☑ **A** and **C** are correct. What tends to happen with a specialized network appliance is that the responsibility for the appliance is overlooked by internal security or it is transferred to a third-party vendor. In this case, its patching requirement might have been overlooked or the vendor has recently lost connectivity to the appliance.

   ☒ **B** and **D** are incorrect. Appliances on the DMZ are every bit as important to patch (if not more so) than internal systems. Also, it's unlikely the system was hacked (yet), but it's a possibility.

38. After a vulnerability scan is completed, what's the "best practice" for prioritizing response actions?

   A. Absolutely start with the highest CVSS rating and work toward the lower-rated vulnerabilities.

   B. Start with the response with the shortest implementation time and work toward the more involved responses.

   C. All scan reports are unique, but in general you should balance least disruption with risk mitigation.

   D. First validate and reconcile all vulnerabilities and then start to remediate.

   ☑ **C** is correct. Scan report findings are unique, ranging from the most critical to more informative findings. Responses will range from quite involved remediations to "quick fixes." Therefore, it's a case-by-case situation of balancing time, budget, and risk mitigation.

   ☒ **A, B,** and **D** are incorrect. **A** is incorrect because working from the highest CVSS to the lowest will most likely use up valuable resources before all the easy, "low-hanging fruit" vulnerabilities are addressed. **B** is incorrect because there will definitely be critical, but somewhat involved, vulnerabilities that you should not wait to fix. **D** is incorrect because it would take too much time to validate every informative finding.

PART III

Cyber Incident Response

The Incident Response Process

This chapter includes questions on the following topics:

- The stakeholders during incident response
- Containment techniques
- Eradication techniques
- Response validation
- Corrective actions
- The purpose of communication processes

The best-case scenario in responding to the unexpected requires a prepared plan and developed process. Inevitably the cybersecurity analyst will need to respond to an incident. An incident could mean discovering a compromised machine from long ago, or the incident could be ongoing, bringing the analyst and adversary face to face in real time. Technical steps, as part of a staged process, must be taken. This chapter covers the entire spectrum of the incident response process, from initial containment to the final response and corrective actions. But perhaps more important than any technical removal or remediation step in incident handling is the communication done all along the way. Key to incident response is communication—from how the incident is first announced to how the lessons learned are shared after the fact. Communication in incident response is multifaceted, with key stakeholders at several levels all wanting to know what's going on, what's being done, and what it will take to not allow the incident happen again.

1. Which of the following is *not* considered an important stakeholder during incident response?

   A. The organization's legal department.

   B. Human resources.

   C. Marketing.

   D. Management.

   E. All are important stakeholders in incident response.

2. In the course of incident response, what phase strives to prevent or reduce the spread of the incident?

   A. Containment

   B. Sanitization

   C. Detection

   D. Patching

3. During incident response, what phase seeks to return all systems to a known-good state?

   A. Eradication

   B. Segmentation

   C. Removal

   D. Scanning

4. During incident response, what phase requires understanding how the incident took place in order to implement countermeasures or controls to prevent the attack from happening again?

   A. Reverse engineering

   B. Sanitization

   C. Reconstruction

   D. Validation

5. Which of the following terms refers to a containment technique to permit cybersecurity analysts to still monitor the system's activity without jeopardizing the whole network?

   A. Removal

   B. Secure disposal

   C. Verifying logging/communication

   D. Isolation

   E. Patching

6. The cybersecurity team just finished recovering from an incident, but within a few days, similar indicators of compromise appear. The cybersecurity team determined that an attacker hijacked an account with elevated privileges. After the team investigated further, it seemed both incidents took advantage of the same attack vector. What was the root cause of the incident that the team failed to address in the earlier incident?

   A. Eradication

   B. Permissions

   C. Patching

   D. Containment

7. In what phase of incident response do cybersecurity team members discuss with stakeholders their experience and understanding of the incident?

   A. During the containment phase through the eradication phase

   B. The validation phase

   C. As the team completes the corrective action phase

   D. Throughout all phases

8. How is any experience gained as a result of the incident being shared among management?

   A. Via constant communication, from start to finish

   B. Through a change control process report

   C. Through a lessons learned report

   D. In the executive summary to the response plan update

9. Performing corrective actions as incident recovery concludes is a vital phase of incident response. What corrective step helps ensure that any procedural gaps identified during the response are fixed in preparation for the next response?

   A. Reviewing the change control process

   B. Publishing a summary report

   C. Updating the incident response plan

   D. Securely disposing of the compromised systems

10. Post-incident, after all corrective actions have been performed, including compiling a full lessons learned report, what is the final documentation step?

   A. New incident response plan

   B. Reverse engineering report

   C. Validation scan and report

   D. Incident summary report

11. A company is dealing with an incident that required involvement with a law enforcement agency (LEA). Cooperation between the cybersecurity team and the LEA was very difficult, given how much the goals and perspectives of the LEA, management, and the cybersecurity team differed. What was the likely reason for this bad experience?

   A. The incident response plan didn't include law enforcement.

   B. The LEA demanded to retain hardware as evidence.

   C. The cybersecurity team had no prior incident practice with the LEA.

   D. Management was unable to lead alongside the LEA.

12. The company Major League Manifolds, Ltd., had an incident, with three main stakeholders involved. Referring to the list of roles and employees, shown in Figure 7-1, you see that Phelps, Brown, and Hayes were the employees involved. From the following possible incidents, which is the probable incident that's occurring.

   A. A senior-level employee's e-mail account was hacked.

   B. The external payroll provider's database server was compromised.

   C. An HR employee was discovered working for a competitor.

   D. An undocumented exception to the patching policy was discovered.

Major League Manifolds, Ltd.	
Roles	**Name**
Owner	R. Phelps
General Manager	L. Brown
Legal	R. Vaughn
HR	J. Jobu
Marketing/PR	P. Cerrano
Analyst	W. Hayes

Figure 7-1 MLM roles and names

13. Referring again to Figure 7-1, consider the roles that should be involved when the company's server for handling payment transactions is compromised by an external hacker. Which of the following list of names includes all the stakeholders?

   A. Brown, Vaughn, Jobu, Cerrano, Hays

   B. Phelps, Brown, Jobu, Hays

   C. Phelps, Brown, Vaughn, Hays

   D. Phelps, Brown, Vaughn, Cerrano, Hays

14. A company recently finished responding to a serious incident of attempted sabotage. The attack seemed suspiciously like it was caused by a current employee. Although the investigation to identify the precise employee is still ongoing, the internal cybersecurity analysts are certain the attack originated from accounts payable in the finance department. The incident summary report has been finished and was sent in encrypted format to the department heads and local managers of admin, HR, finance, manufacturing, and shipping. Select from the following list the one risk that could have been avoided.

   A. Communication disclosure based on regulatory requirements

   B. Extensive communication with management

   C. Insecure method of communication

   D. Inadvertent release of information to the public

15. Allowing for budget, what option does a company have when its lack of technical expertise means the company doesn't have its own internal CSIRT team?

   A. Retain an incident response provider.

   B. Cross-train all employees in incident response techniques.

   C. None. The company has no ability to respond to incidents.

   D. Empower the night security guard to watch over the data center.

16. What are the main challenges for the technical role of incident response? (Choose two.)

   A. Having the necessary technical expertise to address the incident

   B. Licensing the proper software tools

   C. Granting or delegating the authority for unforeseen decisions

   D. Overcoming personality differences and in-house rivalries

17. A company that has grown quickly in size has not yet developed a proper communication escalation process in the event of a security incident. Instead, managers of the cybersecurity team post their analysis and findings on the company's internal blog site. In an effort to maintain confidentiality, the blog posts are kept hidden, with no link on the front page. What is the shortcoming of this communication process?

   A. Disclosure based on legislative requirements

   B. Possible inadvertent release of information

   C. No encryption

   D. Little opportunity for discussion and questions

1. E	**7.** D	**13.** D
2. A	**8.** C	**14.** B
3. A	**9.** C	**15.** A
4. D	**10.** D	**16.** A, C
5. D	**11.** C	**17.** B
6. B	**12.** A	

1. Which of the following is *not* considered an important stakeholder during incident response?

   A. The organization's legal department.

   B. Human resources.

   C. Marketing.

   D. Management.

   E. All are important stakeholders in incident response.

   ☑ **E** is correct. All of the named stakeholders are important and should be involved during the incident response process.

   ☒ **A, B, C,** and **D** are incorrect. Each of these—legal, HR, marketing, and management—is an important stakeholder that should be a part of the incident response process.

2. In the course of incident response, what phase strives to prevent or reduce the spread of the incident?

   A. Containment

   B. Sanitization

   C. Detection

   D. Patching

   ☑ **A** is correct. Containment, the first phase of incident response, includes reducing the spread of the incident.

   ☒ **B, C,** and **D** are incorrect. **B** is incorrect because sanitization, part of eradication phase, involves cleaning up after the incident. **C** is incorrect because detection is not a phase. **D** is incorrect because patching is a corrective action, done long after containment.

3. During incident response, what phase seeks to return all systems to a known-good state?

   A. Eradication

   B. Segmentation

   C. Removal

   D. Scanning

   ☑ **A** is correct. Eradication is the phase where you strive to return the system to a known-good state.

   ☒ **B, C,** and **D** are incorrect. **B** is incorrect because segmentation is a containment tactic for isolating by network segment. **C** is incorrect because removal is the action of taking a known-compromised system completely offline. **D** is incorrect because scanning is a validation technique.

4. During incident response, what phase requires understanding how the incident took place in order to implement countermeasures or controls to prevent the attack from happening again?

  A. Reverse engineering

  B. Sanitization

  C. Reconstruction

  D. Validation

  ☑ **D** is correct. Validation is done to verify the attack vectors and to implement countermeasures.

  ☒ **A, B,** and **C** are incorrect. **A** is incorrect because reverse engineering is an earlier step, a part of containment. **B** is incorrect because sanitization is part of ridding the problem systems of their malware or issues. **C** is incorrect because reconstruction is, like sanitization, part of the eradication phase.

5. Which of the following terms refers to a containment technique to permit cybersecurity analysts to still monitor the system's activity without jeopardizing the whole network?

  A. Removal

  B. Secure disposal

  C. Verifying logging/communication

  D. Isolation

  E. Patching

  ☑ **D** is correct. Isolation means to segregate the system (or systems) but not completely remove it from communicating with others. It's more an exercise of drawing a perimeter around the problem system, rather than removing it entirely.

  ☒ **A, B, C,** and **E** are incorrect. **A** is incorrect because removal means to take the system offline, whereas isolation allows the analyst to still monitor the system. **B** is incorrect because secure disposal describes cleaning or destroying the compromised media. **C** is incorrect because verifying logging and communication is a reference to the validation phase. **E** is incorrect because patching references the corrective actions phase.

6. The cybersecurity team just finished recovering from an incident, but within a few days, similar indicators of compromise appear. The cybersecurity team determined that an attacker hijacked an account with elevated privileges. After the team investigated further, it seemed both incidents took advantage of the same attack vector. What was the root cause of the incident that the team failed to address in the earlier incident?

  A. Eradication

  B. Permissions

  C. Patching

  D. Containment

☑ **B** is correct. Permissions is the corrective action that was missed in the first incident recovery. Seems an account with elevated privileges was compromised and abused, but after the first incident that risk was not adequately mitigated.

☒ **A, C,** and **D** are incorrect. **A** is incorrect because it seems eradication was done correctly in the first incident. **C** is incorrect because patching is not the solution for the compromised account. **D** is incorrect because it seems containment was handled properly in both incidents.

7. In what phase of incident response do cybersecurity team members discuss with stakeholders their experience and understanding of the incident?

   A. During the containment phase through the eradication phase

   B. The validation phase

   C. As the team completes the corrective action phase

   D. Throughout all phases

   ☑ **D** is correct. Communication is critical in all phases.

   ☒ **A, B,** and **C** are incorrect. Communication with the stakeholders is needed in all phases of incident response.

8. How is any experience gained as a result of the incident being shared among management?

   A. Via constant communication, from start to finish

   B. Through a change control process report

   C. Through a lessons learned report

   D. In the executive summary to the response plan update

   ☑ **C** is correct. Concluding the incident response is the "lessons learned" report, where input from everyone involved in the event is used to summarize how the incident response went and how the incident could have been handled better.

   ☒ **A, B,** and **D** are incorrect. **A** is incorrect because although constant communication is important, it is the lessons learned report that focuses on what lessons were gained over the course of the incident. **B** is incorrect because there isn't a change control process report. **D** is incorrect because there isn't an executive summary to the response plan update.

9. Performing corrective actions as incident recovery concludes is a vital phase of incident response. What corrective step helps ensure that any procedural gaps identified during the response are fixed in preparation for the next response?

   A. Reviewing the change control process

   B. Publishing a summary report

   C. Updating the incident response plan

   D. Securely disposing of the compromised systems

☑ **C** is correct. Updating the incident response plan helps improve the process for when (not if) an incident happens again.

☒ **A, B,** and **D** are incorrect. **A** is incorrect because reviewing the change control process is important, but not with the end goal of correcting gaps in incident response. **B** is incorrect because although a summary report might communicate what gaps were identified, it does not directly remediate them. **D** is incorrect because secure disposal does nothing for helping gaps in the IR process.

10. Post-incident, after all corrective actions have been performed, including compiling a full lessons learned report, what is the final documentation step?

    A. New incident response plan

    B. Reverse engineering report

    C. Validation scan and report

    D. Incident summary report

    ☑ **D** is correct. An incident summary report is the final documentation created directly as a result of the incident. Its length and audience vary, depending on the organization.

    ☒ **A, B,** and **C** are incorrect. These answers either are not expected at the conclusion or are not expected at all.

11. A company is dealing with an incident that required involvement with a law enforcement agency (LEA). Cooperation between the cybersecurity team and the LEA was very difficult, given how much the goals and perspectives of the LEA, management, and the cybersecurity team differed. What was the likely reason for this bad experience?

    A. The incident response plan didn't include law enforcement.

    B. The LEA demanded to retain hardware as evidence.

    C. The cybersecurity team had no prior incident practice with the LEA.

    D. Management was unable to lead alongside the LEA.

    ☑ **C** is correct. It is good practice to involve law enforcement when performing incident response practice runs. Only by running through the exercise (or actual incident) can the divergent goals and motivations of different groups be determined.

    ☒ **A, B,** and **D** are incorrect. **A** is incorrect because the incident response plan probably does mention law enforcement. Otherwise, someone wouldn't have involved he LEA during the incident. **B** is incorrect because, although the LEA might want the hardware as evidence, it is not the primary reason for the difficulty. **D** is incorrect because management is likely capable of leading with or without law enforcement being involved.

12. The company Major League Manifolds, Ltd., had an incident, with three main stakeholders involved. Referring to the list of roles and employees, shown in Figure 7-1, you see that Phelps, Brown, and Hayes were the employees involved. From the following possible incidents, which is the probable incident that's occurring.

A. A senior-level employee's e-mail account was hacked.

B. The external payroll provider's database server was compromised.

C. An HR employee was discovered working for a competitor.

D. An undocumented exception to the patching policy was discovered.

Major League Manifolds, Ltd.	
Roles	**Name**
Owner	R. Phelps
General Manager	L. Brown
Legal	R. Vaughn
HR	J. Jobu
Marketing/PR	P. Cerrano
Analyst	W. Hayes

Figure 7-1 MLM roles and names

☑ **A is correct.** Considering the roles involved (owner, general manager, and analyst), it was a "straightforward" incident.

☒ **B, C,** and **D** are incorrect. **B** is incorrect because had an external server been involved, it's much more likely that legal and the public-facing marketing department would be added as stakeholders. **C** is incorrect because if an internal employee were involved, then perhaps HR would be needed. **D** is incorrect because a patching policy breach likely wouldn't involve the owner.

13. Referring again to Figure 7-1, consider the roles that should be involved when the company's server for handling payment transactions is compromised by an external hacker. Which of the following list of names includes all the stakeholders?

A. Brown, Vaughn, Jobu, Cerrano, Hays

B. Phelps, Brown, Jobu, Hays

C. Phelps, Brown, Vaughn, Hays

D. Phelps, Brown, Vaughn, Cerrano, Hays

☑ **D is correct.** Given that the server for handling payment transactions had unauthorized access, this likely means regulatory noncompliance, involving legal and the public-facing marketing department. The other roles should be obvious.

☒ **A, B,** and **C** are incorrect. Again, because of the compromised payment server, both legal and marketing roles would be involved, to handle the regulatory considerations and to address public concerns of identity theft. Given that this is an external attack, not from an internal employee, it's unlikely HR would be called on as a stakeholder.

14. A company recently finished responding to a serious incident of attempted sabotage. The attack seemed suspiciously like it was caused by a current employee. Although the investigation to identify the precise employee is still ongoing, the internal cybersecurity analysts are certain the attack originated from accounts payable in the finance department. The incident summary report has been finished and was sent in encrypted format to the department heads and local managers of admin, HR, finance, manufacturing, and shipping. Select from the following list the one risk that could have been avoided.

    A. Communication disclosure based on regulatory requirements

    B. Extensive communication with management

    C. Insecure method of communication

    D. Inadvertent release of information to the public

    ☑ **B** is correct. As the scenario explains, an employee within the finance department is suspected of causing the incident. However, the incident summary report went to multiple people in finance. This does not demonstrate properly limiting communication to trusted parties.

    ☒ **A, C,** and **D** are incorrect. **A** is incorrect because no regulatory requirements were mentioned. **C** is incorrect because the report was sent in encrypted format. **D** is incorrect because there was no mention of a public release of information.

15. Allowing for budget, what option does a company have when its lack of technical expertise means the company doesn't have its own internal CSIRT team?

    A. Retain an incident response provider.

    B. Cross-train all employees in incident response techniques.

    C. None. The company has no ability to respond to incidents.

    D. Empower the night security guard to watch over the data center.

    ☑ **A** is correct. The choice the company has is to retain an external incident response provider.

    ☒ **B, C,** and **D** are incorrect. **B** is incorrect because cross-training all employees to be an effective IR team is not reasonable. **C** is incorrect because having no ability to respond is unacceptable. **D** is incorrect because the night security guard is likely unable or unwilling to perform incident response.

16. What are the main challenges for the technical role of incident response? (Choose two.)

    A. Having the necessary technical expertise to address the incident

    B. Licensing the proper software tools

    C. Granting or delegating the authority for unforeseen decisions

    D. Overcoming personality differences and in-house rivalries

☑ **A** and **C** are correct. The two challenges are ensuring the technical expertise is at hand, for any reasonably likely incident (depending on what platforms and applications your environment is running) and delegating the authority to members of that team or to immediately accessible managers. Time cannot be wasted waiting for executives to allow a plug to be pulled.

☒ **B** and **D** are incorrect. Software licenses and personality differences are important obstacles but are hardly challenges in overcoming the urgency of responding to an incident.

17. A company that has grown quickly in size has not yet developed a proper communication escalation process in the event of a security incident. Instead, managers of the cybersecurity team post their analysis and findings on the company's internal blog site. In an effort to maintain confidentiality, the blog posts are kept hidden, with no link on the front page. What is the shortcoming of this communication process?

   A. Disclosure based on legislative requirements

   B. Possible inadvertent release of information

   C. No encryption

   D. Little opportunity for discussion and questions

   ☑ **B** is correct. Even though the blog posts are not widely published, their confidentiality is based on the false assurance of "security through obscurity." Anyone who discovers the accessible posts is a potential leaker or abuser of that information.

   ☒ **A, C,** and **D** are incorrect. **A** is incorrect because no legislative requirements were mentioned. **C** is incorrect because encryption would not be the primary issue here. **D** is incorrect because blog posts allow for comments.

CHAPTER 8

Determining the Impact of Incidents

This chapter includes questions on the following topics:
- Criteria for classifying threats to the network
- How to determine the severity level of an incident
- Best practices for prioritizing security incident response
- The most common types of sensitive and protected data

Incident response is very rarely, if ever, a straightforward activity. Like any other job where you are "putting out fires," the job of incident response involves constantly measuring severity and then acting accordingly. That is to say, you fight the fire you determine needs your attention first—you act based on priority.

Prioritizing an incident is a product of several factors, such as the scope of impact (including downtime), what kind of data is affected, and what type of threat you are dealing with. There are other factors as well. How to best identify those factors and thus prioritize your incident response steps are the topics covered in this chapter.

1. In terms of skill and determination, what type of adversary is regarded as the most capable and resourceful?

   A. Script kiddie

   B. Advanced persistent threat

   C. Haxor

   D. Zero-day

2. A company has recently installed an IDS that's capable of detecting a broad set of malicious traffic and operates on signature-based identification. Which of the following types of threats will this IDS identify? (Choose all that apply.)

   A. Zero-day

   B. Threats labeled by CVE

   C. Unknown threats

   D. EICAR file

   E. Known threats

3. A cybersecurity team is responding to an incident. To help prioritize their actions, an analyst requests a list of essential business processes from the CIO. Select from the following factors which one the analyst is most concerned with to help prioritize the team's response.

   A. Downtime

   B. System process criticality

   C. Recovery time

   D. Economic

4. Of the following metrics, which ones rely on a company being able to endure a certain amount of downtime? (Choose all that apply.)

   A. Designated acceptable downtime (DAD)

   B. Key performance indicators (KPIs)

   C. Maximum tolerable downtime (MTD)

   D. Recovery time objective (RTO)

5. Multiple factors can affect the severity of an incident. Which of the following factors does not necessarily impact an incident's severity?

   A. Downtime

   B. Probability of corruption

   C. MTD

   D. System process criticality

   E. None of the above

6. Of the many factors that affect incident severity, which of the following takes the cybersecurity team the longest time to detect issues for or determine the scope of its impact?

   A. Data integrity

   B. System process criticality

   C. Recovery time

   D. Type of data

7. What is the desired relationship when comparing RTO and MTD?

   A. The RTO should be longer than the MTD.

   B. The RTO should be shorter than the MTD.

   C. The MTD and RTO should be roughly the same length.

   D. The MTD should as close to zero as possible.

   E. The RTO needs to be twice the MTD.

   F. The MTD needs to be twice the RTO.

8. The United States Privacy Act of 1974 created rules regarding the collection, storage, and use of what kind of data?

   A. Financial

   B. Intellectual property

   C. PII

   D. Payment card information

9. Which of the following is not a PCI DSS goal or requirement?

   A. Regularly monitor and test networks.

   B. Maintain an information security policy.

   C. Build and maintain a secure network and systems.

   D. Enforce employee security awareness training.

   E. Protect cardholder data.

10. Select from the following the data types that fall under the term "intellectual property." (Choose all that apply.)

    A. The patent behind a company's best-selling product

    B. Your favorite shoe company's trademark

    C. The secret recipe of a chicken flavoring

    D. The details about a company's marketing campaign

11. An analyst is reviewing DLP logs of sensitive documents attached to outgoing e-mails. The analyst discovers a sent document titled "Hilltop Organization Chart," apparently titled after the analyst's own company, Hilltop Cabinets. The document was sent to Hilltop's primary competitor, a company called Sanctuary Sinks. What type of data does this incident cover?

    A. Mergers and acquisitions

    B. Accounting data

    C. Corporate confidential

    D. Intellectual property

12. A new virus called MSB3417, dubbed "Wildfire," is sweeping through organizations, infecting systems by exploiting a previously unknown vulnerability. Wildfire identifies and exfiltrates any spreadsheet documents with large dollar amounts. The documents are then covertly sent to a known and powerful adversarial country. What is this type of malware called?

    A. APT exploit

    B. Zero-day exploit

    C. Financial exfiltration malware

    D. Economic threat

13. What is the particular criminal threat when data related to a company's intent to integrate with another company is mishandled?

    A. Leaked information could lead to trading based on privileged knowledge.

    B. Shareholders of both companies could vote to stop the merger.

    C. Leaked trade secrets could lead to increased competition.

    D. Violations of HIPAA requirements.

14. Which of the following factors determines some noted event will be considered a security incident?

    A. Downtime

    B. Scope of impact

    C. Economic

    D. Types of data affected

15. In the context of long-term effects from a security incident, particularly to a company's reputation and ability to gain potential business, which factor is the most impactful on an incident's severity?

    A. Recovery time

    B. Data integrity

    C. Economic

    D. System process criticality

16. For which of the following types of data is it suggested that a company take additional steps, beyond policy and legal guidance, to protect the data's confidentiality from unauthorized eyes? Not protecting the selected data type might jeopardize the company's sustainability.

    A. HR personnel information

    B. PII

    C. Payment card information

    D. Accounting data

17. Which of the following are possible consequences for unauthorized disclosure of PHI, depending on one's involvement. (Choose all that apply.)

    A. Documented record in employee file

    B. Suspension from employment

    C. Monetary fine

    D. Jail time

    E. Public execution

1. B	**7.** B	**13.** A
2. B, D, E	**8.** C	**14.** B
3. B	**9.** D	**15.** C
4. C, D	**10.** A, B, C	**16.** D
5. B	**11.** C	**17.** A, B, C, D
6. A	**12.** B	

1. In terms of skill and determination, what type of adversary is regarded as the most capable and resourceful?

   A. Script kiddie

   B. Advanced persistent threat

   C. Haxor

   D. Zero-day

   ☑ **B** is correct. The advanced persistent threat (APT) is by far the most skilled, most resourceful of threats.

   ☒ **A, C,** and **D** are incorrect. **A** is incorrect because a script kiddie is the name for someone who is inexperienced, like a child (kiddie), and only knows how to run a script. **C** is incorrect because a "haxor," or hacker, generally is someone who possess some skill, but acts alone, without massive resources behind them. **D** is incorrect because zero-day threats are neither skilled nor resourceful; the zero-day threat is dangerous because it is a new threat with no known mitigation.

2. A company has recently installed an IDS that's capable of detecting a broad set of malicious traffic and operates on signature-based identification. Which of the following types of threats will this IDS identify? (Choose all that apply.)

   A. Zero-day

   B. Threats labeled by CVE

   C. Unknown threats

   D. EICAR file

   E. Known threats

   ☑ **B, D,** and **E** are correct. If an IDS is signature-based, you can assume it's not capable of detecting unknown malware or detecting based on anomalous behavior. Threats with a CVE ID number very likely have a known signature assigned to them. The EICAR file is a well-known test file for malware detection. Known threats, as you can tell by the name, will have a signature.

   ☒ **A** and **C** are incorrect. **A** is incorrect because a zero-day is likely unknown to a signature-based device. **C** is incorrect because unknown threats, as obvious by the name, are unknown to a signature-based device.

3. A cybersecurity team is responding to an incident. To help prioritize their actions, an analyst requests a list of essential business processes from the CIO. Select from the following factors which one the analyst is most concerned with to help prioritize the team's response.

   A. Downtime

   B. System process criticality

C. Recovery time

D. Economic

☑ **B** is correct. System process criticality is the factor that defines whether or not business processes are essential.

☒ **A, C,** and **D** are incorrect. **A** is incorrect because the downtime factor involves how much downtime is allowable. **C** is incorrect because recovery time, which is related to downtime, describes how quickly business processes will be recovered. **D** is incorrect because economic factors include direct and indirect financial impacts.

4. Of the following metrics, which ones rely on a company being able to endure a certain amount of downtime? (Choose all that apply.)

   A. Designated acceptable downtime (DAD)

   B. Key performance indicators (KPIs)

   C. Maximum tolerable downtime (MTD)

   D. Recovery time objective (RTO)

   ☑ **C** and **D** are correct. Both the MTD and RTO presume a company can survive some downtime to some degree. The MTD is the maximum tolerable downtime before an organization's essential systems suffer critically, while the recovery time objective (RTO) describes the period of time when a company strives to recover from a disaster before suffering significant damage.

   ☒ **A** and **B** are incorrect. **A** is incorrect because DAD is a fictional term. **B** is incorrect because KPIs have nothing to do with downtime.

5. Multiple factors can affect the severity of an incident. Which of the following factors does not necessarily impact an incident's severity?

   A. Downtime

   B. Probability of corruption

   C. MTD

   D. System process criticality

   E. None of the above

   ☑ **B** is correct. There is no direct correlation between measuring an incident's severity and the probability of corruption.

   ☒ **A, C, D,** and **E** are incorrect. **A** is incorrect because downtime directly affects the severity of the incident. **C** is incorrect because MTD, or maximum tolerable downtime, affects an incident's severity. **D** is incorrect because system process criticality is how essential a business process is—a direct factor on how severe the impact caused by an incident is. **E** is incorrect because **B** is a correct answer.

6. Of the many factors that affect incident severity, which of the following takes the cybersecurity team the longest time to detect issues for or determine the scope of its impact?

    A. Data integrity

    B. System process criticality

    C. Recovery time

    D. Type of data

    ☑ **A** is correct. Certainly in relation to the other answers, it takes much longer to determine whether data was or wasn't altered by an attacker or incident.

    ☒ **B, C,** and **D** are incorrect. **B** is incorrect because system process criticality is known and discussed immediately after the incident. **C** is incorrect because recovery time is on everyone's mind right away if an incident causes downtime. **D** is incorrect because the type of data (for example, HIPAA or PHI) is known and considered in parallel with incident recovery.

7. What is the desired relationship when comparing RTO and MTD?

    A. The RTO should be longer than the MTD.

    B. The RTO should be shorter than the MTD.

    C. The MTD and RTO should be roughly the same length.

    D. The MTD should as close to zero as possible.

    E. The RTO needs to be twice the MTD.

    F. The MTD needs to be twice the RTO.

    ☑ **B** is correct. The recovery time objective should be shorter than the maximum tolerable downtime.

    ☒ **A, C, D, E,** and **F** are incorrect. Each of these incorrect answers offers a wrong or ridiculous statement about the relationship between RTO and MTD.

8. The United States Privacy Act of 1974 created rules regarding the collection, storage, and use of what kind of data?

    A. Financial

    B. Intellectual property

    C. PII

    D. Payment card information

    ☑ **C** is correct. Personally identifiable information (PII) is protected by the U.S. Privacy Act of 1974.

    ☒ **A, B,** and **D** are incorrect. **A** is incorrect because financial information is not protected by the U.S. Privacy Act of 1974 but instead by Sarbanes-Oxley and the Graham-Leach Bliley Act. **B** is incorrect because intellectual property (IP) is not protected by the U.S. Privacy Act of 1974 but instead by local or state laws regarding IP. **D** is incorrect because payment card information is governed by PCI DSS.

9. Which of the following is not a PCI DSS goal or requirement?

   A. Regularly monitor and test networks.

   B. Maintain an information security policy.

   C. Build and maintain a secure network and systems.

   D. Enforce employee security awareness training.

   E. Protect cardholder data.

   ☑ **D** is correct. Security awareness training is not a PCI DSS requirement.

   ☒ **A, B, C,** and **E** are incorrect. All these answers are requirements of the Payment Card Industry Data Security Standard.

10. Select from the following the data types that fall under the term "intellectual property." (Choose all that apply.)

    A. The patent behind a company's best-selling product

    B. Your favorite shoe company's trademark

    C. The secret recipe of a chicken flavoring

    D. The details about a company's marketing campaign

    ☑ **A, B,** and **C** are correct. **A** is correct because patents are intellectual property. **B** is correct because a trademark is intellectual property. Finally, **C** is correct because a secret recipe is a company's trade secret, which is also intellectual property.

    ☒ **D** is incorrect. A company's marketing campaign is not intellectual property. Instead, a marketing campaign would likely be labeled "corporate confidential."

11. An analyst is reviewing DLP logs of sensitive documents attached to outgoing e-mails. The analyst discovers a sent document titled "Hilltop Organization Chart," apparently titled after the analyst's own company, Hilltop Cabinets. The document was sent to Hilltop's primary competitor, a company called Sanctuary Sinks. What type of data does this incident cover?

    A. Mergers and acquisitions

    B. Accounting data

    C. Corporate confidential

    D. Intellectual property

    ☑ **C** is correct. Given the nature of the document and the fact that it is considered "sensitive," you can assume the e-mailed attachment about the organization chart was marked "corporate confidential."

    ☒ **A, B,** and **D** are incorrect. **A** is incorrect because mergers and acquisitions involves a company's takeover of or union with another company, which the document does not suggest. **B** is incorrect because accounting data wasn't e-mailed. **D** is incorrect because the organization chart doesn't contain intellectual property (IP).

12. A new virus called MSB3417, dubbed "Wildfire," is sweeping through organizations, infecting systems by exploiting a previously unknown vulnerability. Wildfire identifies and exfiltrates any spreadsheet documents with large dollar amounts. The documents are then covertly sent to a known and powerful adversarial country. What is this type of malware called?

A. APT exploit

B. Zero-day exploit

C. Financial exfiltration malware

D. Economic threat

☑ **B** is correct. Malware that works based on exploiting a previously unknown vulnerability is called a zero-day exploit.

☒ **A, C,** and **D** are incorrect. **A** is incorrect because such an exploit is not called an APT exploit just because of the nation from which it supposedly originated. **C** and **D** are incorrect because these are not normal terms, despite what the question's malware did.

13. What is the particular criminal threat when data related to a company's intent to integrate with another company is mishandled?

A. Leaked information could lead to trading based on privileged knowledge.

B. Shareholders of both companies could vote to stop the merger.

C. Leaked trade secrets could lead to increased competition.

D. Violations of HIPAA requirements.

☑ **A** is correct. Leaked information about a merger in progress or even a desired merger could lead to a stockholder deciding to trade their shares. Trading based on that privileged information is a crime called insider trading.

☒ **B, C,** and **D** are incorrect. **B** is incorrect because, even if shareholders somehow became privy to the knowledge, they wouldn't get a chance to vote until the decision was legally eligible to be put up for a vote. **C** is incorrect because trade secrets wouldn't be shared between the companies to be merged until the deal was done. There should be no threat to either company's trade secrets. **D** is incorrect because there was no mention of personal health information (PHI).

14. Which of the following factors determines some noted event will be considered a security incident?

A. Downtime

B. Scope of impact

C. Economic

D. Types of data affected

☑ **B** is correct. Scope of impact is the official determination that has an event crossing the boundary into being a defined security incident.

☒ **A, C,** and **D** are incorrect. **A** is incorrect because downtime is a serious outcome of an incident, but it is not the trait that distinguishes an incident from an event. **C** is incorrect because the economic effects of an incident are typically not measurable in the short term compared to other factors. **D** is incorrect because the types of data, especially those under regulatory protection, often distinguish a severe incident from a moderate one. However, this is not a factor that can push an event into being an incident.

15. In the context of long-term effects from a security incident, particularly to a company's reputation and ability to gain potential business, which factor is the most impactful on an incident's severity?

   A. Recovery time

   B. Data integrity

   C. Economic

   D. System process criticality

   ☑ **C** is correct. The economic factors of an incident affect a company over the long haul, often in terms of its reputation.

   ☒ **A, B,** and **D** are incorrect. **A** is incorrect because recovery time is a short-term factor. **B** is incorrect because even though it takes longer to determine the effects of data integrity, it is still a relatively short-term factor. **D** is incorrect because system process criticality is definitely a short-term, well-defined factor in determining an incident's severity.

16. For which of the following types of data is it suggested that a company take additional steps, beyond policy and legal guidance, to protect the data's confidentiality from unauthorized eyes? Not protecting the selected data type might jeopardize the company's sustainability.

   A. HR personnel information

   B. PII

   C. Payment card information

   D. Accounting data

   ☑ **D** is correct. The security of accounting data is more critical to a business's sustainability, relative to the other answers.

   ☒ **A, B,** and **C** are incorrect. **A** is incorrect because HR personnel information must be kept confidential, but its release wouldn't necessarily threaten the company's well-being. **B** is incorrect because personally identifiable information (PII) is not critical to a company's health. **C** is incorrect because payment card information should be protected as required by PCI DSS. Although its release would certainly jeopardize a company's reputation, it's hardly a significant threat to the business itself.

17. Which of the following are possible consequences for unauthorized disclosure of PHI, depending on one's involvement. (Choose all that apply.)

A. Documented record in employee file

B. Suspension from employment

C. Monetary fine

D. Jail time

E. Public execution

☑ **A, B, C,** and **D** are correct. Depending on the employee's involvement, the consequences can range from a record in the employee's file to possible jail time.

☒ **E** is incorrect. Although disclosing personal health information is a serious offense, it's not worthy of public execution.

CHAPTER 9

Preparing the Incident Response Toolkit

This chapter includes questions on the following topics:
- How digital forensics is related to incident response
- Basic techniques for conducting forensic analysis
- Familiarity with a variety of forensic utilities
- How to assemble a forensic toolkit

When a cybersecurity analyst conducts an incident response, the analyst cannot possibly anticipate whether or not the outcome might lead to legal action or prosecution. As a result, every incident being responded to must be handled as a forensic investigation. A forensic investigation follows specific phases, requiring the analyst to take careful notes and to handle all evidence with complete accountability. To carry this out, the analyst must obviously be prepared and possess the skills required to conduct the investigation.

But perhaps as important as the analyst's skills are the analyst's tools. Only with the kit containing the necessary tools, documentation, and supportive hardware can the analyst progress through the phases of the forensic investigation. This chapter covers the topics concerned with building that forensic kit.

1. What ensures accountability of evidence handling by documenting the handoff from person to person of important forensic material?

   A. Handoff form

   B. Analysis management form

   C. Evidence management log

   D. Chain of custody form

2. Which of the following is developed as part of an incident response plan, but also has practical value in a forensic kit?

   A. Rainbow tables

   B. Call/escalation list

   C. Network map

   D. Acceptable use policy

3. During a forensic investigation, you need to make a bit-for-bit copy of a hard drive called "ops" into a file. To accomplish this, you use the command-line utility **dd** to create the image file CaseCopy.img. The block size will be 2K, and any errors can be disregarded. Which of the following commands does what you need?

   A. dd if=/dev/ops of=CaseCopy.img bs=2048 conv=noerror

   B. dd if=/dev/ops of=casecopy.img bs=2048 conv=noerror

   C. dd if=/dev/casecopy of=ops bs=2048 conv=noerror

   D. dd if=/dev/CaseCopy.img of=ops bs=2048 conv=noerror

4. A junior analyst has two files and needs to verify they are exact duplicates. To do this, the analyst knows to first create hashes from the two files and then compare them. Which of the following tools from the forensic kit is the best tool to use?

   A. dd

   B. sha1sum

   C. eventviewer

   D. BitLocker

5. Including crime tape in a forensic kit might be useful for what purpose?

   A. Securing the chain of custody form to the hard drive.

   B. Acting as a write block on 5 1/4" disks.

   C. Physically cordoning off an area if necessary to prevent tampering.

   D. There is no imaginable use for physical crime tape in a digital forensic investigation.

6. An internal cybersecurity analyst is asked to send a report via e-mail. The analyst plans to send the report from within the company's network. In order to ensure the confidentiality of the report, what is a likely step for the analyst to take?

   A. Create a hash of the report file and send the hash in a second e-mail.

   B. Use the e-mail server, but then wipe it with a cloth or something.

   C. Using a cryptography tool to further protect the report.

   D. None of the above. E-mailing across an internal infrastructure is perfectly safe.

7. An incident involves a legitimate user's account being compromised. Although the company does employ some information security best practices, the analyst notes a few policies missing, including any account lockout policy. The analyst suspects brute-force password guessing was involved. Further, accounts of several machines might have been brute-forced. Which tool should the analyst consider using to gather more information?

   A. Mobile device viewer

   B. Group policy viewer

   C. Password cracker

   D. Log viewer

8. When you're approaching a person's desk or office as a crime scene, essentially everything is potential evidence. Every object's position may be recognized as significant. What is the *most* likely first action an incident handler would perform before moving or handling any object?

   A. Sample the air quality.

   B. Photograph or video the scene.

   C. Dust the scene for fingerprints.

   D. Place obvious digital media in containers with a tamper-proof seal.

9. What is the primary purpose of a notebook in a forensic bag?

   A. To draft a chain of custody

   B. To create an incident log

   C. To amend the incident response plan

   D. To list assets removed from the scene

10. A cybersecurity analyst is investigating a Windows system registry, particularly for malware that might be persistent on reboots. Which of the following registry keys will likely reveal instances of malware? (Choose all that apply.)

    A. HKLM\Software\Microsoft\Windows\CurrentVersion\Run

    B. HKLM\System\Microsoft\Windows\CurrentVersion\Run

    C. HKCU\Software\Microsoft\Windows\CurrentVersion\Run

    D. HKCU\System\Microsoft\Windows\CurrentVersion\Run

11. Which of the following devices burdens the forensics analyst with always having special cables and custom bootloaders with them?

    A. Linux Knoppix 8.1

    B. WOPR SecTran 9.4.3

    C. Asus ZenFone 5Z

    D. Windows Server 2016

12. FTK, EnCase, and The Sleuth Kit are all examples in what category of forensic applications?

    A. Cryptography tools

    B. Password crackers

    C. Hashing utilities

    D. Analysis utilities

13. Which of the following provides a similar benefit to a chain of custody form?

    A. Drive adapter

    B. Tamper-proof seal

    C. Cryptography tool

    D. Drive and media cables

14. Joshua, a junior cybersecurity analyst, is performing his first forensic investigation. He photographs the surrounding scene and then employs tools to analyze the OS and any running processes. After shutting down the system, Joshua pulls the hard drive, attaches a USB drive adapter cable to it, and then connects the cable to his laptop's USB port to start the copying operation. Joshua's supervisor, Dr. Stephen Falken, enters the room. Seeing the hard-drive-copying efforts, Dr. Falken immediately shouts, "You think this is a game? We can't trust what's on that drive!" What did Dr. Falken notice?

    A. Joshua is not using a write blocker.

    B. Joshua should have connected the drive by SATA, not USB.

    C. Dr. Falken believed the system shut down improperly.

    D. Dr. Falken saw nothing wrong. He was playing a game.

15. After the seizure and acquisition phases, where does the next step of a digital forensic investigation likely take place?

    A. The crime scene

    B. The digital forensic workstation

    C. The boardroom

    D. None of the above

16. What's the primary reason for a forensic investigator to wipe the removable media prior to needing it or entering the scene of an investigation?

   A. To save time formatting media

   B. To save on costs

   C. Because clean media is trustworthy media

   D. To comply with the data retention policy

17. Which of the following is a form or documentation that does *not* belong in a forensic kit? (Choose all that apply.)

   A. Chain of custody

   B. Incident response plan

   C. Hash values of forensics application files

   D. Call/escalation list

   E. Incident notes log

1. D	**7.** D	**13.** B
2. B	**8.** B	**14.** A
3. A	**9.** B	**15.** B
4. B	**10.** A, C	**16.** A
5. C	**11.** C	**17.** C
6. C	**12.** D	

1. What ensures accountability of evidence handling by documenting the handoff from person to person of important forensic material?

   A. Handoff form

   B. Analysis management form

   C. Evidence management log

   D. Chain of custody form

   ☑ **D** is correct. The chain of custody form ensures accountability of evidence handling. This document lists the handoff from person to person of evidence to mitigate the risk of unauthorized tampering.

   ☒ **A, B,** and **C** are incorrect. There is no such thing as a handoff form, analysis management form, or evidence management log.

2. Which of the following is developed as part of an incident response plan, but also has practical value in a forensic kit?

   A. Rainbow tables

   B. Call/escalation list

   C. Network map

   D. Acceptable use policy

   ☑ **B** is correct. The call list or escalation list documents who an analyst should call for particular cases. It's originally part of any incident response plan, but it's also a valuable asset in a forensic kit.

   ☒ **A, C,** and **D** are incorrect. **A** is incorrect because rainbow tables relate passwords to their hash values. Although a password cracker might be in your forensic kit, rainbow tables would not come from an incident response (IR) plan. **C** is incorrect because although a network map might be useful, it doesn't come from an IR plan. **D** is incorrect because the acceptable use policy wouldn't be in either the IR plan or the forensic kit.

3. During a forensic investigation, you need to make a bit-for-bit copy of a hard drive called "ops" into a file. To accomplish this, you use the command-line utility **dd** to create the image file CaseCopy.img. The block size will be 2K, and any errors can be disregarded. Which of the following commands does what you need?

   A. dd if=/dev/ops of=CaseCopy.img bs=2048 conv=noerror

   B. dd if=/dev/ops of=casecopy.img bs=2048 conv=noerror

   C. dd if=/dev/casecopy of=ops bs=2048 conv=noerror

   D. dd if=/dev/CaseCopy.img of=ops bs=2048 conv=noerror

   ☑ **A** is correct. This command line shows the correct syntax and spelling to perform the bit-for-bit copy.

☒ **B, C,** and **D** are incorrect. **B** is incorrect because Unix commands are case sensitive. **C** is incorrect because the spelling as well as input and output sources are wrong. **D** is incorrect because the input and output sources are wrong.

4. A junior analyst has two files and needs to verify they are exact duplicates. To do this, the analyst knows to first create hashes from the two files and then compare them. Which of the following tools from the forensic kit is the best tool to use?

   A. dd

   B. sha1sum

   C. eventviewer

   D. BitLocker

   ☑ **B** is correct. The program sha1sum will calculate and check a SHA-1 hash value. The hash value is also known as a message digest. The analyst will use sha1sum to calculate and compare message digests of these two files.

   ☒ **A, C,** and **D** are incorrect. **A** is incorrect because **dd** is a utility for copying, not for creating hash values. **C** is incorrect because eventviewer will not do much good here. **D** is incorrect because BitLocker is a volume encryption tool for Windows systems.

5. Including crime tape in a forensic kit might be useful for what purpose?

   A. Securing the chain of custody form to the hard drive.

   B. Acting as a write block on 5 1/4" disks.

   C. Physically cordoning off an area if necessary to prevent tampering.

   D. There is no imaginable use for physical crime tape in a digital forensic investigation.

   ☑ **C** is correct. It is suggested that you have crime tape on hand in case you need to provide a soft barrier around a physical area.

   ☒ **A, B,** and **D** are incorrect. **A** is incorrect because crime tape is not meant to be adhesive tape. **B** is incorrect because, again, crime tape is not intended to be a sticky tape. What's more, 5 1/4" disks are fairly tough to find. **D** is incorrect because there is a noted use for crime tape, even for a digital forensic investigation.

6. An internal cybersecurity analyst is asked to send a report via e-mail. The analyst plans to send the report from within the company's network. In order to ensure the confidentiality of the report, what is a likely step for the analyst to take?

   A. Create a hash of the report file and send the hash in a second e-mail.

   B. Use the e-mail server, but then wipe it with a cloth or something.

   C. Using a cryptography tool to further protect the report.

   D. None of the above. E-mailing across an internal infrastructure is perfectly safe.

   ☑ **C** is correct. Given that e-mail is open and insecure, encrypting the report first can help ensure the report's confidentiality.

☒ **A**, **B**, and **D** are incorrect. **A** is incorrect because creating a hash doesn't preclude someone from intercepting the report. Having a copy elsewhere doesn't change the file's hash value, so comparing the received copy also doesn't matter. **B** is incorrect because wiping the server afterward (whether with a cloth or something else) doesn't make sending the report by e-mail any more secure. **D** is incorrect because unencrypted e-mail is not safe from prying eyes, regardless of where it happens.

7. An incident involves a legitimate user's account being compromised. Although the company does employ some information security best practices, the analyst notes a few policies missing, including any account lockout policy. The analyst suspects brute-force password guessing was involved. Further, accounts of several machines might have been brute-forced. Which tool should the analyst consider using to gather more information?

   A. Mobile device viewer

   B. Group policy viewer

   C. Password cracker

   D. Log viewer

   ☑ **D** is correct. Using a log viewer is the next step in gathering information on bad password attempts.

   ☒ **A**, **B**, and **C** are incorrect. **A** is incorrect because there's no call for inspecting mobile devices in the question. **B** is incorrect because managing group policy now isn't necessary since the analyst already noted there is no account lockout policy in place. **C** is incorrect because there's no need for a password cracker, unless you're continuing the attacker's effort.

8. When you're approaching a person's desk or office as a crime scene, essentially everything is potential evidence. Every object's position may be recognized as significant. What is the *most* likely first action an incident handler would perform before moving or handling any object?

   A. Sample the air quality.

   B. Photograph or video the scene.

   C. Dust the scene for fingerprints.

   D. Place obvious digital media in containers with a tamper-proof seal.

   ☑ **B** is correct. A camera is a valuable addition to a forensic kit. The camera allows you to photograph or video a crime scene before anything is removed or touched. Although an item's position might seem inconsequential at first, it might become significant later in the investigation.

   ☒ **A**, **C**, and **D** are incorrect. **A** is incorrect because the air quality is likely not important. **C** is incorrect because dusting for fingerprints is unlikely to happen. However, if dusting for fingerprints were to happen, it would follow photographing, not precede it. **D** is incorrect because you want to photograph the scene before placing things in containers.

9. What is the primary purpose of a notebook in a forensic bag?

   A. To draft a chain of custody

   B. To create an incident log

   C. To amend the incident response plan

   D. To list assets removed from the scene

   ☑ **B** is correct. A notebook is critical to have in a forensic kit because the investigator or analyst will be taking constant notes. Those notes create an incident log for the investigator or anyone to refer back to at a later time.

   ☒ **A, C,** and **D** are incorrect. **A** is incorrect because you will have a chain of custody form, in addition to a notebook. **C** is incorrect because any IR plan amendments will happen after the incident is complete, relying on notes taken in the notebook. **D** is incorrect because although listing assets may be part of your notes, this is not the main reason for the notebook.

10. A cybersecurity analyst is investigating a Windows system registry, particularly for malware that might be persistent on reboots. Which of the following registry keys will likely reveal instances of malware? (Choose all that apply.)

    A. HKLM\Software\Microsoft\Windows\CurrentVersion\Run

    B. HKLM\System\Microsoft\Windows\CurrentVersion\Run

    C. HKCU\Software\Microsoft\Windows\CurrentVersion\Run

    D. HKCU\System\Microsoft\Windows\CurrentVersion\Run

    ☑ **A** and **C** are correct. These two are valid registry keys where you will find values of applications loading. If malware has modified registry entries to maintain persistence, then these two entries will likely show the malware intending to run at OS/system startup.

    ☒ **B** and **D** are incorrect. Neither of these is a valid registry key.

11. Which of the following devices burdens the forensics analyst with always having special cables and custom bootloaders with them?

    A. Linux Knoppix 8.1

    B. WOPR SecTran 9.4.3

    C. Asus ZenFone 5Z

    D. Windows Server 2016

    ☑ **C** is correct. Mobile devices are a category of devices where the analyst should be prepared with various cables, connectors, and custom bootloaders. The Asus ZenFone 5Z is obviously just one example of a mobile device the analyst could come across.

    ☒ **A, B,** and **D** are incorrect. **A** is incorrect because Knoppix is a "live" CD and not one where the analyst would need a special cable. **B** is incorrect because the WOPR

SecTran 9.4.3 mainframe is fictitious (that is, to everyone except Professor Stephen Falken and David). **D** is incorrect because a Windows 2016 system wouldn't require any special or particularly unique cables.

12. FTK, EnCase, and The Sleuth Kit are all examples in what category of forensic applications?

   A. Cryptography tools

   B. Password crackers

   C. Hashing utilities

   D. Analysis utilities

   ☑ **D** is correct. FTK, EnCase, and The Sleuth Kit are all analysis utilities.

   ☒ **A, B,** and **C** are incorrect. Although FTK, EnCase, and The Sleuth Kit do have some of these other features, such as computing hash values, they do much more. Therefore, the best answer is that these three applications are generally used for analysis.

13. Which of the following provides a similar benefit to a chain of custody form?

   A. Drive adapter

   B. Tamper-proof seal

   C. Cryptography tool

   D. Drive and media cables

   ☑ **B** is correct. Tamper-proof seals provide protection against unauthorized tampering. Similarly, a chain of custody form helps maintain the integrity of evidence by ensuring accountability.

   ☒ **A, C,** and **D** are incorrect. **A** is incorrect because having a variety of drive adapters helps ensure a physical connection with the variety of drives and storage devices you might encounter. **C** is incorrect because cryptography tools can provide confidentiality through encryption. Although this in turn helps protect integrity, it's not a direct, analogous benefit. **D** is incorrect because drive and media cables provide a physical connection, similar to drive adapters.

14. Joshua, a junior cybersecurity analyst, is performing his first forensic investigation. He photographs the surrounding scene and then employs tools to analyze the OS and any running processes. After shutting down the system, Joshua pulls the hard drive, attaches a USB drive adapter cable to it, and then connects the cable to his laptop's USB port to start the copying operation. Joshua's supervisor, Dr. Stephen Falken, enters the room. Seeing the hard-drive-copying efforts, Dr. Falken immediately shouts, "You think this is a game? We can't trust what's on that drive!" What did Dr. Falken notice?

   A. Joshua is not using a write blocker.

   B. Joshua should have connected the drive by SATA, not USB.

   C. Dr. Falken believed the system shut down improperly.

   D. Dr. Falken saw nothing wrong. He was playing a game.

☑ **A** is correct. By connecting the hard drive directly to the laptop, and not using a write blocker, Joshua jeopardizes the integrity of the hard drive's contents. Joshua should have placed a write blocker between the source and destination, to prevent any writes done to the source disk.

☒ **B, C,** and **D** are incorrect. **B** is incorrect because the physical type of drive connector is irrelevant to the data integrity. **C** is incorrect because there was nothing mentioned to suggest or lead Dr. Falken to believe the system shut down improperly. **D** is incorrect because Joshua's superior obviously noticed something done wrong, something serious enough to believe the copy was not usable.

15. After the seizure and acquisition phases, where does the next step of a digital forensic investigation likely take place?

   A. The crime scene

   B. The digital forensic workstation

   C. The boardroom

   D. None of the above

☑ **B** is correct. The next phase of forensic investigation after seizure and acquisition is analysis. The analysis phase wouldn't be done in the crime scene or the boardroom. Analysis, if possible, should be done on a digital forensics workstation.

☒ **A, C,** and **D** are incorrect. **A** is incorrect because the crime scene, or at least a suspect workstation, is no place to perform analysis. **C** is incorrect because the boardroom is the likely place for delivering a report, but not performing the analysis. **D** is incorrect because the proper answer is the digital forensics workstation, where analysis is conducted.

16. What's the primary reason for a forensic investigator to wipe the removable media prior to needing it or entering the scene of an investigation?

   A. To save time formatting media

   B. To save on costs

   C. Because clean media is trustworthy media

   D. To comply with the data retention policy

☑ **A** is correct. The main advantage of having wiped removable media is that it saves the investigator the time of having to thoroughly wipe the media when it's needed. With the large-sized volumes the investigator may require, wiping the media takes a considerably long time.

☒ **B, C,** and **D** are incorrect. **B** is incorrect because having the equipment is not about saving money, but saving time. **C** is incorrect because, although it's true that clean media is more trustworthy (compared to simply writing on top of data), the main advantage is having the media wiped ahead of time. **D** is incorrect because the wiped media on hand does not necessarily comply with a data retention policy.

17. Which of the following is a form or documentation that does *not* belong in a forensic kit? (Choose all that apply.)

A. Chain of custody

B. Incident response plan

C. Hash values of forensics application files

D. Call/escalation list

E. Incident notes log

☑ **C** is correct. The hash values of your applications are the least likely thing to have in your forensics kit.

☒ **A, B, D,** and **E** are incorrect. **A** is incorrect because the chain of custody is an absolute necessity to have available, either as an already prepared form or to be drafted as needed. **B** is incorrect because having a copy of the incident response plan is a valuable addition to the forensic kit. **D** is incorrect because the call/escalation list is certainly necessary to have available in order to know who to call for any unexpected events. **E** is incorrect because a notebook or incident log is absolutely necessary to have because taking notes is critical to incident response and forensics.

Selecting the Best Course of Action

This chapter includes questions on the following topics:
- How to diagnose incidents by examining network symptoms
- How to diagnose incidents by examining host symptoms
- How to diagnose incidents by examining application symptoms

Unfortunately, in the real world, when issues appear, they are not isolated but rather mixed together with the routine chaos and normal "buzz" of a production environment. Moreover, issues might not come at you one at a time. Instead, one issue might overlap with another, at least partly due to symptoms and timing. Your challenge, should you choose to accept it as a certified CySA+, is to diagnose those issues. This chapter is focused on diagnosing problems and determining the myriad of symptoms that point us to them.

Diagnosing a problem, or incident, starts with identifying what's wrong or different in your environment. Obviously, to be able to identify what's different, you must first have a solid understanding of what's right or normal in your environment. That "normal" is also called the *baseline*. The steps on how to get a baseline are not covered in detail in this chapter, because it's assumed that the baseline for your environment is already established and understood. This should be done before an incident occurs in order for you to have a point of comparison. So, on the assumption you have something to compare it to, you can diagnose your incident by what's changed in your environment.

What this chapter *does* cover is diagnosing your full environment, including the network, the hosts, and their applications. Each of these areas offers a variety of telltale behaviors and points to examine. This chapter focuses on the assortment of symptoms found in these areas.

1. Which of the following bandwidth-consumption behaviors strongly indicates something suspicious?

   A. Higher-than-normal bandwidth, every day, at the same time

   B. Higher-than-normal bandwidth once, during off-peak hours

   C. Lower-than-normal bandwidth used during peak hours

   D. Higher-than-normal bandwidth used during peak hours

2. Your SIEM alerts you to an unusual amount of ARP queries. This is indicative of what sort of behavior?

   A. Rogue device on the network

   B. Scan sweeps

   C. Unauthorized privileges

   D. Unauthorized software

3. What is a property of network usage that suggests a rogue device on the network?

   A. Repeated failed remote logins

   B. Beaconing

   C. Failed connection attempts on the legitimate wireless access points

   D. Unrecognized MAC addresses logged on legitimate access points

4. With regard to peer-to-peer network communication, which of the following observations should a cybersecurity analyst be concerned with as abnormal? (Choose all that apply.)

   A. Host-to-host connections using an unprivileged account

   B. Host-to-host connections using a privileged account

   C. Local user connecting to a print server on another subnet

   D. Client/server connections with high numbered client ports

5. A network engineer is responding to users complaining the network is slow. Looking at the blinking lights, the engineer notices considerable activity from the HR file server. What would be the network engineer's next step?

   A. Unplug the network cable at the switch going to the file server.

   B. Monitor usage and compare it against the baseline.

   C. Alert the CIO to the traffic spike.

   D. Sample the traffic using a packet analyzer.

6. A cybersecurity analyst has a suspicion about a system's behavior, but reviewing logs and baseline performance of that system has proven nothing. Finally, the analyst decides to investigate network traffic, based on a hunch. The analyst starts with an endpoint analysis. The analyst sorts the traffic log first by internal source address, then by destination address, and finally by time. What evidence is the analyst clearly searching for?

A. Beaconing.

B. Anomalous activity.

C. Network memory consumption.

D. This is not a search; rather, the analyst is creating a new baseline.

7. A user notices the workstation seems louder than normal—not necessarily fan noise, but the hard drive is constantly "working" without the user installing or moving any files. When the analyst asks if any other system behavior is occurring, the user replies the system seems a bit slower as well. What might be an issue the system is experiencing?

A. Processor consumption

B. Drive capacity consumption

C. Memory consumption

D. Network bandwidth consumption

8. Figure 10-1 shows a portion of active connections on the author's desktop. The output is presented in the following order: protocol, local address, foreign address, connection state, and process ID. At the same time, the author opens Task Manager and takes note of a few running applications and their processes' IDs, as detailed in Figure 10-2. Which of these processes might the author want to investigate further?

A. Dropbox.exe

B. chrome.exe

C. notepad.exe

D. WINWORD.EXE

```
Command Prompt                                                         —  □  ✕
TCP     127.0.0.1:50151        127.0.0.1:50152        ESTABLISHED    9708   ^
TCP     127.0.0.1:50152        127.0.0.1:50151        ESTABLISHED    9708
TCP     127.0.0.1:50264        127.0.0.1:50265        ESTABLISHED    1652
TCP     127.0.0.1:50265        127.0.0.1:50264        ESTABLISHED    1652
TCP     127.127.127.127:3939   0.0.0.0:0              LISTENING      4
TCP     169.254.128.67:139     0.0.0.0:0              LISTENING      4
TCP     169.254.128.67:5040    0.0.0.0:0              LISTENING      7588
TCP     192.168.2.240:139      0.0.0.0:0              LISTENING      4
TCP     192.168.2.240:5040     0.0.0.0:0              LISTENING      7588
TCP     192.168.2.240:49158    81.161.59.85:80        ESTABLISHED    1652
TCP     192.168.2.240:49164    162.125.18.133:443     ESTABLISHED    9612
TCP     192.168.2.240:49176    162.125.18.133:443     ESTABLISHED    9612
TCP     192.168.2.240:49245    131.253.34.236:443     ESTABLISHED    2840
TCP     192.168.2.240:49302    50.116.51.249:443      ESTABLISHED    5864
TCP     192.168.2.240:49990    81.161.59.132:80       ESTABLISHED    4248
TCP     192.168.2.240:49991    162.125.4.3:443        CLOSE_WAIT     9612
TCP     192.168.2.240:49993    52.1.221.21:443        CLOSE_WAIT     9612
TCP     192.168.2.240:50028    162.125.34.137:443     CLOSE_WAIT     9612
TCP     192.168.2.240:50034    52.1.29.190:443        TIME_WAIT      0
TCP     192.168.2.240:50035    81.161.59.94:80        ESTABLISHED    9708
TCP     192.168.2.240:50036    52.1.29.190:443        TIME_WAIT      0
TCP     192.168.2.240:50054    172.217.12.165:443     ESTABLISHED    16640
TCP     192.168.2.240:50055    52.1.29.190:443        ESTABLISHED    1652   v
```

Figure 10-1   Outbound connections

Figure 10-2

Running
processes

Output from Task Manager			
Name	**PID**	**Status**	**User name**
Dropbox.exe	9612	Running	admin
chrome.exe	2840	Running	admin
notepad.exe	16640	Running	admin
WINWORD.EXE	3461	Running	admin

9. The cybersecurity analyst hears of recent news about a new worm traveling through the company network, installing a bot that mines digital currency. Because the mining software is installed under a random name, running as a random process, there are few known signatures to search for. What might be a likely symptom that could point to infected systems?

A. Processor consumption

B. Unexpected output

C. Unusual traffic spikes

D. Introduction of new accounts

10. In regard to stopping unauthorized software from being installed on a system, which approach is the most effective?

A. Software blacklisting

B. Standardized desktop images and privileges

C. Software whitelisting

D. Host-based intrusion detection and antivirus

11. An application is experiencing apparent memory issues. The symptoms are fairly straightforward, resulting in the application terminating. Occasionally an error pop-up appears with a vague message about a buffer address. From what you see, what is the next course of action?

A. Perform a memory dump

B. Back up the disk

C. Ensure drivers are up to date

D. Capture a packet sample

12. After recovering from an incident, a company decides to invest in a data loss prevention (DLP) solution as well as printers to subtly watermark documents from certain workstations. What do you think was the host-related issue the company experienced during the incident?

A. Unauthorized privileges

B. Service interruption

C. Unusual traffic spikes

D. Data exfiltration

13. A new file server is made available to employees. The server's capacity is expected to be sufficient for three years. Within two weeks, users complain the file server isn't as responsive as it used to be. What's more, a file called MB2TB.exe has been spotted in every folder. What might be a likely issue?

A. Bandwidth consumption

B. Processor consumption

C. Drive capacity consumption

D. Memory consumption

14. A user has raised a support ticket because of an unexpected dialog box on his Windows 10 laptop. He wasn't concerned at first, because the pop-up seems a legitimate Windows prompt, as seen in Figure 10-3. However, the user cannot understand why the pop-up appears, given there seems no connection to his actions. Treating this as an incident, where would you investigate further?

A. User account "Randy."

B. Admin account.

C. Application's publisher.

D. This is not an incident but rather a legitimate User Access Control prompt.

Figure 10-3 User Access Control dialog box

15. A contractor has borrowed an older company laptop and has been using it with no issues for months. Recently the contractor came in, asking for a new laptop because his is "acting weird." When asked for specifics, the contractor mentioned his application sometimes freezes, the browser goes to different websites, and other strange things start happening. What might be the best course of action?

   A. Ensure the OS and applications are patched.

   B. Increase the size of the hard drive; add more memory.

   C. Create the contractor a new account.

   D. Back up his data and perform a fresh, updated system install.

16. A security team member alerts you that a new domain account has been created, but there is no documented account request. Further, there is no legitimate way the account could be created without you or the team member's assistance. In fact, a quick look shows you the new user account has a session active now on a local host. What is your first step?

   A. Fire the team member.

   B. Log off the user session.

   C. Isolate the host.

   D. Reset the account password.

17. An important file that lists numbered bank accounts is tightly controlled, including a process for making any changes to that file. Although the file has no documented changes made in months, an analyst has determined its hashed value was changed sometime between today and last week. What would cause a different hash?

   A. New account added

   B. Unauthorized changes made

   C. Different hash generator used

   D. Drive capacity increased

1. B	**7.** C	**13.** C
2. B	**8.** C	**14.** A
3. D	**9.** A	**15.** D
4. A, B	**10.** C	**16.** D
5. B	**11.** A	**17.** B
6. A	**12.** D	

1. Which of the following bandwidth-consumption behaviors strongly indicates something suspicious?

   A. Higher-than-normal bandwidth, every day, at the same time

   B. Higher-than-normal bandwidth once, during off-peak hours

   C. Lower-than-normal bandwidth used during peak hours

   D. Higher-than-normal bandwidth used during peak hours

   ☑ **B** is correct. A single instance of higher-than-normal bandwidth consumption outside the "work day" is the most suspect. However, although it doesn't necessarily guarantee suspicious behavior, such bandwidth consumption is worth investigating further.

   ☒ **A, C,** and **D** are incorrect. **A** is incorrect because if such higher bandwidth consumption is happening every day, then that has become the new normal. Investigating further is prudent but unlikely necessary. **C** is incorrect because lower-than-normal bandwidth could point to other issues, such as network disruption. **D** is incorrect because higher bandwidth consumption during the work day is not necessarily abnormal.

2. Your SIEM alerts you to an unusual amount of ARP queries. This is indicative of what sort of behavior?

   A. Rogue device on the network

   B. Scan sweeps

   C. Unauthorized privileges

   D. Unauthorized software

   ☑ **B** is correct. A spike in ARP queries would indicate someone or some process is conducting a scan. This would warrant additional action and investigation.

   ☒ **A, C,** and **D** are incorrect. The ARP queries indicate a scan, which may or may not be originating from a rogue device, unauthorized software, or unauthorized privileges.

3. What is a property of network usage that suggests a rogue device on the network?

   A. Repeated failed remote logins

   B. Beaconing

   C. Failed connection attempts on the legitimate wireless access points

   D. Unrecognized MAC addresses logged on legitimate access points

   ☑ **D** is correct. Unrecognized MAC addresses indicate unrecognized or unauthorized devices.

   ☒ **A, B,** and **C** are incorrect. **A** is incorrect because repeated failed logins don't suggest a rogue device. **B** is incorrect because beaconing indicates a possibly compromised system keeping in contact with a malicious actor or system outside the network. **C** is incorrect because failed connection attempts don't indicate a rogue device, except perhaps in the case where connections are only allowed from whitelisted MAC addresses.

4. With regard to peer-to-peer network communication, which of the following observations should a cybersecurity analyst be concerned with as abnormal? (Choose all that apply.)

   A. Host-to-host connections using an unprivileged account

   B. Host-to-host connections using a privileged account

   C. Local user connecting to a print server on another subnet

   D. Client/server connections with high numbered client ports

   ☑ **A** and **B** are correct. Host-to-host connections are fairly uncommon. Such peer-to-peer communication can suggest an attacker moving laterally from one compromised system to another.

   ☒ **C** and **D** are incorrect. **C** is incorrect because a local workstation connecting to any print server is hardly abnormal. **D** is incorrect because client/server connections typically originate with the client using a high port number.

5. A network engineer is responding to users complaining the network is slow. Looking at the blinking lights, the engineer notices considerable activity from the HR file server. What would be the network engineer's next step?

   A. Unplug the network cable at the switch going to the file server.

   B. Monitor usage and compare it against the baseline.

   C. Alert the CIO to the traffic spike.

   D. Sample the traffic using a packet analyzer.

   ☑ **B** is correct. The network engineer's next step is to consider whether or not the activity is normal by monitoring usage and comparing it against the baseline.

   ☒ **A, C,** and **D** are incorrect. **A** is incorrect because unplugging the network cable is clearly wrong. **C** is incorrect because it's far too early to escalate the issue to the CIO. **D** is incorrect because sampling the traffic is likely the course of action after comparing traffic against the baseline.

6. A cybersecurity analyst has a suspicion about a system's behavior, but reviewing logs and baseline performance of that system has proven nothing. Finally, the analyst decides to investigate network traffic, based on a hunch. The analyst starts with an endpoint analysis. The analyst sorts the traffic log first by internal source address, then by destination address, and finally by time. What evidence is the analyst clearly searching for?

   A. Beaconing.

   B. Anomalous activity.

   C. Network memory consumption.

   D. This is not a search; rather, the analyst is creating a new baseline.

☑ **A** is correct. Judging by the analyst's traffic analysis, the intention is to identify any beaconing.

☒ **B, C,** and **D** are incorrect. **B** is incorrect because the analyst is sorting traffic a particular way. **C** is incorrect because the analyst wouldn't be sorting traffic to identify network memory consumption. **D** is incorrect because the analyst is searching for a particular clue.

7. A user notices the workstation seems louder than normal—not necessarily fan noise, but the hard drive is constantly "working" without the user installing or moving any files. When the analyst asks if any other system behavior is occurring, the user replies the system seems a bit slower as well. What might be an issue the system is experiencing?

   A. Processor consumption

   B. Drive capacity consumption

   C. Memory consumption

   D. Network bandwidth consumption

   ☑ **C** is correct. The scenario is evidence of disk paging, a sign of extreme memory consumption.

   ☒ **A, B,** and **D** are incorrect. **A** is incorrect because the user mentioned the system is running somewhat slower, but not so much to point to processor consumption. **B** is incorrect because the drive sounds like it is "paging" due to a memory shortage, not drive capacity shortage. **D** is incorrect because there was no mention of network issues.

8. Figure 10-1 shows a portion of active connections on the author's desktop. The output is presented in the following order: protocol, local address, foreign address, connection state, and process ID. At the same time, the author opens Task Manager and takes note of a few running applications and their processes' IDs, as detailed in Figure 10-2. Which of these processes might the author want to investigate further?

   A. Dropbox.exe

   B. chrome.exe

   C. notepad.exe

   D. WINWORD.EXE

```
Command Prompt                                                    —  □  ×
TCP    127.0.0.1:50151        127.0.0.1:50152        ESTABLISHED    9708
TCP    127.0.0.1:50152        127.0.0.1:50151        ESTABLISHED    9708
TCP    127.0.0.1:50264        127.0.0.1:50265        ESTABLISHED    1652
TCP    127.0.0.1:50265        127.0.0.1:50264        ESTABLISHED    1652
TCP    127.127.127.127:3939   0.0.0.0:0              LISTENING      4
TCP    169.254.128.67:139     0.0.0.0:0              LISTENING      4
TCP    169.254.128.67:5040    0.0.0.0:0              LISTENING      7588
TCP    192.168.2.240:139      0.0.0.0:0              LISTENING      4
TCP    192.168.2.240:5040     0.0.0.0:0              LISTENING      7588
TCP    192.168.2.240:49158    81.161.59.85:80        ESTABLISHED    1652
TCP    192.168.2.240:49164    162.125.18.133:443     ESTABLISHED    9612
TCP    192.168.2.240:49176    162.125.18.133:443     ESTABLISHED    9612
TCP    192.168.2.240:49245    131.253.34.236:443     ESTABLISHED    2840
TCP    192.168.2.240:49302    50.116.51.249:443      ESTABLISHED    5864
TCP    192.168.2.240:49990    81.161.59.132:80       ESTABLISHED    4248
TCP    192.168.2.240:49991    162.125.4.3:443        CLOSE_WAIT     9612
TCP    192.168.2.240:49993    52.1.221.21:443        CLOSE_WAIT     9612
TCP    192.168.2.240:50028    162.125.34.137:443     CLOSE_WAIT     9612
TCP    192.168.2.240:50034    52.1.29.190:443        TIME_WAIT      0
TCP    192.168.2.240:50035    81.161.59.94:80        ESTABLISHED    9708
TCP    192.168.2.240:50036    52.1.29.190:443        TIME_WAIT      0
TCP    192.168.2.240:50054    172.217.12.165:443     ESTABLISHED    16640
TCP    192.168.2.240:50055    52.1.29.190:443        ESTABLISHED    1652
```

Figure 10-1   Outbound connections

Figure 10-2
Running
processes

Output from Task Manager			
Name	**PID**	**Status**	**User name**
Dropbox.exe	9612	Running	admin
chrome.exe	2840	Running	admin
notepad.exe	16640	Running	admin
WINWORD.EXE	3461	Running	admin

☑ **C** is correct. There's little doubt that notepad.exe maintaining an outbound connection, on port 443 no less, is suspicious. That outbound communication should be investigated further.

☒ **A, B,** and **D** are incorrect. Dropbox and Chrome are expected to have outbound connections. Microsoft Word is not shown in the display of Figure 10-1, but it also might have an outbound connection.

9. The cybersecurity analyst hears of recent news about a new worm traveling through the company network, installing a bot that mines digital currency. Because the mining software is installed under a random name, running as a random process, there are few known signatures to search for. What might be a likely symptom that could point to infected systems?

   A. Processor consumption

   B. Unexpected output

   C. Unusual traffic spikes

   D. Introduction of new accounts

☑ **A** is correct. Because the executable and process names are random, the worm is difficult to locate by name. However, mining software tends to be processor intensive, so that's a good place for the analyst to start.

☒ **B, C,** and **D** are incorrect. **B** is incorrect because there was no mention of unexpected output. **C** is incorrect because mining software isn't likely to produce much network traffic. **D** is incorrect because no new accounts were mentioned in this scenario.

10. In regard to stopping unauthorized software from being installed on a system, which approach is the most effective?

    A. Software blacklisting

    B. Standardized desktop images and privileges

    C. Software whitelisting

    D. Host-based intrusion detection and antivirus

    ☑ **C** is correct. Whitelisting, or allowing only explicitly listed applications, is the most restrictive method.

    ☒ **A, B,** and **D** are incorrect. **A** is incorrect because blacklisting particular software as "bad" or unauthorized is effective, but this method relies on knowing every potential piece of software. **B** is incorrect because having a standard image is good at the start, but if privileges are not restricted, any software could be installed. **D** is incorrect because using a host-based IDS and antivirus is very effective at stopping known malware, but not necessarily at restricting safe-but-unauthorized software.

11. An application is experiencing apparent memory issues. The symptoms are fairly straightforward, resulting in the application terminating. Occasionally an error pop-up appears with a vague message about a buffer address. From what you see, what is the next course of action?

    A. Perform a memory dump

    B. Back up the disk

    C. Ensure drivers are up to date

    D. Capture a packet sample

    ☑ **A** is correct. In a case where an application is experiencing memory issues, possibly memory overflow, performing a memory dump is a prudent measure. Memory overflow is symptomatic of a malicious attempt at exploiting the application or system.

    ☒ **B, C,** and **D** are incorrect. **B** is incorrect because backing up the disk will not capture anything memory related. **C** is incorrect because it's unlikely unstable drivers are the issue. **D** is incorrect because capturing packets from the network is not useful because it's a "shotgun" approach to investigating. Packet analysis is really only effective when you have a good idea of what you're looking for.

12. After recovering from an incident, a company decides to invest in a data loss prevention (DLP) solution as well as printers to subtly watermark documents from certain workstations. What do you think was the host-related issue the company experienced during the incident?

    A. Unauthorized privileges

    B. Service interruption

    C. Unusual traffic spikes

    D. Data exfiltration

    ☑ **D** is correct. Given the mention of DLP and watermarks, you can assume there was an incident of sensitive information being removed or exfiltrated.

    ☒ **A, B,** and **C** are incorrect. **A** is incorrect because an incident of unauthorized privileges would result in better account and authorization management. **B** is incorrect because service interruption, which can also be an application-related issue, would have been handled with added layers of redundancy, fault tolerance, or high availability. **C** is incorrect because unusual traffic spikes might have affected network design or application control.

13. A new file server is made available to employees. The server's capacity is expected to be sufficient for three years. Within two weeks, users complain the file server isn't as responsive as it used to be. What's more, a file called MB2TB.exe has been spotted in every folder. What might be a likely issue?

    A. Bandwidth consumption

    B. Processor consumption

    C. Drive capacity consumption

    D. Memory consumption

    ☑ **C** is correct. The performance and mysterious file "MB2TB" suggests malware, which greatly consumes drive space.

    ☒ **A, B,** and **D** are incorrect. There's no suggestion that the network bandwidth, processor, or memory is experiencing a bottleneck. However, the drive capacity does seem tight.

14. A user has raised a support ticket because of an unexpected dialog box on his Windows 10 laptop. He wasn't concerned at first, because the pop-up seems a legitimate Windows prompt, as seen in Figure 10-3. However, the user cannot understand why the pop-up appears, given there seems no connection to his actions. Treating this as an incident, where would you investigate further?

    A. User account "Randy."

    B. Admin account.

    C. Application's publisher.

    D. This is not an incident but rather a legitimate User Access Control prompt.

Figure 10-3 User Access Control dialog box

☑ **A** is correct. Investigation should start with the local account "Randy," as it appears to be the account initiating the attempted install.

☒ **B, C,** and **D** are incorrect. **B** is incorrect because the administrator account likely isn't compromised. If it were, the software likely would not require the credentials prompt. **C** is incorrect because the UAC pop-up shows a "verified" publisher. The software appears legitimate. **D** is incorrect because something is certainly amiss given that the UAC pop-up appears for no reason.

15. A contractor has borrowed an older company laptop and has been using it with no issues for months. Recently the contractor came in, asking for a new laptop because his is "acting weird." When asked for specifics, the contractor mentioned his application sometimes freezes, the browser goes to different websites, and other strange things start happening. What might be the best course of action?

   A. Ensure the OS and applications are patched.

   B. Increase the size of the hard drive; add more memory.

   C. Create the contractor a new account.

   D. Back up his data and perform a fresh, updated system install.

☑ **D** is correct. Given the older system was probably poorly managed and behind on patch management, the system might have been compromised. Best approach is to wipe it and start with a new, up-to-date install if the system has the resources.

☒ **A, B,** and **C** are incorrect. **A** is incorrect because although the OS and/or applications are likely not up to date on patching, it might be too late for that course of action. **B** is incorrect because increasing the hard drive and memory space is a good idea once the system has a fresh install. **C** is incorrect because creating a new account will not solve the system performance problems.

16. A security team member alerts you that a new domain account has been created, but there is no documented account request. Further, there is no legitimate way the account could be created without you or the team member's assistance. In fact, a quick look shows you the new user account has a session active now on a local host. What is your first step?

   A. Fire the team member.

   B. Log off the user session.

   C. Isolate the host.

   D. Reset the account password.

☑ **D** is correct. Your first step is to reset that account's password, quickly followed by logging off the session.

☒ **A, B,** and **C** are incorrect. **A** is incorrect because there's certainly no evidence to suggest the team member is behind this. **B** is incorrect because this is your second step. If you log off the session, the unauthorized account would probably immediately log back on. Resetting the password first stops the user. **C** is incorrect because isolating the host would likely cause the unauthorized user to log in from another host.

17. An important file that lists numbered bank accounts is tightly controlled, including a process for making any changes to that file. Although the file has no documented changes made in months, an analyst has determined its hashed value was changed sometime between today and last week. What would cause a different hash?

   A. New account added

   B. Unauthorized changes made

   C. Different hash generator used

   D. Drive capacity increased

☑ **B** is correct. Whether the contextual change in the file was due to a new account being added or the account being changed, the file was changed. That change, given the process, was unauthorized and creates a different hash value when calculated.

☒ **A, C,** and **D** are incorrect. **A** is incorrect because regardless how the file was different, the change to the file was unlikely authorized. **C** is incorrect because the tool used to generate the hash value should not matter, provided the same hashing algorithm (for example, MD5) is used. **D** is incorrect because changing the drive capacity would not change the file.

PART IV

Security Architecture and Tool Sets

Frameworks, Policies, Controls, and Procedures

This chapter includes questions on the following topics:
- Common information security management frameworks
- Common policies and procedures
- Considerations in choosing controls
- How to verify and validate compliance

Before a security analyst can complain they are too busy, the analyst needs to understand *why* they are busy. Before the first configuration change is made and before any management tool is used, the organization needs to know what it wants to enforce and monitor. Before the environment can be secured, there needs to be documented steps on how to carry that out. These answers and much more are provided by the organization's policies and procedures. The policies state the "why," while the procedures specify the "how."

When an organization is tackling the question of how best to marry security and business in the environment, frameworks can provide an overarching approach. Other frameworks can be used that focus on service management or security for government systems, for example. A variety of frameworks is available, as you will find in this chapter as we delve into policies and procedures.

1. The Cyber Security Framework published by NIST includes the CSF Core. The Core organizes cybersecurity activities into five main functions. Which of the following answers lists these five functions in the correct order?

   A. Identify, Protect, Detect, Respond, Recover

   B. Detect, Identify, Respond, Recover, Protect

   C. Identify, Detect, Respond, Recover, Protect

   D. Detect, Identify, Recover, Respond, Protect

   E. Identify, Protect, Detect, Recover, Respond

2. Which of the following frameworks is an architectural framework that defines business requirements from a security perspective, and then continues building levels of detail for the practical implementation?

   A. ITL

   B. TOGAF

   C. SABSA

   D. COBIT

3. A company wants to protect its information according to the varied levels of how sensitive the information is as well as the potential for damage if that information is lost. What sort of policy would most benefit the company?

   A. Data classification

   B. Data backup

   C. Data ownership

   D. Data retention

4. Which of the following requirements would you *not* expect to find in a password policy?

   A. Prohibited types of words

   B. Minimum password age

   C. Technology solution

   D. Types of characters to be used

5. Which of the following comprises and presents the Information Security Management System (ISMS) standards?

   A. The Open Group Architecture Framework

   B. IT Governance Institute

   C. NIST Cyber Security Framework

   D. ISO/IEC 27000 series

6. Which type of procedure is considered synonymous with the term *e-discovery*?

   A. Evidence production

   B. Continuous monitoring

   C. Control-testing procedures

   D. E-mail and fax discovery

7. A company is experiencing several unrelated cases of misused user accounts. The user accounts are either created new as privileged accounts or created as new accounts and then elevated to privileged accounts. In either case, the creation of unauthorized accounts must be stopped. After ensuring policy and procedures are being properly carried out, the company determines that the abuse points to a shortcoming in the policy. Which policy most likely needs to be updated to stop this misuse of accounts?

   A. Acceptable use policy

   B. Account management policy

   C. Data ownership policy

   D. Password policy

8. After a routine vulnerability scan of their servers, the Bushwood Country Club discovers 18 holes to be patched. Carl, a junior analyst, asks to perform the patching. However, he seems confused on how move forward with the patching. What is the highest authority and proper documentation for Carl to follow?

   A. The organization's patch management procedures

   B. ISO 27002

   C. NIST SP 800-53

   D. ITIL

9. Companies make use of security controls with different parameters. Which of the following would not influence the choice of security controls and how those controls are implemented?

   A. Local or federal law

   B. Regulatory requirements

   C. Technical expertise to implement

   D. The organization's risk appetite

10. What type of control is a hardware-based firewall?

   A. Administrative control

   B. Physical control

   C. Test control

   D. Logical control

11. Carnegie Mellon University developed the Capability Maturity Model Integration, a set of guidelines for establishing a maturity level as well as evaluating security engineering practices. Maturity levels are defined from the Initial level to the most mature, the Optimizing level. Which of the following is the level at which an organization has formal processes in place to collect and analyze quantitative data, and metrics are defined and fed into the process-improvement program?

A. Repeatable

B. Defined

C. Managed

D. Optimizing

12. Which of the following describes a comprehensive technical evaluation of a system's security components, with regard to applicable regulations? In some cases, if formal assurance of the system meeting all requirements is needed, management or some responsible entity grants accreditation.

A. Certification

B. Assessment

C. Audit

D. Evaluation

13. On occasion, a system has a vulnerability that cannot be closed because the fix is either too costly or there is no feasible way to fix it directly. At such times, a security control could still be implemented to mitigate the vulnerability, at least partially. Risk assessment combined with additional requirements set by law, regulations, and a company's policy would govern the control choice. What sort of documentation would an analyst consult to implement such a control?

A. Control-testing procedures

B. Evidence production procedures

C. Remediation plan procedures

D. Compensating control development procedures

14. Which of the following is *not* an essential element of exception management procedures?

A. Involving the correct people

B. Listing all stakeholders

C. Ensuring access to the necessary information

D. Documenting steps on how to handle decision disagreements

1. A
2. C
3. A
4. C
5. D

6. A
7. B
8. A
9. C
10. D

11. C
12. A
13. D
14. B

1. The Cyber Security Framework published by NIST includes the CSF Core. The Core organizes cybersecurity activities into five main functions. Which of the following answers lists these five functions in the correct order?

   A. Identify, Protect, Detect, Respond, Recover

   B. Detect, Identify, Respond, Recover, Protect

   C. Identify, Detect, Respond, Recover, Protect

   D. Detect, Identify, Recover, Respond, Protect

   E. Identify, Protect, Detect, Recover, Respond

   ☑ **A** is correct. The five main functions of the CSF Core are Identify, Protect, Detect, Respond, and Recover.

   ☒ **B, C,** and **D** are incorrect. The order of each of these options is wrong.

2. Which of the following frameworks is an architectural framework that defines business requirements from a security perspective, and then continues building levels of detail for the practical implementation?

   A. ITL

   B. TOGAF

   C. SABSA

   D. COBIT

   ☑ **C** is correct. The Sherwood Applied Business Security Architecture (SABSA) is a layered model where business requirements from a security perspective make up the first and most abstract layer. Each subsequent layer is more detailed, ending with the sixth layer detailing practical implementation.

   ☒ **A, B,** and **D** are incorrect. **A** is incorrect because ITIL is the Information Technology Infrastructure Library, the de facto standard for best practices for IT service management. **B** is incorrect because TOGAF is The Open Group Architecture Framework, which originates from the U.S. Department of Defense and provides an iterative and cyclic process to approach building enterprise architectures for businesses, data, technologies, or applications. **D** is incorrect because COBIT is the Control Objectives for Information and related Technology, a framework developed by ISACA to define goals and controls for managing IT.

3. A company wants to protect its information according to the varied levels of how sensitive the information is as well as the potential for damage if that information is lost. What sort of policy would most benefit the company?

   A. Data classification

   B. Data backup

   C. Data ownership

   D. Data retention

☑ **A** is correct. A data classification policy is the formal document to define and enforce how information is protected by levels of sensitivity.

☒ **B, C,** and **D** are incorrect. Policies about backup requirements, ownership, and retention would all protect information, but not based on varying sensitivity levels. Data ownership is often coupled with data classification, but the data ownership policy specifies the roles and responsibilities of the information owner—particularly how they are responsible for protecting the information. A data retention policy specifies for how long each type of information should be kept—typically to satisfy regulatory requirements. Backup policy would enforce the best practice for backing up valuable information if the need for restoring it ever arose.

4. Which of the following requirements would you *not* expect to find in a password policy?

   A. Prohibited types of words

   B. Minimum password age

   C. Technology solution

   D. Types of characters to be used

   ☑ **C** is correct. A password policy, or any policy, would not specify the technology to be used for enacting its requirements.

   ☒ **A, B,** and **D** are incorrect. A password policy would likely specify the minimum and maximum age per password, the types of characters that must be used, and the minimum length. It might even prohibit certain easily guessable words, such as the organization's name.

5. Which of the following comprises and presents the Information Security Management System (ISMS) standards?

   A. The Open Group Architecture Framework

   B. IT Governance Institute

   C. NIST Cyber Security Framework

   D. ISO/IEC 27000 series

   ☑ **D** is correct. The ISMS is a set of global information security standards, developed by the International Organization for Standardization (ISO) and the International Electrotechnical Commission (IEC).

   ☒ **A, B,** and **C** are incorrect. TOGAF, ITGI, and the NIST CSF do not provide the Information Security Management System, or ISMS. The ISMS is a set of global information security standards developed by ISO and IEC.

6. Which type of procedure is considered synonymous with the term *e-discovery*?

   A. Evidence production

   B. Continuous monitoring

   C. Control-testing procedures

   D. E-mail and fax discovery

☑ **A** is correct. Evidence production is a legal term describing the production of electronic evidence, also known as "e-discovery."

☒ **B, C,** and **D** are incorrect. **B** is incorrect because continuous monitoring procedures refer to the practice of maintaining the awareness of security controls and how they are mitigating known threats, vulnerabilities, and other security activities in the organization. **C** is incorrect because control-testing procedures refer to the process of verifying and validating security controls, a process intended to avoid a control being unknowingly ineffective. **D** is incorrect because e-mail and fax discovery is not an actual term.

7. A company is experiencing several unrelated cases of misused user accounts. The user accounts are either created new as privileged accounts or created as new accounts and then elevated to privileged accounts. In either case, the creation of unauthorized accounts must be stopped. After ensuring policy and procedures are being properly carried out, the company determines that the abuse points to a shortcoming in the policy. Which policy most likely needs to be updated to stop this misuse of accounts?

   A. Acceptable use policy

   B. Account management policy

   C. Data ownership policy

   D. Password policy

   ☑ **B** is correct. The account management policy would include requirements about the creation, modification, and deletion of user accounts, as well as how to handle the misuse of accounts.

   ☒ **A, C,** and **D** are incorrect. The acceptable use policy specifies what behavior from the employee the company finds acceptable. The data ownership policy specifies the roles and responsibilities of the information owner, particularly how they are responsible for protecting the information. A password policy specifies detailed requirements for passwords, such as the minimum and maximum age per password, the types of characters that must be used, and the minimum length of the password.

8. After a routine vulnerability scan of their servers, the Bushwood Country Club discovers 18 holes to be patched. Carl, a junior analyst, asks to perform the patching. However, he seems confused on how move forward with the patching. What is the highest authority and proper documentation for Carl to follow?

   A. The organization's patch management procedures

   B. ISO 27002

   C. NIST SP 800-53

   D. ITIL

   ☑ **A** is correct. Several best practice standards exist, but because every organization has different needs, manages a different environment, and has a different risk tolerance, the overruling procedure is the organization's own patch management procedure.

☒ **B, C,** and **D** are incorrect. ISO 27002 is a best practice standard for security management, but it does not overrule the organization's own patch management procedures. NIST SP 800-53, "Security and Privacy Controls for Federal Information Systems and Organizations," provides specific guidance on security controls, but it still does not take precedence over an organization's own patch management procedures. ITIL is a comprehensive best practice standard for service management, but it's not the authority on patch management.

9. Companies make use of security controls with different parameters. Which of the following would not influence the choice of security controls and how those controls are implemented?

   A. Local or federal law

   B. Regulatory requirements

   C. Technical expertise to implement

   D. The organization's risk appetite

   ☑ **C** is correct. Technical expertise might be a requirement for implementing a security control, but it would not generally dissuade a company from using a needed control.

   ☒ **A, B,** and **D** are incorrect. Laws, regulatory requirements, and especially an organization's risk appetite all strongly influence what controls are needed and what organizationally defined parameters are placed on that control.

10. What type of control is a hardware-based firewall?

    A. Administrative control

    B. Physical control

    C. Test control

    D. Logical control

    ☑ **D** is correct. A firewall is an example of a logical or technical control.

    ☒ **A, B,** and **C** are incorrect. Examples of a physical control include a fence, a door lock, and the environmental controls in the data center. Examples of an administrative control are a password policy and the procedures for hiring and firing. There is no such thing as a "test control."

11. Carnegie Mellon University developed the Capability Maturity Model Integration, a set of guidelines for establishing a maturity level as well as evaluating security engineering practices. Maturity levels are defined from the Initial level to the most mature, the Optimizing level. Which of the following is the level at which an organization has formal processes in place to collect and analyze quantitative data, and metrics are defined and fed into the process-improvement program?

    A. Repeatable

    B. Defined

    C. Managed

    D. Optimizing

☑ **C** is correct. The fourth of five levels, "Managed," is defined as when an organization has formal processes in place to collect and analyze quantitative data, and metrics are defined and fed into the process-improvement program.

☒ **A, B,** and **D** are incorrect. The "Repeatable" level is described as when a formal management structure may be in place, but no formal process models are defined. The level "Defined," which is just below "Managed," is described as having formal procedures in place, and the organization has defined a way for quantitative process improvement, but it's not implemented. The final level, "Optimizing," is when a company budgets and integrates plans for continuous process improvement.

12. Which of the following describes a comprehensive technical evaluation of a system's security components, with regard to applicable regulations? In some cases, if formal assurance of the system meeting all requirements is needed, management or some responsible entity grants accreditation.

    A. Certification

    B. Assessment

    C. Audit

    D. Evaluation

    ☑ **A** is correct. Certification is the technical evaluation and verification that security components are meeting requirements, often in the context of a regulation or law.

    ☒ **B, C,** and **D** are incorrect. **B** is incorrect because an assessment is some process that gathers information, and a determination is made based on that assessment. **C** is incorrect because an audit is a systematic inspection by a third party, typically due to needing to meet regulatory compliance requirements. **D** is incorrect because an evaluation is generally another form of an assessment, both of which isn't as formal or comprehensive a process as a certification.

13. On occasion, a system has a vulnerability that cannot be closed because the fix is either too costly or there is no feasible way to fix it directly. At such times, a security control could still be implemented to mitigate the vulnerability, at least partially. Risk assessment combined with additional requirements set by law, regulations, and a company's policy would govern the control choice. What sort of documentation would an analyst consult to implement such a control?

    A. Control-testing procedures

    B. Evidence production procedures

    C. Remediation plan procedures

    D. Compensating control development procedures

    ☑ **D** is correct. In the case where employing a compensating control is the best action to take, having compensating control development procedures will help guide the decisions to be made.

☒ **A, B,** and **C** are incorrect. **A** is incorrect because control-testing procedures would handle how to test a control to validate its intended effectiveness. **B** is incorrect because evidence production procedures manage how to fulfill a legal request for evidence. **C** is incorrect because remediation plan procedures specify how an organization handles operations if its security posture worsens.

14. Which of the following is *not* an essential element of exception management procedures?

    A. Involving the correct people

    B. Listing all stakeholders

    C. Ensuring access to the necessary information

    D. Documenting steps on how to handle decision disagreements

    ☑ **B** is correct. The listing of all stakeholders would likely change too often to be feasibly maintained in the procedure. Even a listing of all the potential roles cannot be reasonably managed. Instead, the stakeholders must be identified when an exception is raised.

    ☒ **A, C,** and **D** are incorrect. **A** is incorrect because involving the correct people is critical to managing an exception. **C** is incorrect because ensuring the stakeholders have access to the necessary information is critical. **D** is incorrect because procedures should also include how to handle irreconcilable differences between decision-makers.

Identity and Access Management

This chapter includes questions on the following topics:

- Various parameters for context-based authentication
- Security issues and best practices for using common authentication protocols
- Security issues with various components of the network environment
- Commonly used exploits against authentication and access systems

Authentication and authorization are the gatekeepers between users and the resources they need. The one key component that's necessary is the identity; whether it's a user, an application, a service, or a system, the identity commands a level of trust that the subject is who or what it claims to be. In this chapter, we cover methods for protecting identity, issues involved with sharing identity, and some common methods to exploit identity sharing.

1. Which of the following context-based authentication methods is the most difficult to forge or falsify?

   A. Time

   B. Frequency

   C. Location

   D. Behavior

2. Your company plans to employ single sign-on for services and web-based applications. It needs to choose a federated identity technology for authorization and, if possible, authentication. Which of the following technologies satisfy the company's needs? (Choose all that apply.)

   A. SAML

   B. Active Directory Federated Services

   C. OAuth2

   D. OpenID

3. When you're securing endpoints, what is their main vulnerability in comparison to other identities with regard to authentication?

   A. Relative to servers, securing the endpoints is difficult to scale.

   B. Compared to applications, endpoints can only rely on token-based authentication.

   C. Relative to services, endpoints are vulnerable to replay attacks.

   D. Compared to personnel, endpoints are more difficult to lock down.

4. Which of the following context-based authentication methods is likely to reveal someone attempting to brute-force an account using an automated script?

   A. Time

   B. Frequency

   C. Location

   D. Behavior

5. A company utilizes a resource for storing employee credentials, otherwise known as an identity repository. In general, all employees have their network access validated by a central server. Although most employees work in the headquarters building, a small set of users work in locations that provide all their needed productivity services locally, except for the authentication. Communications between headquarters and these other locations either rely on a dedicated but unreliable low-bandwidth connection or occur across the Internet. All of the following identity repositories, except one, would be acceptable as a solution. Which repository must use a fully reliable and secure network?

   A. RADIUS

   B. TACAS+

C. LDAP

D. XTACACS

6. Figure 12-1 shows a hierarchical relationship of organizational resources and users. According to RFC 1779, which of the following is a correctly represented distinguished name (DN)?

A. cn=Bowmani,ou=Temple,o=Galactic Empire

B. cn=Bowmani,ou=Temple,ou=Coruscant,o=Galactic Empire

C. cn=Offee,ou=Coruscant,o=Galactic Empire

D. cn=Vader,ou=Killun Station,ou=Killun 71,o=Galactic Empire

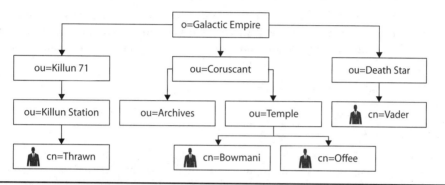

Figure 12-1 RFC 1779 organization

7. What type of identity is unique in that its authorizations can vary in multiple ways?

A. Services

B. Roles

C. Endpoints

D. Applications

8. A few employees have fallen victim to having their passwords compromised. The users claim it is happening after visiting the company's own internal hourly billing website. The cybersecurity analyst verifies the website code and web server as clean. However, you witness the attack yourself after watching a user click through a text message that reminds them to update their timesheet. What sort of attack seems to be happening here?

A. Man-in-the-middle

B. Cross-site scripting

C. Rootkit

D. Privilege escalation

9. A vice president's workstation is acting erratically, so you investigate the laptop personally. You carefully review the system's application and security logs. You confirm the antivirus is running and nothing is quarantined. You evaluate the running processes and find nothing out of the ordinary. After using command-line utilities to confirm no strange network connections, you feel somewhat frustrated to find nothing to report. What action should you take next?

   A. Return the laptop to the vice president and report that all is fine.

   B. Reinstall and update the antivirus to rescan the system.

   C. Assume the laptop has a rootkit and wipe the system immediately.

   D. Use tools external to the laptop to explore the suspicion of a rootkit.

10. Manual provisioning of accounts takes considerable time, but still allows a genuine person to exercise due diligence. With regard to auto-provisioning accounts, what is the most critical piece in the identity and access request process never to be compromised?

    A. Consumer

    B. Identity provider

    C. Service provider

    D. Network access

11. A company recently implemented a self-service password reset mechanism. Although this saves the administrators hours of time dealing with forgotten passwords, a new problem has started. Administrators have noticed brute-force attacks on the password reset page. Even though the password reset page is visible outside the company, the attacks are always against valid e-mails only, so the administrator suspects an insider is responsible. What might be the source of the problem on the reset page?

    A. Error messages for invalid input

    B. Website source code

    C. Constant availability

    D. Instructions on reset page usage

12. Knowing the root cause and mechanics behind session hijacking, what is the most effective way to mitigate this specific attack?

    A. Employing extremely long session keys

    B. Using special character sets within sessions

    C. Encrypting the session key

    D. Ensuring sessions have a very short timeout

13. Because the user appreciates how important security is when banking online, they carefully type the bank's website address, beginning with HTTPS. However, when the browser resolves the address, the user sees a puzzling pop-up message about a certificate server. Moving past the message, the user is at a website that appears familiar, so they feel safe enough to enter their credentials. Unfortunately, the account funds are emptied shortly thereafter. What was the likely attack used, even though the user tried hard to avoid it?

A. Privilege escalation

B. Rootkit

C. Cross-site scripting

D. Man-in-the-middle

1. C	**6.** B	**11.** A
2. A, B, C	**7.** B	**12.** C
3. C	**8.** B	**13.** D
4. B	**9.** D	
5. A	**10.** B	

1. Which of the following context-based authentication methods is the most difficult to forge or falsify?

   A. Time

   B. Frequency

   C. Location

   D. Behavior

   ☑ **C** is correct. Location is understood to be the most difficult techniques to falsify of the four context-based approaches to authentication. Context-based authentication by location means using someone physical location, presumably via GPS, to determine whether that person should be authenticated.

   ☒ **A, B,** and **D** are incorrect. Time-based authentication would be fairly straightforward to forge. Frequency is determined by a reasonable assessment of how often someone attempts to authenticate. Naturally, if someone attempts 30 times a second, this couldn't possibly be the correct person. Behavior-based authentication is possible after learning someone's routine and expected performance. It would be difficult, but not impossible if you knew the target user very well.

2. Your company plans to employ single sign-on for services and web-based applications. It needs to choose a federated identity technology for authorization and, if possible, authentication. Which of the following technologies satisfy the company's needs? (Choose all that apply.)

   A. SAML

   B. Active Directory Federated Services

   C. OAuth2

   D. OpenID

   ☑ **A, B,** and **C** are correct. Security Assertion Markup Language (SAML) is commonly used for both authentication and authorization. AD Federated Services is used for both authentication and authorization, primarily in Windows environments. The OAuth2 protocol is used generally for authorization, commonly for services. Although OAuth2 is used inside of authentication protocols, it's technically not a standalone replacement. In any case, the company requires authorization, not authentication.

   ☒ **D** is incorrect. OpenID is commonly used for authentication. However, unlike SAML, OAuth2, and AD Federated Services, OpenID cannot be used for authorization.

3. When you're securing endpoints, what is their main vulnerability in comparison to other identities with regard to authentication?

   A. Relative to servers, securing the endpoints is difficult to scale.

   B. Compared to applications, endpoints can only rely on token-based authentication.

C. Relative to services, endpoints are vulnerable to replay attacks.

D. Compared to personnel, endpoints are more difficult to lock down.

☑ **C** is correct. In terms of authentication, endpoints are particularly vulnerable to replay attacks.

☒ **A, B,** and **D** are incorrect. Servers are typically authenticated by certificates, as defined by the X.509 standard. The use of PKI certificates makes authenticating servers fairly straightforward, but not on a massive scale. Endpoints do not require authentication by token. Also, endpoints are not more difficult to secure when dealing with larger numbers. An administrator might argue that with volume licensing, standardized images, and group policy, a large number of workstations can be relatively simple to lock down. Personnel are by far the most difficult to "lock down" when you consider that human error and the tendency to want to help are constant vulnerabilities to personnel.

4. Which of the following context-based authentication methods is likely to reveal someone attempting to brute-force an account using an automated script?

A. Time

B. Frequency

C. Location

D. Behavior

☑ **B** is correct. If someone is using an automated script to guess someone's credentials via brute force, the frequency of attempts will be far greater than a person could reasonably perform.

☒ **A, C,** and **D** are incorrect. Whether by script or not, the time of those attempts isn't mentioned. The location may or may not be the same, meaning the brute-force attack could be performed locally or remotely. The behavior aspect does not apply here, because the attacker hasn't logged on yet. Behavior means monitoring a user's activity, such as websites visited and applications used.

5. A company utilizes a resource for storing employee credentials, otherwise known as an identity repository. In general, all employees have their network access validated by a central server. Although most employees work in the headquarters building, a small set of users work in locations that provide all their needed productivity services locally, except for the authentication. Communications between headquarters and these other locations either rely on a dedicated but unreliable low-bandwidth connection or occur across the Internet. All of the following identity repositories, except one, would be acceptable as a solution. Which repository must use a fully reliable and secure network?

A. RADIUS

B. TACAS+

C. LDAP

D. XTACACS

☑ **A** is correct. The Remote Authentication Dial-In User Service (RADIUS) uses UDP, not TCP. Additionally, RADIUS allows the use of a "shared secret" across the network. For both these reasons, using an unreliable or untrusted network is highly discouraged if the company is wanting to use RADIUS.

☒ **B, C,** and **D** are incorrect. **B** is incorrect because Terminal Access Controller Access Control System Plus (TACAS+) uses TCP, so it is a viable solution for the low-bandwidth network. However, because TACAS+ does not use encryption, it is vulnerable to reply attacks. Therefore, authenticating across the Internet is not recommended. **C** is incorrect because Lightweight Directory Access Protocol (LDAP) is an option over the dedicated line. **D** is incorrect because XTACACS is a later, extended version of TACACS and also uses encryption, so the untrusted network is not a big risk.

6. Figure 12-1 shows a hierarchical relationship of organizational resources and users. According to RFC 1779, which of the following is a correctly represented distinguished name (DN)?

A. cn=Bowmani,ou=Temple,o=Galactic Empire

B. cn=Bowmani,ou=Temple,ou=Coruscant,o=Galactic Empire

C. cn=Offee,ou=Coruscant,o=Galactic Empire

D. cn=Vader,ou=Killun Station,ou=Killun 71,o=Galactic Empire

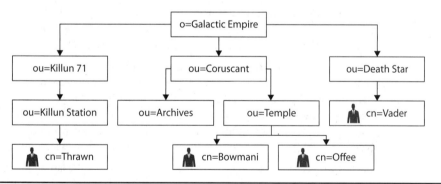

Figure 12-1 RFC 1779 organization

☑ **B** is correct. Directory services are a central repository for storing and managing information and resources. The hierarchical naming convention for resources is the user name (common name, or cn), the organizational unit (ou), and then the organization (o), separated by a special character, typically a comma.

☒ **A, C,** and **D** are incorrect. The distinguished name must include all levels from common name to organization.

7. What type of identity is unique in that its authorizations can vary in multiple ways?

   A. Services

   B. Roles

   C. Endpoints

   D. Applications

   ☑ **B** is correct. Roles are unique in that there is often a many-to-one relationship between roles and users. A user can have multiple roles, and so the challenge to administrators is to grant access according to the task fitting the role at the time.

   ☒ **A, C,** and **D** are incorrect. Services, endpoints, and applications would all generally have one defined set of access. This contrasts with a role or a user, which might have multiple levels of access.

8. A few employees have fallen victim to having their passwords compromised. The users claim it is happening after visiting the company's own internal hourly billing website. The cybersecurity analyst verifies the website code and web server as clean. However, you witness the attack yourself after watching a user click through a text message that reminds them to update their timesheet. What sort of attack seems to be happening here?

   A. Man-in-the-middle

   B. Cross-site scripting

   C. Rootkit

   D. Privilege escalation

   ☑ **B** is correct. Considering that the problem might be originating from a link provided by text, which is extra difficult for users to scrutinize, and that the web server was verified as clean, then cross-site scripting is the likely attack method.

   ☒ **A, C,** and **D** are incorrect. There doesn't seem to be any indication of a man-in-the-middle attack. Rootkits would be significantly harder to detect or witness without specialized tools, and privilege escalation isn't the primary issue. However, after the XSS attack, perhaps the session information gleaned from the attack might contribute to privilege escalation later, meaning the attacker might use the opportunity to elevate the privileges to a higher level, or to somehow gain access to others' accounts.

9. A vice president's workstation is acting erratically, so you investigate the laptop personally. You carefully review the system's application and security logs. You confirm the antivirus is running and nothing is quarantined. You evaluate the running processes and find nothing out of the ordinary. After using command-line utilities to confirm no strange network connections, you feel somewhat frustrated to find nothing to report. What action should you take next?

   A. Return the laptop to the vice president and report that all is fine.

   B. Reinstall and update the antivirus to rescan the system.

C. Assume the laptop has a rootkit and wipe the system immediately.

D. Use tools external to the laptop to explore the suspicion of a rootkit.

☑ **D** is correct. Despite suspicious behavior, local tools reporting nothing wrong is a strong suggestion to explore deeper with offline tools. Using tools stored on media outside the system, and if possible without the OS running, can improve visibility without allowing the potential rootkit to mask itself.

☒ **A, B,** and **C** are incorrect. Returning the laptop might be what the VP would like, but this is not acceptable until after some closer examination. Because a rootkit is resident under the operating system and running applications, reinstalling the antivirus would only give you a false sense of security. Although a rootkit might be the suspicion, such a suspicion is typically not enough to warrant wiping the system.

10. Manual provisioning of accounts takes considerable time, but still allows a genuine person to exercise due diligence. With regard to auto-provisioning accounts, what is the most critical piece in the identity and access request process never to be compromised?

A. Consumer

B. Identity provider

C. Service provider

D. Network access

☑ **B** is correct. Because auto-provisioning means creating an account on the fly, the service provider (SP) is completely trusting the identity provider's assertion that the user is allowed to hold an account. Therefore, the identity provider (IDP) cannot be compromised; otherwise, that trust is easily abused.

☒ **A, C,** and **D** are incorrect. It's best to never completely trust the consumer or user. The service provider is of course important, but the burden falls much more on the identity provider to be trustworthy. Network access is important to keep secure, as always, but no more so when auto-provisioning is used.

11. A company recently implemented a self-service password reset mechanism. Although this saves the administrators hours of time dealing with forgotten passwords, a new problem has started. Administrators have noticed brute-force attacks on the password reset page. Even though the password reset page is visible outside the company, the attacks are always against valid e-mails only, so the administrator suspects an insider is responsible. What might be the source of the problem on the reset page?

A. Error messages for invalid input

B. Website source code

C. Constant availability

D. Instructions on reset page usage

☑ **A** is correct. Having different error messages for an invalid username and invalid password only serves to ensure a username is valid. Confirming for the attacker that a username is valid means they can spend more time brute-forcing the password.

☒ **B, C,** and **D** are incorrect. Learning that only valid usernames are being attacked tells you that the website source code and availability are not the weakness. Also, it's unlikely the instructions are written so poorly to cause users to keep attempting bad passwords.

12. Knowing the root cause and mechanics behind session hijacking, what is the most effective way to mitigate this specific attack?

    A. Employing extremely long session keys

    B. Using special character sets within sessions

    C. Encrypting the session key

    D. Ensuring sessions have a very short timeout

    ☑ **C** is correct. Encrypting the session keys would certainly stop the keys from being captured or stolen.

    ☒ **A, B,** and **D** are incorrect. Session hijacking generally happens because the session key was captured and replayed to impersonate the valid client. Regardless of whether session keys are very long or contain any special characters, they can and will be captured. Only encryption between the client and server can thwart the key being captured. Having a very short timeout would likely only result in frustrated clients.

13. Because the user appreciates how important security is when banking online, they carefully type the bank's website address, beginning with HTTPS. However, when the browser resolves the address, the user sees a puzzling pop-up message about a certificate server. Moving past the message, the user is at a website that appears familiar, so they feel safe enough to enter their credentials. Unfortunately, the account funds are emptied shortly thereafter. What was the likely attack used, even though the user tried hard to avoid it?

    A. Privilege escalation

    B. Rootkit

    C. Cross-site scripting

    D. Man-in-the-middle

    ☑ **D** is correct. The user likely typed in HTTPS correctly but might have accidentally visited a malicious website designed to appear like their bank. The certificate error was warning of an invalid or untrusted certificate server.

    ☒ **A, B,** and **C** are incorrect. Privilege escalation wasn't involved because the user provided credentials high enough to carry out the attack and withdrawal. No rootkit was necessary in this attack, and no cross-site scripting was involved because the user went to the malicious website directly.

CHAPTER 13

Putting in Compensating Controls

This chapter includes questions on the following topics:

- Best practices for security analytics using automated methods
- Techniques for basic manual analysis
- Applying the concept of "defense in depth" across the network
- Processes to continually improve your security operations

Implementing the right compensating control is the focus of this chapter. The purpose of a compensating control is to mitigate the risk already assessed in your environment. But how do you know the control is providing the value you desired? You measure a control's effectiveness through analysis of the affected systems or area. Depending on the actual system or type of control, you might be analyzing logs, gauging the difference between prior to the control being implemented and afterward. Being able to analyze data—whether in the form of logs, alerts or automated reports—is key to making informed decisions for your environment's security.

1. You're the manager of a small team of information security specialists. The team recently ended a challenging period of a few incidents and one forensic investigation involving law enforcement. Given that the incidents and investigation are finished, the team seems to be struggling considerably. In fact, you notice that the patch rollout cycle is inconsistent, occasionally taking twice as long as it should. What might you consider to be most helpful to the team?

   A. Succession planning

   B. Awarding team members for dedication

   C. Mandatory vacation

   D. Cross-training

2. Over time, the specific needs on systems, applications, and business processes will change. How an organization approaches and accomplishes these changes depends on the maturity of the organization. In the context of continual changes, what distinguishes a mature organization from other organizations?

   A. Process improvement

   B. Process definition

   C. Process documentation

   D. Process management

3. An incoming CIO starts their first day on the job by reading and becoming familiar with the company's security policies. The CIO dusts off policies about the management of pagers, fax machines, and CRT monitors, among other policies that seem to apply to technology no longer applicable to the business's goals and operations today. What might the incoming CIO add to their to-do list to address this issue?

   A. Retirement of processes

   B. Automated reporting

   C. Deputy CIO

   D. Scheduled reviews

4. What software approach can ensure that the security and management functions of an organization can operate and cooperate together?

   A. Cross-training

   B. Custom APIs

   C. Security suites

   D. Security appliances

5. A company has recently implemented Elasticsearch, Logstash, and Kibana (ELK) as a central part of its SIEM. Which features has the company gained in their SIEM that were likely missing before? (Select two.)

   A. Data outsourcing

   B. Data aggregation

   C. Data correlation

   D. Data automation

6. Which of the following is not a key concern for organizations relying on an outsourcing firm?

   A. Sufficient vetting

   B. Access to sensitive data by non-employees

   C. Redundancy of efforts

   D. Agreement on incident-handling responsibilities and decision-making

7. A recent incident at a company revealed that a normal employee has been using special network-analyzing software to capture and read internal e-mails. What control could be put in place to immediately stop this?

   A. E-mail signatures

   B. Cryptography

   C. Two-factor login authentication

   D. Network segmentation between departments

8. Compensating controls are available from both personnel and technology categories. Which of the following are technology-based controls? (Choose all that apply.)

   A. Automated log review and reporting

   B. Load balancers

   C. Dual control

   D. Cross-training

   E. Network design

Use the following scenario to answer questions 9–13:

The government bureau of Urban Development and Enrichment (UDE) has three information security personnel: two analysts and a director. The analysts, Donnie and Walter, divide up the typical information security responsibilities for the bureau. Today's duties include reviewing several logs and creating a few accounts. Regarding the review of logs, an analyst reviews only the logs of systems that once belonged to internal departments the analyst has been qualified by (a procedure dating back before all departments were merged). The procedure for creating a new account begins with an analyst filling in account information in the directory service and then submitting the account request to the director. The Director of UDE will log in to approve and activate the new account.

9. On this particular day, Walter has invited a vendor to come demonstrate a log review tool. At the last minute, the vendor mentions he will need a specially named account. Walter assures the vendor that the account will be ready in time for their 3:00 p.m. appointment. Walter informs the Director of UDE (DUDE) that the account is needed urgently and thus requests that he handle both steps of filling in the account info and the account approval. The DUDE abides. What particular security control is Walter breaking by circumventing the change request?

    A. Dual control

    B. Outsourcing

    C. Succession planning

    D. Separation of duties

10. Donnie regularly reviews the event logs on the Windows desktop systems. However, a few Linux systems are missed because Donnie is not familiar with them. What similar feature on the Linux systems is he missing?

    A. L.Event log

    B. Linux logs

    C. Messages

    D. Syslogs

11. Some network perimeter devices have been experiencing denial of service attempts over the past several months. Even though the attempts are increasing, Donnie is confident the firewall can handle the added load for the immediate future. However, by Walter's analysis, the bureau should consider purchasing a more robust firewall soon. What type of analysis is Walter performing to come to this conclusion?

    A. Firewall log analysis

    B. Historical analysis

    C. Trend analysis

    D. Data correlation

12. As mentioned earlier, Walter and Donnie need to be "qualified" to review logs of particular departmental systems, even though all of the bureau's departments are now merged together. This causes added administrative overhead for each new system brought online. What change control process is failing?

    A. Retirement of process

    B. Separation of duties

    C. Procedural training

    D. Scheduled reviews

13. The bureau has procured the new log review application. However, the task of integrating this application in with current systems is apparently quite challenging and specialized. Integration requires a high level of experience in database optimization, which only Walter possesses, at an intermediate level. The integration process is described by the vendor as "quick and painless" because all their sales engineers are both skilled and experienced in the requisite knowledge. What might be the best action to take, and who will be involved?

    A. Training (vendor trains Donnie)

    B. Dual control (vendor and Walter)

    C. Separation of duties (Donnie and Walter)

    D. Consultant (vendor)

14. Recent news articles on hacker sites mention a new type of scanning seen in the wild in recent weeks. The articles say the only way to confirm such a scan is occurring is to collect data from devices already aware of a particular packet signature and compare those events to the logs of the network perimeter gateway for the internal network. Besides the IDS, where else could you look?

    A. Syslog

    B. Firewall log

    C. Switch log

    D. IPS log

1. C
2. A
3. D
4. C
5. B, C

6. C
7. B
8. A, B, E
9. D
10. D

11. C
12. A
13. D
14. B

1. You're the manager of a small team of information security specialists. The team recently ended a challenging period of a few incidents and one forensic investigation involving law enforcement. Given that the incidents and investigation are finished, the team seems to be struggling considerably. In fact, you notice that the patch rollout cycle is inconsistent, occasionally taking twice as long as it should. What might you consider to be most helpful to the team?

   A. Succession planning

   B. Awarding team members for dedication

   C. Mandatory vacation

   D. Cross-training

   ☑ **C is correct.** After the described recent workload, the team is likely tired and weary. Further, as the narrative explained about the inconsistent patch management cycle, the team has grown complacent. In this case, mandatory vacation is required to ensure team members get the needed rest.

   ☒ **A, B,** and **D** are incorrect. **A** is incorrect because succession planning is an organization's planned transition of responsibilities from the current person to the successor. In this case, succession planning would be useful if current personnel decided to leave, but such planning should have already been done. **B** is incorrect because recognition, while nice and appreciated, will do little to subside the team's exhaustion and complacency. **D** is incorrect because cross-training is certainly useful in order to mitigate the loss of skills when a specialist is absent (such as on mandatory vacation), but implementing training at this time would only add to the team's workload. Mandatory vacation should come first.

2. Over time, the specific needs on systems, applications, and business processes will change. How an organization approaches and accomplishes these changes depends on the maturity of the organization. In the context of continual changes, what distinguishes a mature organization from other organizations?

   A. Process improvement

   B. Process definition

   C. Process documentation

   D. Process management

   ☑ **A is correct.** Continual process improvement is a defining characteristic of a mature organization.

   ☒ **B, C,** and **D** are incorrect. These wrong answers are worded to mirror the maturity levels of the process appraisal program, Capability Maturity Model Integration (CMMI). When an organization's maturity is evaluated, the program's representative levels, escalating in increasing maturity, are as follows: Initial, Managed, Defined, Quantitatively Managed, and Optimizing. Optimizing, as the final, most mature level, represents the practice of continually improving processes.

3. An incoming CIO starts their first day on the job by reading and becoming familiar with the company's security policies. The CIO dusts off policies about the management of pagers, fax machines, and CRT monitors, among other policies that seem to apply to technology no longer applicable to the business's goals and operations today. What might the incoming CIO add to their to-do list to address this issue?

    A. Retirement of processes

    B. Automated reporting

    C. Deputy CIO

    D. Scheduled reviews

    ☑ **D** is correct. Given the outdated policies, it seems the organization is lacking any review of security policies. Holding regularly or periodically scheduled security reviews helps validate policies as effective and relevant.

    ☒ **A, B,** and **C** are incorrect. **A** is incorrect because the retirement of processes is correct concerning the relevance and practicality of processes, but not when dealing with policies. **B** is incorrect because automated reporting addresses the feature of sending alerts or notifications by a security monitoring product after its analysis shows a team's attention is warranted. **C** is incorrect because although having a deputy CIO might be useful, adding another management level wouldn't directly affect the outdated policies.

4. What software approach can ensure that the security and management functions of an organization can operate and cooperate together?

    A. Cross-training

    B. Custom APIs

    C. Security suites

    D. Security appliances

    ☑ **C** is correct. Security suites are a type of software that offers multiple security and management-related functions. Also called "multilayered security," security suites ensure a level of consistency and interoperability that having several disparate, single-function applications cannot offer.

    ☒ **A, B,** and **D** are incorrect. **A** is incorrect because cross-training helps employees be effective at tasks normally performed by their peers. This helps personnel, but systems need to be more "interoperable." **B** is incorrect because developing custom APIs is not a practical or sustainable solution to ensuring several security functions working together. **D** is incorrect because although a security appliance performs multiple security functions, it is a hardware solution, not a software one.

5. A company has recently implemented Elasticsearch, Logstash, and Kibana (ELK) as a central part of its SIEM. Which features has the company gained in their SIEM that were likely missing before? (Select two.)

    A. Data outsourcing

    B. Data aggregation

C. Data correlation

D. Data automation

☑ **B** and **C** are correct. The aggregation and correlation of data are both well handled by ELK, or the three applications known fully as Elasticsearch, Logstash, and Kibana. With so many varied types of data, from a myriad of source applications and devices, it becomes quickly overwhelming to a person to collect, review, and analyze all this data to glean actionable information from it.

☒ **A** and **D** are incorrect. **A** is incorrect because data outsourcing is not what's being done. **D** is incorrect because although "data automation" could describe what is being done, this is not the recognized term.

6. Which of the following is not a key concern for organizations relying on an outsourcing firm?

   A. Sufficient vetting

   B. Access to sensitive data by non-employees

   C. Redundancy of efforts

   D. Agreement on incident-handling responsibilities and decision-making

   ☑ **C** is correct. When you're dealing with outsourcing, the redundancy of efforts is not the problem.

   ☒ **A, B,** and **D** are incorrect. **A** is incorrect because it is difficult to sufficiently vet and clear the presumed many outsourced employees. **B** is incorrect because outsourcing means granting access to sensitive data and access to internal networks, both of which mean strict access control is required. **D** is incorrect because an organization and the outsourcing firm may both attempt to handle an event or incident, without considerable planning and practice for a variety of events.

7. A recent incident at a company revealed that a normal employee has been using special network-analyzing software to capture and read internal e-mails. What control could be put in place to immediately stop this?

   A. E-mail signatures

   B. Cryptography

   C. Two-factor login authentication

   D. Network segmentation between departments

   ☑ **B** is correct. If cryptography were in place to protect e-mail while in transit, attempts to capture and read it would prove futile.

   ☒ **A, C,** and **D** are incorrect. E-mail signatures, such as inserting contact information at the bottom of every message, do no good in ensuring confidentiality. Two-factor login authentication is an improvement in protecting logging in to the system. However, e-mail would continue to be sent in the clear. Network segmentation would be an improvement to some degree, such as segmenting network traffic between departments. However, we don't know if the snooping employee is reading their own department's e-mail.

8. Compensating controls are available from both personnel and technology categories. Which of the following are technology-based controls? (Choose all that apply.)

A. Automated log review and reporting

B. Load balancers

C. Dual control

D. Cross-training

E. Network design

☑ **A, B,** and **E** are correct. Automated log review and reporting, load balancers, and network design are technology-based compensating controls. Technology-based controls provide the speed, automation, and opportunities to minimize the impact of human error and complacency.

☒ **C** and **D** are incorrect. Dual control and cross-training are two personnel-based compensating controls. Personnel-based controls, and personnel in general, provide what computers cannot do (yet), such as making judgment calls and adding the "human" element to make businesses valued by their customers.

Use the following scenario to answer questions 9–13:

The government bureau of Urban Development and Enrichment (UDE) has three information security personnel: two analysts and a director. The analysts, Donnie and Walter, divide up the typical information security responsibilities for the bureau. Today's duties include reviewing several logs and creating a few accounts. Regarding the review of logs, an analyst reviews only the logs of systems that once belonged to internal departments the analyst has been qualified by (a procedure dating back before all departments were merged). The procedure for creating a new account begins with an analyst filling in account information in the directory service and then submitting the account request to the director. The Director of UDE will log in to approve and activate the new account.

9. On this particular day, Walter has invited a vendor to come demonstrate a log review tool. At the last minute, the vendor mentions he will need a specially named account. Walter assures the vendor that the account will be ready in time for their 3:00 P.M. appointment. Walter informs the Director of UDE (DUDE) that the account is needed urgently and thus requests that he handle both steps of filling in the account info and the account approval. The DUDE abides. What particular security control is Walter breaking by circumventing the change request?

A. Dual control

B. Outsourcing

C. Succession planning

D. Separation of duties

☑ **D** is correct. Separation of duties means it takes two people to perform a task, each performing their own part, to mitigate the risk of abuse of power. In this case,

Walter has assumed the responsibility, given no technical restraint or control, to both create and approve a new account. Therefore, he has circumvented the separation of duties.

☒ **A, B,** and **C** are incorrect. Dual control involves requiring two people to accomplish one task. Although dual control does not prevent collusion or mitigate the risk of conflict of interest like separation of duties can, it does minimize human error or individual fraud. Outsourcing is incorrect because both Walter and the DUDE are employees, not external parties to be outsourced. Succession planning is incorrect because Walter's actions do not undermine his succession, meaning his role's successor is not disadvantaged because of Walter escaping the separation of duties.

10. Donnie regularly reviews the event logs on the Windows desktop systems. However, a few Linux systems are missed because Donnie is not familiar with them. What similar feature on the Linux systems is he missing?

    A. L.Event log

    B. Linux logs

    C. Messages

    D. Syslogs

    ☑ **D** is correct. As Donnie knows, the Windows Event log reports an assortment of system-related messages for the administrator. The logging feature synonymous with the Windows Event log on Linux systems is syslog. Syslog is the common system message protocol used by most network devices, appliances, and UNIX/Linux systems.

    ☒ **A, B,** and **C** are incorrect. The other options do not exist as recognized log or message protocol names.

11. Some network perimeter devices have been experiencing denial of service attempts over the past several months. Even though the attempts are increasing, Donnie is confident the firewall can handle the added load for the immediate future. However, by Walter's analysis, the bureau should consider purchasing a more robust firewall soon. What type of analysis is Walter performing to come to this conclusion?

    A. Firewall log analysis

    B. Historical analysis

    C. Trend analysis

    D. Data correlation

    ☑ **C** is correct. Trend analysis is the process of analyzing what has been happening, in order to foresee what will happen. Trend analysis is similar to historical analysis but should be considered forward-looking analysis.

    ☒ **A, B,** and **D** are incorrect. Walter is looking at the firewalls, but the type of analysis is trend analysis. Historical analysis is more concerned about past events and the trend of events leading up to the present. Data correlation means analyzing data to find the connection between two or more events, but not necessarily continuing that over a time period.

12. As mentioned earlier, Walter and Donnie need to be "qualified" to review logs of particular departmental systems, even though all of the bureau's departments are now merged together. This causes added administrative overhead for each new system brought online. What change control process is failing?

A. Retirement of process

B. Separation of duties

C. Procedural training

D. Scheduled reviews

☑ **A** is correct. Because the reasoning behind the process is outdated, and the process serves little value today, that process should be retired. This activity of reviewing and removing obsolete processes is called "retirement of process."

☒ **B, C,** and **D** are incorrect. Separation of duties helps prevent collusion and conflict of interests. Procedural training is not a real term to be used here. Scheduled reviews describe a review of policies to ensure they are still relevant and effective for their purpose and for the business.

13. The bureau has procured the new log review application. However, the task of integrating this application in with current systems is apparently quite challenging and specialized. Integration requires a high level of experience in database optimization, which only Walter possesses, at an intermediate level. The integration process is described by the vendor as "quick and painless" because all their sales engineers are both skilled and experienced in the requisite knowledge. What might be the best action to take, and who will be involved?

A. Training (vendor trains Donnie)

B. Dual control (vendor and Walter)

C. Separation of duties (Donnie and Walter)

D. Consultant (vendor)

☑ **D** is correct. Hiring the application vendor as a consultant for the purpose of integrating the application is the correct solution. Hiring a consultant is often done because they possess specialized knowledge. In this case, the vendor knows how to integrate the software far more easily than the bureau's own staff does. This makes the software vendor a third party, in service to the bureau for the time period necessary to install the application. In this temporary role, no doubt the vendor will need to sign an NDA to mitigate the risk of sensitive information being exposed during their service.

☒ **A, B,** and **C** are incorrect. Training Donnie to perform the integration is likely well beyond his abilities. Additionally, training an internal employee would have the integration take much longer. Donnie is out of his element here. Dual control between the vendor and Walter is unnecessary. Separation of duties between the two analysts will not get the application installed.

14. Recent news articles on hacker sites mention a new type of scanning seen in the wild in recent weeks. The articles say the only way to confirm such a scan is occurring is to collect data from devices already aware of a particular packet signature and compare those events to the logs of the network perimeter gateway for the internal network. Besides the IDS, where else could you look?

A. Syslog

B. Firewall log

C. Switch log

D. IPS log

☑ **B** is correct. You need to collect logs from your IDS and the firewall, according to the articles. The benefit of having multiple protective devices, such as a firewall and an IDS/IPS, is to provide defense in depth, or a layered approach to security.

☒ **A, C,** and **D** are incorrect. Entries in the syslog will likely not help for this analysis. Switches are not the perimeter gateway device the articles are referring to. The IPS may be helpful, but the question makes it clear that you are already using an IDS.

14

Secure Software Development

This chapter includes questions on the following topics:

- The software development lifecycle (SDLC)
- General principles for secure software development
- How to ensure the security of software
- Best practices for secure coding

As often as we hear about software vulnerabilities and security incidents related to software, we should wonder why common security flaws continue to appear in new applications. The answer is because discussing security requirements during software development is still not a common priority. Too often security needs are considered far along into the software development lifecycle, if at all, prior the application's launch. As a CySA+, you will need to take an active approach to ensuring security needs are met during software development.

To be engaged with meeting security requirements during software development, you do not need to be a software developer yourself. You only need to appreciate the importance of information security (which undoubtedly you do) and understand several best practices in secure software development. Your ability to communicate these with developer peers will make both your lives much easier in the end.

1. A developer has just finished modifying an application—specifically, how input is processed. As part of the development cycle, their application must go through testing to determine what, if any, security vulnerabilities might exist as a result. What technique should a tester use to find any flaws in the developer's changes?

   A. Web application vulnerability scanning

   B. SQL injection

   C. User acceptance

   D. Fuzzing

2. The finance application seems to operate fine, so long as only a few people are connected to it. However, at the end of the month, when nearly everyone in the company connects to this application, it actually freezes. Even after people stop trying, the application is locked up until an administrator resets it. What type of software testing should have caught this problem?

   A. Input validation testing

   B. Fuzzing

   C. Regression testing

   D. Stress testing

3. What organization, best known for its Top Ten list, specializes in web security issues?

   A. SANS Institute

   B. CMMI

   C. OWASP

   D. CIS

4. To reduce the number of modifications soon after an application's release, what practice is done to verify the application will be used as developers expected?

   A. Stress testing

   B. Static code analysis

   C. User acceptance testing

   D. Manual peer review

Use the following scenario to answer Questions 5–7:

Tywin is the CEO of a factory where most employees are paid hourly. Employees must submit on paper all their expected hours for the week by Tuesday to get paid on Friday. Jon, the factory floor manager, shares with Tywin that every week he hears the same complaints from employees: "How do I know by Tuesday that my schedule won't change by Friday?" Understanding the need for a quicker way to submit hours, Tywin remembers that his neighbor's son, Sam, has been taking web development courses at a university for a few semesters. Therefore, Tywin offers Sam an opportunity to help.

After a few weeks of development, Sam launches a web application. Employees are told to authenticate and enter their hours using this application. The application then submits the hours to the Finance department and tells employees how much they can expect to get paid on Friday. Hours can be submitted as late as Thursday night. Jon reports to Tywin that employees are happy with the web application and it seems to be the subject of a constant buzz around the break room.

5. A very honest user tells Jon that if a user enters a single quote, followed by "OR 1=1" in the password field, they can make the application reply with the hours of any employee. What part of software development did Sam likely overlook?

   A. Parameter validation

   B. Input validation

   C. Stress testing

   D. Session tokens not randomized

6. Another honest user, Arya, reports that if she changes the user ID in the URL to someone else's ID number, she can get the paycheck total for that other person's week. The same user claims by changing other parameters in the URL, she can make the server reveal much information about itself and the application. If you could hire this Arya to perform security analysis work, what type of work does her experience seem to match?

   A. Regression testing

   B. Interception proxy

   C. User acceptance testing

   D. Vulnerability scanning

7. Considering the issues discovered to date, what phase of software development was likely missing during the application lifecycle?

   A. Security requirements definition

   B. Stress testing

   C. Security regression testing

   D. Operations and Maintenance

   E. User acceptance testing

8. What detailed guides published by the CIS are equivalent to the Security Technical Implementation Guides published by the Defense Information System Agency and other government entities?

   A. Regression reports

   B. Benchmarks

   C. Security requirements definitions

   D. Secure coding best practice guides

9. The Center for Internet Security has organized focus groups and built consensus to formulate a group of 20 "CIS Controls." These controls are separated in groups of Basic, Foundational, and Organizational. What is the intended aim of these controls?

   A. Employee-controlled access

   B. Software development best practices

   C. Wireless access control

   D. System design recommendations

1. D	**4.** C	**7.** A
2. D	**5.** B	**8.** B
3. C	**6.** D	**9.** D

1. A developer has just finished modifying an application—specifically, how input is processed. As part of the development cycle, their application must go through testing to determine what, if any, security vulnerabilities might exist as a result. What technique should a tester use to find any flaws in the developer's changes?

   A. Web application vulnerability scanning

   B. SQL injection

   C. User acceptance

   D. Fuzzing

   ☑ **D** is correct. Fuzzing, or fuzz testing, is specifically intended to create invalid input or unexpected amounts of input, hoping to trigger an unexpected response. Given a way to monitor that response, security testers can explore how that response could be leveraged into an exploit.

   ☒ **A, B,** and **C** are incorrect. There was no mention of the application being a web application, so web app vulnerability scanning wouldn't apply here. Also, there was no mention of a SQL database, so there's likely no opportunity for a SQL injection attack. Although user acceptance testing can reveal different ways a user will enter input, it's not the best technique for identifying possible input vulnerabilities.

2. The finance application seems to operate fine, so long as only a few people are connected to it. However, at the end of the month, when nearly everyone in the company connects to this application, it actually freezes. Even after people stop trying, the application is locked up until an administrator resets it. What type of software testing should have caught this problem?

   A. Input validation testing

   B. Fuzzing

   C. Regression testing

   D. Stress testing

   ☑ **D** is correct. From the narrative, it sounds like the application functions so long as it is not under too much demand. Stress testing would have caught that issue, had it been done.

   ☒ **A, B,** and **C** are incorrect. The application seems to operate so long as it isn't pushed to its limits. Input validation was probably performed to ensure the application functioned as expected. The same can be said for fuzzing. Regression testing is intended to discover newly introduced issues due to a change in coding, not necessarily targeted to the problem.

3. What organization, best known for its Top Ten list, specializes in web security issues?

    A. SANS Institute

    B. CMMI

    C. OWASP

    D. CIS

    ☑ **C** is correct. The Open Web Application Security Project is an organization that specifically addresses web security issues. What most people know OWASP from is its Top Ten common web application security concerns, published almost every year.

    ☒ **A, B,** and **D** are incorrect. SANS Institute is an authority on security—be it web, application, system, or network—but does not specialize in web security. CMMI is the Capability Maturity Model Integration, the well-known, five-level maturity model from the Software Engineering Institute, a federally funded research and development center at Carnegie-Mellon University. The Center for Internet Security (CIS) is a nonprofit organization that excels in enhancing security with its collaborative approach.

4. To reduce the number of modifications soon after an application's release, what practice is done to verify the application will be used as developers expected?

    A. Stress testing

    B. Static code analysis

    C. User acceptance testing

    D. Manual peer review

    ☑ **C** is correct. Before an application gets released, it's common to have it tested by a handful of users. These early users will report on what should be changed before the application goes to a wider audience. This is called user acceptance testing.

    ☒ **A, B,** and **D** are incorrect. Stress testing involves pushing the application to its limits to see what breaks or fails first. Static code analysis is an automated form of reviewing code without having to run the program. This is typically performed by a specialized application. Manual peer review is a slower but methodical code review done by the developers' peers. This code review allows others to catch the simple errors or typos that developers might too easily skip over from being so familiar with the code.

Use the following scenario to answer Questions 5–7:

Tywin is the CEO of a factory where most employees are paid hourly. Employees must submit on paper all their expected hours for the week by Tuesday to get paid on Friday. Jon, the factory floor manager, shares with Tywin that every week he hears the same complaints from employees: "How do I know by Tuesday that my schedule won't change by Friday?" Understanding the need for a quicker way to submit hours, Tywin remembers that his neighbor's son, Sam, has been taking web development courses at a university for a few semesters. Therefore, Tywin offers Sam an opportunity to help.

After a few weeks of development, Sam launches a web application. Employees are told to authenticate and enter their hours using this application. The application then submits the hours to the Finance department and tells employees how much they can expect to get paid on Friday. Hours can be submitted as late as Thursday night. Jon reports to Tywin that employees are happy with the web application and it seems to be the subject of a constant buzz around the break room.

5. A very honest user tells Jon that if a user enters a single quote, followed by "OR 1=1" in the password field, they can make the application reply with the hours of any employee. What part of software development did Sam likely overlook?

   A. Parameter validation

   B. Input validation

   C. Stress testing

   D. Session tokens not randomized

   ☑ **B** is correct. Input validation is the coding practice of verifying that a user's input falls within the expected range in size, character types, and format.

   ☒ **A, C,** and **D** are incorrect. Parameter validation is the coding practice of verifying that the information passed is what the application expects. It's similar to input validation, but parameter validation might also check input from another portion of the application or another application entirely. Stress testing involves pushing the application to its limits to see what breaks or fails first. Lastly, session tokens not being randomized is incorrect as session tokens aren't mentioned nor are relevant to the attack.

6. Another honest user, Arya, reports that if she changes the user ID in the URL to someone else's ID number, she can get the paycheck total for that other person's week. The same user claims by changing other parameters in the URL, she can make the server reveal much information about itself and the application. If you could hire this Arya to perform security analysis work, what type of work does her experience seem to match?

   A. Regression testing

   B. Interception proxy

   C. User acceptance testing

   D. Vulnerability scanning

   ☑ **D** is correct. Arya seems determined to find vulnerabilities in this web application. She successfully attempted URL manipulation as well as found information leaks. In this case, URL manipulation was able to make the application return another person's paycheck amount. Web application vulnerability scanning would encompass these and many other checks, including cross-site scripting (XSS), improper use of HTTPS, improper user authentication, and more.

☒ **A, B,** and **C** are incorrect. Regression testing is applicable, but because this is the first release of the app, we would not call this regression testing. Interception proxy is a software tool, not a person's role, used to discover similar vulnerabilities by being inserted between two devices. The interception proxy will act as a go-between monitoring device. An analyst can examine the traffic for any vulnerabilities. Up to now, Arya has been a user determined to discover issues. If Arya transitions to the security team, she would no longer be "just a user" but as a team member to validate issues discovered by user testing. Normally, before an application is released, it is tested by a handful of users. These early users will report on what should be changed before the application goes to a wider audience.

7. Considering the issues discovered to date, what phase of software development was likely missing during the application lifecycle?

   A. Security requirements definition

   B. Stress testing

   C. Security regression testing

   D. Operations and Maintenance

   E. User acceptance testing

   ☑ **A** is correct. It seems the developer did very little security testing prior to the application's release. If security requirements had been submitted and followed closely over the course of development, many of these issues could have been avoided. Truly, these are dark times.

   ☒ **B, C, D,** and **E** are incorrect. Stress testing involves trying to break an application by making it work far harder than intended. Regression testing is testing the application after a modification to ensure new vulnerabilities were not introduced. Operations and Maintenance is the continued care of the application after its release, so this option doesn't actually apply to the question. User acceptance testing describes how an application gets tested by a handful of users, prior to release. Early users can report what should be changed before the application goes to a wider audience.

8. What detailed guides published by the CIS are equivalent to the Security Technical Implementation Guides published by the Defense Information System Agency and other government entities?

   A. Regression reports

   B. Benchmarks

   C. Security requirements definitions

   D. Secure coding best practice guides

   ☑ **B** is correct. The Center for Internet Security Benchmarks are detailed configuration guides that are comparable to the STIGs published by the DISA and other government agencies. These guides are free to download, are available for desktop, mobile, server, and network devices, and cover both hardware and virtual platforms. They are highly recommended for anyone to review and understand.

☒ **A, C,** and **D** are incorrect. A regression report would detail what, if any, security vulnerabilities had appeared due to a modification to software. A security requirements definition is a key document that details the security expectations for software. Ideally, this should be drafted in parallel to the software's early requirements and definitions documents. Secure coding best practice guides are not a particular publication of CIS.

9. The Center for Internet Security has organized focus groups and built consensus to formulate a group of 20 "CIS Controls." These controls are separated in groups of Basic, Foundational, and Organizational. What is the intended aim of these controls?

   A. Employee-controlled access

   B. Software development best practices

   C. Wireless access control

   D. System design recommendations

   ☑ **D** is correct. The CIS Controls are system design recommendations, grouped into three categories: Basic, Foundational, and Organizational. These consensus-based best practices provide a set of actionable recommendations, intended for anyone responsible for information security.

   ☒ **A, B,** and **C** are incorrect. Although employee-controlled access, software development, and wireless access controls are all very important, they each represent just one area to be covered by the CIS Controls.

Tool Sets

This chapter includes questions on the following topics:
- The major cybersecurity tools and technologies for analysts
- When and how you might use different tools and technologies
- How to choose among similar tools and technologies

There is that old adage that "knowledge is power." But even the most knowledgeable information security analysts still require tools to apply that power. As with any skilled trade, an analyst can't get far without the use of tools. What sets the analyst apart from everybody else is that the infosec analyst will know which tool is required for a given scenario.

When preparing for the CySA+ exam, you should be able to at least recognize nearly a 100 different tools, applications, frameworks, and tool suites. Although you are not required to be proficient with every tool, you should recognize each tool's general purpose and perhaps some basic functionality.

1. Which of the follow tools are considered exploit tools? (Choose all that apply.)

   A. Nagios

   B. Splunk

   C. OSSIM

   D. Burp Suite

   E. Metasploit

2. According to firewall logs, an external, known malware server has tried communicating with a few workstations. A relevant sample log entry is shown in Figure 15-1. You quickly determine those workstations are beaconing to that server. Quick assessment shows the workstations are infected by a popular Trojan. After you isolate those workstations, your concern is what other workstations might be infected. What tool should you use to identify other workstations?

   A. Nessus

   B. MRTG

   C. nmap

   D. netstat

   E. QRadar

Date	Priority	Description	Source	S.port	Destination	D.port	Protocol	Event
2018-10-31	2	Orca Response	72.247.244.88	25278	192.168.175.10	5297	udp	Alert
2018-10-31	2	Orca Response	72.247.244.88	25278	192.168.175.27	5297	udp	Alert
2018-10-31	2	Orca Response	72.247.244.88	25278	192.168.175.18	5297	udp	Alert
2018-10-31	2	Orca Response	72.247.244.88	25278	192.168.175.83	5297	udp	Alert

Figure 15-1 Firewall log entry

3. Which of the following command-line utilities is capable of reporting interface statistics like those found in Figure 15-2?

   A. netstat

   B. ping

   C. tracert/traceroute

   D. nslookup/dig

   E. ipconfig/ifconfig

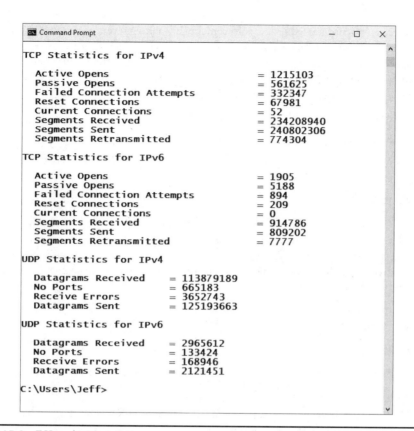

```
Command Prompt                                          —   □   ×

TCP Statistics for IPv4

    Active Opens                     = 1215103
    Passive Opens                    = 561625
    Failed Connection Attempts       = 332347
    Reset Connections                = 67981
    Current Connections              = 52
    Segments Received                = 234208940
    Segments Sent                    = 240802306
    Segments Retransmitted           = 774304

TCP Statistics for IPv6

    Active Opens                     = 1905
    Passive Opens                    = 5188
    Failed Connection Attempts       = 894
    Reset Connections                = 209
    Current Connections              = 0
    Segments Received                = 914786
    Segments Sent                    = 809202
    Segments Retransmitted           = 7777

UDP Statistics for IPv4

    Datagrams Received    = 113879189
    No Ports              = 665183
    Receive Errors        = 3652743
    Datagrams Sent        = 125193663

UDP Statistics for IPv6

    Datagrams Received    = 2965612
    No Ports              = 133424
    Receive Errors        = 168946
    Datagrams Sent        = 2121451

C:\Users\Jeff>
```

Figure 15-2   TCP and UDP statistics

4. Which of the following vulnerability scanners is the open source and free version of the commercially licensed scanner Nessus?

   A. Nikto

   B. OpenVAS

   C. Nexpose

   D. Qualys

   E. Microsoft Baseline Security Analyzer

5. A recent incident has led to law enforcement (LE) taking several employees' mobile devices. LE requires data extraction from these devices, while ensuring no changes to the data can be made during extraction. Given the scope of their effort, and how it's done on company-managed devices, LE asks for your suggestion on the proper forensic tool for the job. What forensic tool suite would you recommend?

   A. EnCase

   B. FTK Imager

   C. Sysinternals

   D. Cellebrite

   E. Helix

6. As a safety measure, a finance manager has been archiving the small company's finance folder every evening, keeping the backup off the server. One early morning, the manager asks you if there is any way to ensure that the files have not changed since they were archived the night before. What tools can you use to demonstrate no changes have been made? (Choose all that apply.)

   A. md5sum

   B. tcpdump

   C. shasum

   D. Vega

   E. ZAP

7. The in-house development team is proud of their newest XML application. They claim that if you can break the application just by entering data in it like a user would, they will buy you lunch. Seeing how you are quite hungry, what tool do you reach for?

   A. ModSecurity

   B. Kiwi Syslog

   C. Cain & Abel

   D. Untidy

8. Your CEO recently read an article titled "Security Information and Event Management—How You Can Know Everything." The CEO has always been interested in alerts you receive from the company's vast array of systems, but he now is willing to invest in real-time analysis of those alerts. Which tool would you suggest the CEO invest in?

   A. ArcSight

   B. Bro

   C. Cacti

   D. tcpdump

Use the following scenario to answer Questions 9 and 10:

In the Department of Research and Development, one of the Windows servers goes offline once or twice a day. Each outage lasts only three to five minutes. The server drops offline and restores connectivity with no apparent cause or pattern. Every outage is temporary, but it's disruptive enough that the department manager has finally demanded an investigation. After a network engineer diagnosed the routing table and wiring as fine and a system admin was unable to replicate the problem, they then turn to security.

9. Although the networking and routing have been determined to be good, there could still be a networking issue to detect on the system. What command-line utility could be used to display open sockets and network connections?

   A. nslookup

   B. nmap

   C. netstat

   D. tracert

10. The networking connections display one external, foreign IP address with an active connection. What device or application would be the first choice to corroborate this finding as well as to stop it?

   A. Antivirus

   B. Firewall

   C. Antimalware

   D. IPS

11. What Next-Generation Firewall (NGFW) company released "Wildfire," a cloud-based malware-detection service?

   A. Cisco

   B. Check Point

   C. Palo Alto

   D. Sourcefire

Use the following scenario to answer Questions 12 and 13:

A special-purpose workstation connects with several external hosts during the normal workday. On the rare occasion, a connection triggers an alert on a network intrusion detection system or some other security device because malicious traffic is detected. This is because none of the external nodes are under the company's control or security policy. Because this is a necessary function of this particular workstation, the potential for malicious traffic is an acceptable risk.

12. What should be the first line of defense to protect the workstation from a security incident?

    A. Antivirus

    B. Firewall

    C. HIDS

    D. Network-based IDS

13. The new CISO has decided the workstation must connect via VPN to improve security. What, if any, change in controls should be considered?

    A. Adding an HIPS

    B. Ensuring the CA is up to date

    C. Capturing packet headers

    D. No change in controls needed

14. What network-monitoring application is the following rule useful for?

```
alert tcp $ $EXTERNAL_NET any -> $HOME_NET any (msg: "You're gonna need
a bigger boat"; content: "dun_dun"; depth:5; nocase; detection_filter:
track by_src, count 3, seconds 2;)
```

    A. Metasploit

    B. Web proxy

    C. Network General

    D. Snort

    E. Most firewalls

1. D, E	**6.** A, C	**11.** C
2. C	**7.** D	**12.** A
3. A	**8.** A	**13.** A
4. B	**9.** C	**14.** D
5. D	**10.** B	

1. Which of the follow tools are considered exploit tools? (Choose all that apply.)

   A. Nagios

   B. Splunk

   C. OSSIM

   D. Burp Suite

   E. Metasploit

   ☑ **D** and **E** are correct. Both Burp Suite and Metasploit are exploitative tools. Burp Suite is a web application testing platform, able to provide analysis of a web application's vulnerabilities. The Metasploit Framework is an exploit tool that includes a large array of modular-like exploit code that a user can execute against a target.

   ☒ **A, B,** and **C** are incorrect. Nagios is an analytical tool useful for monitoring. Splunk is a collective tool used for log file searching and analysis. OSSIM, or the Open Source Security Information Manager, is a set of tools primarily used for monitoring and integrating with the company security information and event management (SIEM) solution.

2. According to firewall logs, an external, known malware server has tried communicating with a few workstations. A relevant sample log entry is shown in Figure 15-1. You quickly determine those workstations are beaconing to that server. Quick assessment shows the workstations are infected by a popular Trojan. After you isolate those workstations, your concern is what other workstations might be infected. What tool should you use to identify other workstations?

   A. Nessus

   B. MRTG

   C. nmap

   D. netstat

   E. QRadar

Date	Priority	Description	Source	S.port	Destination	D.port	Protocol	Event
2018-10-31	2	Orca Response	72.247.244.88	25278	192.168.175.10	5297	udp	Alert
2018-10-31	2	Orca Response	72.247.244.88	25278	192.168.175.27	5297	udp	Alert
2018-10-31	2	Orca Response	72.247.244.88	25278	192.168.175.18	5297	udp	Alert
2018-10-31	2	Orca Response	72.247.244.88	25278	192.168.175.83	5297	udp	Alert

Figure 15-1   Firewall log entry

   ☑ **C** is correct. Given that the port number is known from the firewall log, it would be best to scan the network for workstations listening on port 5297. This can be done quickly and easily with the port scanner utility nmap.

   ☒ **A, B, D,** and **E** are incorrect. Nessus is a popular vulnerability scanner with tens of thousands of plug-ins available for searching vulnerabilities. While Nessus would likely be able to identify the vulnerabilities that allowed the malware to get installed, it isn't the ideal tool for identifying which systems are already infected. The monitoring tool Multi Router Traffic Grapher (MRTG) is for graphing network utilization, but it is not able to identify individual workstation behavior. The command-line utility netstat would report on network connections and listening sockets, but it wouldn't identify all the systems with port 5297 open as quickly as nmap can. The commercially licensed SIEM QRadar from IBM might report on strange behavior originating from other systems. However, as a security information and event management tool, much of its value depends on how it is configured. QRadar would not be as practical as nmap for identifying the infected systems.

3. Which of the following command-line utilities is capable of reporting interface statistics like those found in Figure 15-2?

A. netstat

B. ping

C. tracert/traceroute

D. nslookup/dig

E. ipconfig/ifconfig

Figure 15-2 TCP and UDP statistics

☑ **A** is correct. The command-line utility netstat is the utility used to produce those statistics.

☒ **B, C, D,** and **E** are incorrect. The ping utility is excellent for a quick network connection and availability check, but it's not a utility for producing statistics. The utility traceroute (Linux/Unix) or tracert (Windows) is used for mapping the path taken by network hops, but it produces little information apart from listing the individual route stops along the way. The utility dig (Linux/Unix) or nslookup (Windows) is for DNS resolution and information, but it provides little information outside of DNS-related statistics. The utility ifconfig (Linux/Unix) or ipconfig (Windows) will provide configuration and static information about the network interface, but it provides little information related to packets.

4. Which of the following vulnerability scanners is the open source and free version of the commercially licensed scanner Nessus?

   A. Nikto

   B. OpenVAS

   C. Nexpose

   D. Qualys

   E. Microsoft Baseline Security Analyzer

   ☑ **B** is correct. OpenVAS is open source and free to use. Originally forked from the Nessus project, OpenVAS is similarly structured and capable.

   ☒ **A, C, D,** and **E** are incorrect. All of the vulnerability scanners collect and analyze the data, but their scope and pricing differs. Nikto is also a vulnerability scanner, but unlike Nessus, Nikto is a command-line utility and specific to web servers. As such, Nikto works very quickly but is not as intuitive as GUI-based tools. Nexpose, like Nessus and Nikto, is also a vulnerability scanner. While Nexpose is more useful for managing vulnerabilities, it can integrate directly with Metasploit, making Nexpose something of an exploitative tool as well. Qualys commercially licenses its vulnerability scanner QualysGuard. Lastly, the Microsoft Baseline Security Analyzer is free, but only capable of scanning Windows endpoints and servers.

5. A recent incident has led to law enforcement (LE) taking several employees' mobile devices. LE requires data extraction from these devices, while ensuring no changes to the data can be made during extraction. Given the scope of their effort, and how it's done on company-managed devices, LE asks for your suggestion on the proper forensic tool for the job. What forensic tool suite would you recommend?

   A. EnCase

   B. FTK Imager

   C. Sysinternals

   D. Cellebrite

   E. Helix

☑ **D** is correct. Cellebrite's flagship product, the Universal Forensic Extraction Device (UFED), is a handheld device for facilitating data extraction while also employing write blocking.

☒ **A, B, C,** and **E** are incorrect. EnCase is by far the most popular forensic product used by law enforcement. However, its mobile device capabilities are not close to those of UFED. The tool FTK Imager is another well-known forensic tool for law enforcement for data preview and volume imaging, but is not useful for mobile devices. As a side note, FTK does have a utility—the Mobile Phone Examiner Plus (MPE+)—that would apply here, but MPE+ wasn't given as an answer option. The Windows utilities originally created by Sysinternals (now owned by Microsoft) are a powerful set of tools for security analysts, but their capabilities offer nothing particular to mobile devices. Helix is the only forensic tool suite that provides value specific to mobile devices. However, to date, Helix's mobile utilities are still not as robust and versatile as those offered by Cellebrite.

6. As a safety measure, a finance manager has been archiving the small company's finance folder every evening, keeping the backup off the server. One early morning, the manager asks you if there is any way to ensure that the files have not changed since they were archived the night before. What tools can you use to demonstrate no changes have been made? (Choose all that apply.)

A. md5sum

B. tcpdump

C. shasum

D. Vega

E. ZAP

☑ **A** and **C** are correct. To verify the collection of files remain the same as the archive, the finance manager should archive the files again and then compare hashes made from the two archives. A hash is a value computed from the precise structure of a file. Only if the archives are exactly alike will the two hash values be exactly alike. The two utilities shown that create such hash values are md5sum and shasum.

☒ **B, D,** and **E** are incorrect. The utility tcpdump is a command-line-based packet capture and analysis tool. For use on different platforms, but arguably best on Linux/Unix systems, tcpdump is ideal for capturing packets off the network, not for comparing files and archives. Vega offers nothing to compare file versions. Instead, Vega is an interception proxy, so it sits between a user and the resources the user seeks to access. The proxy will monitor access requests and possibly act on them, depending what its user wants to do. Vega, written in Java, offers automated scanning, injection discovery, and XSS vulnerability discovery. ZAP is an interception proxy much like Vega. However, ZAP is considerably more popular because of its easier learning curve and more intuitive interface. Interception proxies are a special type of tool in that they act both as an analyzer and as an exploit tool, much like a man-in-the-middle attack.

7. The in-house development team is proud of their newest XML application. They claim that if you can break the application just by entering data in it like a user would, they will buy you lunch. Seeing how you are quite hungry, what tool do you reach for?

   A. ModSecurity

   B. Kiwi Syslog

   C. Cain & Abel

   D. Untidy

   ☑ **D** is correct. Untidy is a fuzzing tool, meaning its purpose is to send unexpected input to an application with the intent of breaking or crashing it. Input varies in type and size, from slightly "off" to vastly different from what the application expects. Untidy works with XML and modifies it before inputting it. Currently, Untidy is part of the Peach Fuzzer project. Peach Fuzzer is a suite of fuzzing tools that rely on XML-based modules, which their designers call "pits." The pits are what configure the tool concerning how to conduct the test.

   ☒ **A, B,** and **C** are incorrect. ModSecurity is a monitoring and control toolkit that benefits from the OWASP Core Rule Set (CRS), a set of detection rules tailored for web application attacks. Kiwi Syslog, like ModSecurity, is also a monitoring tool. However, Kiwi functions just short of an actual SIEM, and instead concentrates on regulatory compliance issues. Cain & Abel is a password-cracking tool, and although it does perform brute-force attempts, it would not be able to operate with the developer's new XML input.

8. Your CEO recently read an article titled "Security Information and Event Management—How You Can Know Everything." The CEO has always been interested in alerts you receive from the company's vast array of systems, but he now is willing to invest in real-time analysis of those alerts. Which tool would you suggest the CEO invest in?

   A. ArcSight

   B. Bro

   C. Cacti

   D. tcpdump

   ☑ **A** is correct. ArcSight is a powerful trio of platforms, intended for medium to large companies. Its correlation and analytics engines are mature and well-respected in the field of SIEM solutions. The CEO would be quite proud and pleased with ArcSight integrated into the current fold of alert management systems.

   ☒ **B, C,** and **D** are incorrect. The IDS Bro is a monitoring and detection tool. Given a strong, flexible scripting language, Bro is nearly an intrusion prevention system, able to respond to certain alerts. But Bro can hardly be considered a comprehensive SIEM. Cacti, also a monitoring tool, is a free front end to a network logging and graphic tool based on MRTG. Unlike Bro, Cacti just monitors and makes nice graphs—again, far from functioning as a SIEM. The packet capture and analysis tool tcpdump excels at capturing packets, but not at responding to or reporting findings in a particularly useful way.

Use the following scenario to answer Questions 9 and 10:

In the Department of Research and Development, one of the Windows servers goes offline once or twice a day. Each outage lasts only three to five minutes. The server drops offline and restores connectivity with no apparent cause or pattern. Every outage is temporary, but it's disruptive enough that the department manager has finally demanded an investigation. After a network engineer diagnosed the routing table and wiring as fine and a system admin was unable to replicate the problem, they then turn to security.

9. Although the networking and routing have been determined to be good, there could still be a networking issue to detect on the system. What command-line utility could be used to display open sockets and network connections?

   A. nslookup

   B. nmap

   C. netstat

   D. tracert

   ☑ **C** is correct. The command-line utility netstat will display current sockets and network connections.

   ☒ **A, B,** and **D** are incorrect. The utility nslookup is for DNS resolution and information, but it provides little information outside of DNS-related statistics. Incidentally, if the server had been a Linux system, the equivalent utility is dig. The protocol scanner nmap would be great to show what ports are open, closed, or filtered (through a firewall), but it will not show what connections are currently open. Lastly, the tracert utility is used for mapping the path taken by network hops, but it produces little information about currently open connections. If the system had been a Linux system, the command would be traceroute.

10. The networking connections display one external, foreign IP address with an active connection. What device or application would be the first choice to corroborate this finding as well as to stop it?

    A. Antivirus

    B. Firewall

    C. Antimalware

    D. IPS

    ☑ **B** is correct. If there is a connection between an internal system and an external system, the connection passes through the firewall. The firewall is a network perimeter device that will either deny or allow a connection to take place, depending on the rules you instruct the firewall to follow.

    ☒ **A, C,** and **D** are incorrect. Antivirus would stop certain malware, such as a virus or worm, from spreading from your machine or infecting your machine. Antimalware stops more pervasive and insidious malware. An intrusion prevention system (IPS) would detect bad traffic on the network and possibly respond by blocking the traffic.

11. What Next-Generation Firewall (NGFW) company released "Wildfire," a cloud-based malware-detection service?

   A. Cisco

   B. Check Point

   C. Palo Alto

   D. Sourcefire

   ☑ **C** is correct. Wildfire is a subscription service from Palo Alto. With Wildfire, Palo Alto moves malware detection to the cloud.

   ☒ **A, B,** and **D** are incorrect. Sounding fairly similar, FirePOWER is Cisco's NGFW product. It's a subscription-based service that brings an NGFW-level solution to a traditional ASA firewall. Check Point is popularly recognized as the pioneer of stateful packet inspection, but it did not produce Wildfire. Finally, Sourcefire is not a firewall company. Instead, Sourcefire is the original producer of FirePOWER appliances, which Cisco absorbed as part of its acquisition of Sourcefire in 2013.

Use the following scenario to answer Questions 12 and 13:

A special-purpose workstation connects with several external hosts during the normal workday. On the rare occasion, a connection triggers an alert on a network intrusion detection system or some other security device because malicious traffic is detected. This is because none of the external nodes are under the company's control or security policy. Because this is a necessary function of this particular workstation, the potential for malicious traffic is an acceptable risk.

12. What should be the first line of defense to protect the workstation from a security incident?

   A. Antivirus

   B. Firewall

   C. HIDS

   D. Network-based IDS

   ☑ **A** is correct. Antivirus (AV) on the host should be an obvious first line of defense. AV should be already present, at a minimum.

   ☒ **B, C,** and **D** are incorrect. A perimeter-based firewall is the first line of defense from a packet's perspective. In this case, the workstation is initiating connections, and traffic (malicious or not) is already past the firewall. Unless the firewall were an application-layer firewall or an NGFW, we can assume malware might make it to the workstation unblocked. If an HIDS was installed on the workstation or an IDS was in line between the firewall and workstation, either of them would catch the malware. But either is also only a monitoring device, with no response. We have to assume someone is monitoring IDS alerts and, if warranted, would terminate any connection at the firewall or provide some similar response. However, whether host-based or network-based, an IDS will not actively defend the workstation like an antivirus application.

13. The new CISO has decided the workstation must connect via VPN to improve security. What, if any, change in controls should be considered?

A. Adding an HIPS

B. Ensuring the CA is up to date

C. Capturing packet headers

D. No change in controls needed

☑ **A** is correct. If a VPN is used between the workstation and a foreign node (which is a very dangerous idea, by the way), then all traffic is now encrypted and unviewable by the company's own network security devices. Only a host-based IDS or IPS can view the traffic as it leaves or enters the endpoint. Therefore, adding an HIPS is the correct choice.

☒ **B, C,** and **D** are incorrect. Ensuring the Certificate Authority (CA) is up to date is fine regarding the certificate's validity and strength, but it does nothing to help control security on the workstation. Capturing packet headers, presumably from the host, would only document the source and destination address information. No payload or possibly malicious traffic would be monitored.

14. What network-monitoring application is the following rule useful for?

```
alert tcp $ $EXTERNAL_NET any -> $HOME_NET any (msg: "You're gonna need
a bigger boat"; content: "dun_dun"; depth:5; nocase; detection_filter:
track by_src, count 3, seconds 2;)
```

A. Metasploit

B. Web proxy

C. Network General

D. Snort

E. Most firewalls

☑ **D** is correct. The provided example is a Snort rule. Functionally, the rule will detect and alert on packets containing "dun_dun" in their content at a depth of five octets, and sensing three such packets within two seconds from a single source. (Although this rule is likely not practical in the real world, I think coastal data centers should include it in their Snort rule set.) Snort installations come with close to 2000 stock rules in various readable text files. Various sets of rules are available for use depending on your environment, OS platform, or applications running.

☒ **A, B, C,** and **E** are incorrect. The Metasploit framework is every bit as powerful and flexible as Snort, but it relies on commands and modules (not rules) to exploit the identified target. A web proxy functions more like a caching server, but monitors traffic for the likely purpose of content filtering. Network General is the original commercial packet sniffer product, from back in the late 1980s. Packet sniffers, as they were back then, did not employ rules, but today's most common sniffers are also packet analyzers. Firewalls, in general, use rules to determine what type of traffic and what response to take if such traffic is detected. However, the structure and parameters of the provided rule in the question are unique to Snort.

About the Digital Content

This book comes complete with TotalTester Online customizable practice exam software containing 200 multiple-choice practice exam questions, a pre-assessment test, and ten performance-based questions.

If you purchased the print book, a link to the online software is provided on the CD-ROM that accompanies the print book, and you'll also get a secured PDF version of the book.

If you purchased the ebook or you do not have a CD-ROM drive, see the "Your Total Seminars Training Hub Account" section in this Appendix for details.

CD-ROM

Accessing the CD-ROM content requires Windows Vista or later and 30MB of hard disk space for full installation, in addition to a current or prior major release of Chrome, Firefox, Internet Explorer, or Safari. To run, the screen resolution must be set to 1024×768 or higher.

From the main screen of the CD-ROM menu, you may link to the TotalTester Online and then follow the instructions in the "Your Total Seminars Training Hub Account" section in this Appendix.

As a unique benefit of the CD-ROM, you will also receive a secured PDF of the book that you can view on your computer or various devices with Adobe Reader or the Adobe Acrobat Reader mobile app.

 NOTE If you are unable to access the software from the CD-ROM, please see the following sections for details on accessing the online test engine.

Your Total Seminars Training Hub Account

To get access to the online content you will need to create an account on the Total Seminars Training Hub. Registration is free and you will be able to track all your online content using your account. You may also opt in if you wish to receive marketing information from McGraw-Hill Education or Total Seminars, but this is not required for you to gain access to the online content.

Privacy Notice   McGraw-Hill Education values your privacy. Please be sure to read the Privacy Notice available during registration to see how the information you have provided will be used.

You may view our Corporate Customer Privacy Policy by visiting the McGraw-Hill Education Privacy Center. Visit the mheducation.com site and click on "Privacy" at the bottom of the page.

Single User License Terms and Conditions

Online access to the digital content included with this book is governed by the McGraw-Hill Education License Agreement outlined next. By using this digital content you agree to the terms of that license.

Duration of License   Access to your online content through the Total Seminars Training Hub will expire one year from the date the publisher declares the book out of print.

Your purchase of this McGraw-Hill Education product, including its access code, through a retail store is subject to the refund policy of that store.

The Content is a copyrighted work of McGraw-Hill Education and McGraw-Hill Education reserves all rights in and to the Content. The Work is © 2019 by McGraw-Hill Education, LLC.

System Requirements   The current and previous major versions of the following desktop browsers are recommended and supported: Chrome, Microsoft Edge, Firefox, and Safari. These browsers update frequently and sometimes an update may cause compatibility issues with the TotalTester Online or other content hosted on the Training Hub. If you run into a problem using one of these browsers, please try using another until the problem is resolved.

Access   To access TotalTester Online, follow the instructions below to register and activate your Total Seminars Training Hub account. When you register you will be taken to the Total Seminars Training Hub.

Here are the steps to register and activate your Total Seminars Training Hub account:

1. Go to **hub.totalsem.com/mheclaim**.

2. To Register and create a new Training Hub account, enter your e-mail address, name, and password. No further information (such as credit card number) is required to create an account.

3. If you already have a Total Seminars Training Hub account, select "Log in" and enter your email and password.

4. Enter your Product Key: `3mkk-tn7n-f2b0`

5. Click to accept the user license terms.

6. Click "Register and Claim" to create your account. You will be taken to the Training Hub and have access to the content for this book.

 NOTE   Once you have registered, you may access the exam at any time by going to **hub.totalsem.com** and logging in.

Using the TotalTester Online Content

The TotalTester Online provides you with a simulation of the CompTIA CySA+ Cybersecurity Analyst (CS0-001) exam. Exams can be taken in Practice Mode or Exam Mode. Practice Mode provides an assistance window with hints, references to the book, explanations of the correct and incorrect answers, and the option to check your answer as you take the test. Exam Mode provides a simulation of the actual exam. The number of questions, the types of questions, and the time allowed are intended to be an accurate representation of the exam environment. If you choose to customize your test, you can create custom exams from selected domains or chapters, and you can further customize the number of questions and time allowed. All exams provide an overall grade and a grade broken down by domain. You will also have the option to take a pre-assessment quiz and get an additional ten performance-based questions to further support your exam preparation.

From the Training Hub Home page, select **CompTIA CySA+ Practice Exams (CS0-001) Total-Tester** from the "Your Topics" list on the Home page or from the Study drop-down menu at the top of the page. You can then select the **Pre-Assessment TotalTester** or the full **TotalTester** option and begin testing yourself. All exams provide an overall grade and a grade broken down by domain.

Pre-Assessment Test

The TotalTester Online includes a CompTIA CySA+ pre-assessment test with 25 questions to help you assess your understanding of the topics before reading the book. To launch the pre-assessment test, select **Pre-Assessment TotalTester**. When you complete the exam and select **Grade Test**, you can review your results by domain and even choose to review the questions with your answers and in-depth explanations. Set priorities for additional study based on the score you receive for each exam domain.

Performance-Based Questions

Ten simulated performance-based questions are also included to allow you to practice with this question type. To access the performance-based questions, return to the Training Hub Home page and select **Additional Resources for CompTIA CySA+ Practice Exams (CS0-001)** or go to the **Resources** tab of the TotalTester.

Performance-based questions are mostly graphical in nature and require the test taker to understand the concepts of the question or case study from a practical and graphical aspect. For example, you may need to identify the correct component within a graphic, arrange a sequence of steps into the correct order, or match a set of terms with the correct definitions. It is not as easy to memorize answers for these types of questions, and they in turn make passing the exam more challenging.

Technical Support

For questions regarding the TotalTester software or operation of the CD-ROM included with the print book, visit **www.totalsem.com** or e-mail **support@totalsem.com**.

For questions regarding book content, e-mail **hep_customer-service@mheducation.com**. For customers outside the United States, e-mail **international_cs@mheducation.com**.